Penguin Business
The Anatomy of Decisions

Professor Peter Moore is Principal of the London Business School and also holds the Chair of Decision Sciences. He is President elect of the Royal Statistical Society, a recent Past President of the Institute of Actuaries, a former member of the University Grants Committee and a current member of the Council of the new University of Science and Technology in Hong Kong. Before joining the Business School, Professor Moore worked for Reed International and spent some time in the United States. He has received an Honorary D.Sc from Heriot-Watt University, a Guy Medal from the Royal Statistical Society, and the Scaife Medal from the Institution of Production Engineers. His books include *Principles of Statistical Techniques, Basic Operation Research* and *The Business of Risk*.

Howard Thomas is James F. Towey Professor of Strategic Management and Policy and Director of the Strategic Management Research Program at the University of Illinois at Urbana-Champaign. He holds degrees from the Universities of Chicago, London and Edinburgh, and has held faculty appointments at the Australian Graduate School of Management, Edinburgh University, London Business School, Massachusetts Institute of Technology, the University of British Columbia and the University of Southern California. Professor Thomas is the author (or co-author) of many articles and books in the areas of risk and decision analysis, strategic management and competitive strategy.

Peter G. Moore and Howard Thomas

The Anatomy of Decisions

SECOND EDITION

PENGUIN BOOKS

PENGUIN BOOKS

Published by the Penguin Group
Penguin Books Ltd, 27 Wrights Lane, London W8 5TZ, England
Viking Penguin, a division of Penguin Books USA Inc.
375 Hudson Street, New York, New York 10014, USA
Penguin Books Australia Ltd, Ringwood, Victoria, Australia
Penguin Books Canada Ltd, 2801 John Street, Markham, Ontario, Canada L3R 1B4
Penguin Books (NZ) Ltd, 182–190 Wairau Road, Auckland 10, New Zealand

Penguin Books Ltd, Registered Offices: Harmondsworth, Middlesex, England

First published 1976
Second edition 1988
10 9 8 7 6 5 4 3 2

Printed in England by Clays Ltd, St Ives plc
Filmset in 10/12 Times

Contents

Preface

In recent years interest in the quality of decisions made in both the public and private sectors of the economy has grown tremendously. Two dramatic examples amongst many, namely the collapse of the Pennsylvania Railroad, and the acceptance of the ill-fated RB 211 contract with the Lockheed Corporation for the L1011 Tristar aircraft that led to the Rolls-Royce collapse, bear witness to the intense concern felt amongst managers about the procedures by which decisions are reached. Traditional approaches to decision-making are clearly lacking, particularly in their common failure to link together initial and consequential alternatives and the informal bases on which uncertainties are commonly dealt with.

This book develops an analytical approach to the consideration of risk in management decisions that is both consistent and of general applicability. It is argued that this enables the relevant expertise of advisers and managers to be properly utilized and hence better decisions made. No method, short of eliminating uncertainty, will guarantee success in every situation, but an increase in the percentage of good decisions made can have a dramatic effect on an organization's overall results. In a period that has seen the collapse of so many household names in business throughout the more developed economies, it cannot be denied that a more rational approach to uncertainty is needed. This is contrary, however, to a widely held view that intuition and judgement form the crucial elements for success in management. Of course, the truth lies somewhere in between the two extremes. Analysis will not generate, in itself, the possible ideas for action in the first place – these must be derived from the creativity and vision of those concerned. Rational analysis will, however, enable the accepted scarce availability of creativity and judgement amongst managers to be better exploited.

The way in which the material in this book is developed contains some features which will be novel to many readers, although few of the ideas are themselves new. In particular Thomas Bayes, the Nonconformist clergyman from Tunbridge Wells who died in 1761, would be amazed to find that his essay on probability is now a cornerstone of modern thinking on the formal incorporation of uncertainty in business, medicine, the law and elsewhere. Howard Raiffa at Harvard, and Dennis Lindley at University College London, are responsible for many of the developments discussed in this book, but our own debt is much wider and includes those from many professions with whom we have discussed these ideas, and who have consciously or unconsciously provided us with illustrative material. The text has been aimed at an international audience and the widely based selection of illustrative material reflects this aim.

The mathematics in the text has been kept to the lowest possible level consistent with the adequate development and illustration of the appropriate conceptual arguments. As such, it should be within the competence of all those seriously interested in the subject. The examples and exercises have been drawn from (or suggested by) a wide variety of sources in a number of different countries, many connected with consulting work carried out by the authors over recent years. The bulk of the examples use US dollars but, where it seemed more appropriate to retain the original currency, this has been done. Certain exercises, marked with an asterisk*, are of greater difficulty than the others and could be omitted on a first reading.

A general bibliography is given at the end of the book for further study, whilst a number of journal references to specific topics are given at the end of individual chapters.

It is a pleasure to acknowledge the help received from many quarters in the preparation of this book. Mrs Sonja Moore has given valuable assistance with the proof reading. The ultimate responsibility for the contents must, however, rest with the authors and comments from readers will be welcomed. For ease of reading we refer to the decision-makers as males, but this should be taken equally to include female decision-makers.

London Business School and
Sloan School of Management (M1T)   P.G.M.
September 1987   H.T.

1 Decision Situations

Introduction

In the past twenty years, a number of new techniques have been developed for the use of business managers, while many existing techniques have been broadened almost beyond recognition through the extensive development of electronic computing. Although many, if not most, of these techniques are essentially simple in concept, they have often been sponsored by over-enthusiastic specialists, and managers have consequently some-times regarded them with a certain degree of suspicion and dis-comfort. Part of this reaction is related to the attitude of mind which regards judgement and intuition as the primary elements in solving a business or administrative problem. The intense and sustained effort that is required for progress in subjects like phys-ics, it is argued, would not be worthwhile in business, because the relevant data in the business problem would never be known with sufficient accuracy or certainty to justify hard thought. To make this line of argument is to overlook two pertinent factors.

First, the inaccuracies or uncertainties in the data could per-haps themselves be precisely specified, so that their very exist-ence would provide an incentive for hard thinking. Uncertainty exists in virtually all problem situations. We need to be able to cope with it, to eliminate it where possible, but to live with it in the most efficient manner possible where it cannot be eliminated and not to pretend that it does not exist. Many executives think of themselves as individuals whose greater grasp of the available information and greater insights remove the uncertainties from the situation. Even casual observation of most business decisions usually reveals the fallacy of this view; substantial uncertainty is more often the rule than the exception. 'The only sure thing in this world is the past,' wrote Auguste Detoeuf, 'but all we have to work with is the future.' Our primitive ancestors sought to avoid the dilemma by consulting soothsayers and cranks who would reveal to them the uncertainty of the future in all its majesty. The methods have changed, astrology and the reading of sheep entrails being somewhat out of fashion today, but predictions of the future still abound – many of them of dubious value. A formal theory of decision-making must take uncertainty as its departure point and regard precise knowledge of ultimate outcomes as an unobtainable ideal.

Second, hard thought should enable the manager to reduce a large messy problem with many variables and factors to one where the issues, although not soluble by the use of techniques alone, are focused on fewer variables and factors. The area within which judgement is required is then more sharply defined. Of course, this means that judgement on specific issues becomes more important and more observable. But such an approach ensures that a top manager's task is not cluttered up with matters that can be resolved in other ways. This reserves his energy, time and expertise for issues which cannot readily be delegated. Pursuing the lines of argument discussed here, a much greater number of situations than is commonly admitted can bring the promise of substantial reward through applying basic scientific methods such as decision analysis.

Descriptive methods have been used, by social psychologists and other behaviouralists, to evolve general theories of decision-making through observing the way in which people currently make decisions. Results of such studies in the past, usually of limited scope, suggest that managers do not always make decisions on any coherent or logical principles and reinforce our belief that there is a positive contribution to be made by mathematicians and statisticians to the development of the subject – not merely confirming managers in their present ways. We therefore approach decision situations not by descriptive methods, but by inviting readers to sit back and think about the decision process, thereby deducing that it must have certain features. These features are then built upon to provide a rational, coherent and consistent framework that can provide us with the necessary guides to action.

The term *decision analysis* is both an approach to decision-making and a set of techniques. Above all, it is a guide to the taking of decisions in an environment of risk and uncertainty. In carrying out such an analysis, the decision-maker will commonly proceed via a number of stages to enable him both to think about the problem and resolve its solution in his mind. The three basic stages involved are *decomposing and structuring* the problem, assessing the *uncertainties and values* of the possible outcomes, and determining the *optimal strategy*. Decision analysis provides a framework in which all available information is used to deduce which of the decision-maker's alternatives is 'best' according to his stated preferences.

Choosing an alternative that is consistent with these preferences and present knowledge does not guarantee that we will choose the alternative which, with hindsight, turns out to have been the best. A distinction must be drawn between a good *decision* and a good *outcome*. We are all familiar with situations in which careful management and extensive planning produced poor results, whilst a disorganized and badly managed competitor produced a spectacular success. As an extreme example, place yourself in the position of the company chief executive who has just discovered that a valuable and trusted subordinate, whose numerous judgements in the past have proved unfailingly accurate, had actually based his decisions upon the advice of a gypsy fortune-teller. Would you promote this man, or fire him? (The answer, of course, is to fire him and hire the gypsy as a consultant!) The availability of such a clairvoyant to provide perfect information would make decision theory unnecessary. But we should not confuse the two possibilities. The procedure outlined in this book is not a substitute for the fortune-teller. It is rather a procedure that takes account of all available information to give us the best possible logical decision. It will minimize the consequences of getting an unfavourable outcome, but we cannot expect our theory to shield us from all 'bad luck'. The best insurance we have against a bad outcome is a good decision.

Thumb Nail Sketches

To illustrate the kinds of situation to which these principles can be applied, a number of brief sketches are given of problems that have been analysed using this decision analysis framework. Some of these problems will be treated in rather greater depth in later chapters of the book. Meanwhile, they provide illustrations of the width of activities to which the principles can be applied, both in the private enterprise sector of an economy and, increasingly, by governments and public sector agencies.

Oil Exploration

An oil company has an option on an area of sea and must decide whether or not to drill at this location before its option expires. The executive making this decision is uncertain about many things: the cost of drilling, the extent of the oil at the location, the cost of raising the oil, the standard of the oil, etc. He has available to him objective records of similar drillings in the same area and he has discussed the peculiar features of this particular site with his geologist, his geophysicist and his surveyor. He can, at a substantial cost, gain further relevant, but still not perfect, information about the underlying geophysical structure at this site by having seismic soundings conducted. Since the information is costly and still somewhat imperfect, the executive's problem is to decide whether or not to have the seismic soundings carried out before he makes his final decision as to whether to drill or to abandon the site.

Plant Modernization

Decisions regarding automation or modernization programmes illustrate the close interplay of technical and marketing uncertainty. This type of issue can pose serious problems of conflict of interest amongst executives. For example, a company management must decide on a proposal by its engineering staff who want to install a computer-based control system in the company's major plant. The expected cost of the control system is some $10 million. The claimed advantages of the system are a reduction in labour costs and an improved product yield. These benefits depend on the level of product output, which is expected to rise over the next decade. It is anticipated that the installation programme will take about two years and involve a substantial sum besides the cost of the equipment itself. The engineer calculates that the project will yield 20 per cent return on investment after taxes: this projection has been based on a ten-year forecast of product demand by the market research department, with the assumption of an eight-year life for the process control system.

The proposal involves a number of obvious uncertainties. The actual product sales may be higher or lower than forecast. The process may not work as intended, nor achieve the economies expected, whilst the costs may also be overspent. Other competitors may follow suit if the company is successful, or fresh products may be developed that will make the new plant obsolete before the investment can be recovered, whilst the system itself may not last eight years.

Diagnosis of Illness

An American doctor is faced with a sick patient and, before carrying out any detailed examination, believes that he is suffering from one or other of three possible diseases. The treatment he would give depends upon correct diagnosis of the particular disease concerned, and incorrect diagnosis could have dangers through wrong treatment. The doctor can carry out tests on the patient, which will indicate which of the three diseases is the most likely. These tests, however, are imperfect in that positive reactions to the tests could occur with all three diseases although with very varying degrees of likelihood. Futhermore, the doctor need not consider just one test or symptom. He can look, and commonly will look, at a whole battery of tests, and the information from each of these needs to be combined in some form. Finally, the doctor needs to take into account any initial beliefs that he has as to the likelihood of each disease arising in this particular patient. For example, his initial belief will be coloured by where he is working – the likelihood of a patient having beriberi is different in the USA and in Tanzania. In the USA the doctor would not diagnose beriberi unless the symptoms are very emphatic indeed, even though it is theoretically one of the three possible diseases from which his patient is suffering. It is, therefore, useful for the doctor to have some formal mechanism for combining his prior beliefs as to the likelihood of the diseases with the additional information that can be obtained from one or more tests that are carried out on the patient.

Nuclear Power Plant Siting

An investor who was the principle investor in an electric power company on the west coast of the USA retained consultants to develop and apply a methodology to recommend a site for a nuclear power plant. There were a number of challenging features involved in the decision. The geology of the area included seismic consideration, whilst the power plant would require large quantities of cooling water, both of which incorporated different degrees of uncertainty in any possible location selected. Siting concerns also included licensing requirements, public health and safety, environmental and socio-economic effects and public acceptance.

The electric company has responsibilities to its shareholders and its customers, its workers and local residents as well as other groups concerned with nuclear power matters. Requirements imposed by the US Nuclear Regulatory Commission have to be observed and, finally, there were data limitations, either because of non-availability or because of time constraints. The consultants had to meld the various objectives and use a form of risk analysis to determine the effects of major uncertainties on a range of possible sites.

Price Setting

The UC Company is considering the introduction of a new type of soap powder with miracle cleaning properties. A major reason for launching the product at the present time is to provide an alternative to an existing product of similar chemical composition introduced by the PG Company nine months ago.

The UC and PG Companies are the major manufacturers in the soap-powder market and together they account for the greater proportion of the total market for soap powder in Western Europe. Both UC and PG have faced considerable criticism in the past from consumers because of the high price of soap powder.

In discussion, UC executives felt there were three initial pricing alternatives, viz: set the price at PG's level; raise it above PG to establish a quality image; cut the price below PG to try to establish an initial foothold. There were obviously variations possible within the latter two options. All these alternatives contain varying degrees of risk, and there was, moreover, some disagreement amongst executives as to the time horizon which ought to be considered. Management viewed this as a situation where it would be possible to use decision analysis both to structure the alternatives and possible outcomes, as well as to focus attention on the relevant quantities whose estimation was pertinent to the decision. These quantities would be related both to the value to the company of the various alternatives, as well as to the uncertainties surrounding the attainment of that value.

The analysis made showed that price-cutting by 10 per cent was the optimal decision in the sense that the expected profits on a discounted basis were thereby maximized. It also pointed out those areas of the analysis where it was important to obtain accurate estimates of the inputs involved.

Tourism

Tropica Realtors, an American property development company, was looking at the possibilities of various property development packages within the Caribbean area. With the rapid growth of tourism and the increasing wealth of the area a number of possibilities had been identified:

 (i) A mix of office and apartment development activity.
 (ii) Residential developments: apartments and homes.
(iii) Hotel and leisure park development.

The major uncertainties which the company felt were important in its decision-making revolved around the political risks involved, i.e. the possibilities of governmental stability, of revolution, of subsequent military takeover, of changes in laws and, ultimately, the chance of appropriation of assets. Quite apart from this very crucial source of uncertainty it was also concerned about the chances of obtaining suitable short- and long-term financing, the likely development costs, the speed of obtaining planning permission and the number of potential users of the proposed developments. In addition, the development of a good transport infrastructure and a willingness of the international airlines to route more airlines to this area would assist the profitability of the operation considerably. The company realized that, in coming to a conclusion, it needed to explore ways of measuring and handling the very considerable range of uncertainties inherent to the situation.

Government Investment in R and D

A governmental agency must decide whether to undertake a ten-year R and D (research and development) programme to develop fast-breeder reactors. Presently known supplies of low-cost uranium are sufficient for only eight years, in which time the demand for nuclear power plants will rise rapidly. The basis of a breeder reactor is that it acts as a source of fissionable fuel and generates more fuel than it consumes: therefore it reduces the dependence on natural ore. The use of breeder reactors would allow maintenance of present low electricity costs, even if cheap ores were to become scarce. Private industrial sources have suggested several different innovations for the construction of such reactors, all of which depend on different heat transfer materials. The agency is uncertain, however, whether a fast-breeder reactor can be built which is both safe and cost effective.

The chief executive of the agency must decide whether to launch a crash programme of breeder development, with the option of halting it later if new low-cost ore is discovered, or whether to launch a modest R and D programme having a more distant completion date in the expectation that there will be substantial ore discoveries. He must also decide whether to concentrate all research on one innovation or to divide funds among several parallel projects until more information is available about the ultimate success of each.

Television Series Production

The Television Division of Movie International Artistes (MIA) is considering a new twelve-episode film series for television based on a recently published novel that is an exposé of the workings of high finance. MIA has approached one of the major US TV networks for financial backing.

The network concerned is considering whether, and how much, to invest in the series, and faces a number of uncertainties in reaching a decision. These relate primarily to the costs of production, the availability of outside financial backing, the level of viewing audience that will be attracted, the pulling power of such a series to potential advertisers, the availability of certain artistes to play the lead roles in the series, and the possible sales potential of the series to networks outside the United States.

Faced with such uncertainties, the network is considering yet another option, namely to contract for one or two pilot episodes only, and to use these to evaluate more clearly the likely viewing audience and advertising potential of the complete series. With the large sums of money involved, and the inherent high risks, the management is anxious to make a rational evaluation of this and related proposals.

Plan of the Book

The plan of this book is as follows. Chapter 2 describes in some detail a case-history derived from a real-life situation in manufacturing industry. Later chapters in the book contain more detailed and generalized considerations of the diverse issues that are raised by the various stages in this case-history. Chapters 3 and 4, which are the kernel of the book, develop a foundation for the formal analysis of decisions and discuss decision trees. Chapters 5 and 6 deal with the incorporation of fresh information in decision situations and with the analysis of increasingly complex decision trees, derived mainly from case-histories. Chapters 7 and 8 deal with formal assessments of uncertainties in decision analysis, whilst chapters 9 and 10 are concerned with the measurement of the consequences of various alternative outcomes and the appropriate decision criteria to be used. In chapter 11 risk analysis, which has been widely used in capital investment analysis, is discussed in terms of illustrative situations. Finally, chapter 12 gives some further applications of the methodology described in the book, and discusses some of the problems that arise in implementing the concepts.

2   The Rev Counter Decision

Introduction

This case arose out of a decision tree analysis carried out for a well-known industrial firm. The company's identity and the actual product manufactured have been altered for reasons of confidentiality. The various discussions outlined in the case are reported in the same order in which they occurred within the firm when the problem was originally under study. The case should be read through quickly to get a general, rather than a detailed, grasp of the subject matter which is developed more fully in later chapters, references being made back to this chapter where appropriate.

Part I

It is 10.30 a.m. and a meeting is in progress in the office of Pethow Inc. This firm, which makes car components, believes there is going to be increased demand for one of its products, a revolution counter for cars. The managing director and four of his executives are considering ways of coping with this new level of demand. Existing plant in the company is working at full capacity on normal shifts, and the firm is considering two alternative options to meet the demand. The first is to expand capacity by putting all its employees on overtime, whilst the second is to purchase an additional revolution counter assembly machine. The managing director has ruled out subcontracting the work to another supplier, because this might result in the subcontractor marketing his own competitive instrument with similar technical features. Furthermore, a price change, except one linked directly to inflation, is ruled out by the marketing manager because of various undertakings that have been given to customers.

Once the options have been outlined, the meeting gets down

to a discussion of what might happen under each of them. First of all, they decide that they ought to base their decision upon the gains to Pethow over a one-year planning period. The marketing manager feels that the projected rise in demand in this period will probably be 15 per cent (if present trends continue), but he adds that there is some possibility of a fall of 5 per cent if the market turns sour. Other possibilities are, he feels, so unlikely that they can be excluded from further consideration. Pressed by the others, the marketing manager admits that he and his staff have accumulated a considerable body of information on future levels of demand and, as a synthesis of this information, he puts the relative likelihoods of the two possible outcomes at something a little different from evens, say 3:2 in favour of increased sales.

Next, the accountant is asked to cost the various options according to the possible outcomes. This he does, after discussions with the production manager on material and equipment costs, and with the personnel manager on wage rates. The new equipment option is costed to include a fair market rent for the use of equipment in the year concerned. The managing director now puts all the data together into a payoff table given below (Table 2.1), giving the net cash flows for each possible action and outcome combination, converting the likelihoods to probabilities that sum to unity over all possible outcomes. After a few moments' thought he includes a further alternative, namely that they do not accept any orders that would take them beyond a level that could be met with their present capacity, working no overtime.

The managing director asks how they should best handle the information contained in this table, whereupon the production manager suggests that it should be put out in the form of a 'decision tree' (Figure 2.1). In explaining to the others the relevance of the decision tree, he points out that each path along the tree represents a route along which the decision-maker could drive. Along each route he may have to pay a toll, such as the cost of some capital investment, and will attain different outcomes or rewards through following each route. These outcomes are not always certain, and there is a chance element as to which branch

Table 2.1 Payoffs and probabilities

	demand (probabilities in parentheses)	
action	5 per cent fall (0·4)	15 per cent rise (0·6)
new equipment (S_1)	260	440
overtime (S_2)	300	420
existing level (S_3)	300	340

figures in $000

is followed. Obviously the tree simplifies even this particular problem, but 'we can always', the production manager states, 'add these complexities later'.

The marketing manager next takes up the story, pointing out that the current decision is but one of a whole range of decisions about various products that the company makes, and that their company philosophy is to achieve the highest expected overall gain. This would be satisfied through using expected monetary value (EMV) as a choice criterion at every stage in a project, always choosing that action for which the EMV was highest. To implement the EMV approach they need to look at each possible option in turn. Thus for S_1 (which is to install new equipment) there is a payoff of 440 with probability 0·6, or an alternative payoff of 260 with probability 0·4. The EMV would accordingly be:

$$0·6 \times 440 + 0·4 \times 260 = 368.$$

A similar calculation shows that the EMV for the decision S_2 (to have overtime working) is 372. Finally, S_3 (to do nothing, but continue with present production level and no overtime working) has an EMV of 324. The Pethow company ought, under the EMV approach, to choose the action which gives the highest expectation, namely to work overtime. In this instance, of course, the EMVs for overtime and new equipment are so close that the results are virtually indistinguishable. On seeing this

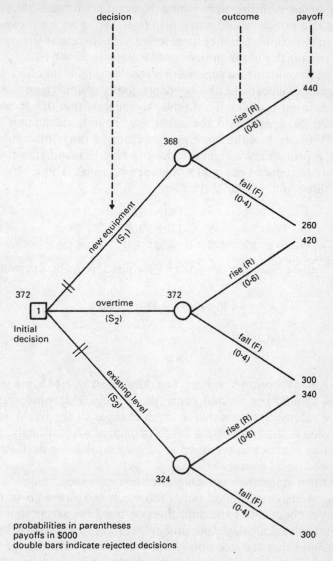

decision   outcome   payoff

440

rise (R)
(0·6)

368 ◯

fall (F)
(0·4)

260

new equipment
(S₁)

420

rise (R)
(0·6)

372 ▢   overtime   372 ◯
[1]   (S₂)

fall (F)
(0·4)

300

340

rise (R)
(0·6)

existing level
(S₃)

324 ◯

fall (F)
(0·4)

300

Initial
decision

probabilities in parentheses
payoffs in $000
double bars indicate rejected decisions

2.1 Initial decision tree

result, the personnel manager points out that overtime would be popular with the men, whilst the accountant states that the overtime option would make his life easier as no fresh capital has to be obtained. Hence there seems to be no reason to reverse the strict order of the options produced by the analysis.

The accountant now suggests they should examine the effect that the precise values of the likelihoods previously assumed have had on the decision reached. To do this, he suggests that the decision should be approached the other way round, calculating the EMV for each of the three options against a range of values of p, the probability assigned to having high demand (the probability of reduced demand would then be $1-p$). The EMV for the three options would then be:

$$
\begin{array}{ll}
S_1 & 180p+260, \\
S_2 & 120p+300, \\
S_3 & 40p+300.
\end{array}
$$

Thus option S_2 always dominates S_3; whilst S_1 is the best provided that:

$$180p+260 > 120p+300$$

or

$$p > \tfrac{2}{3}.$$

If p is $< \frac{2}{3}$, option S_2 is best. The differences in EMV are very small around $p = \frac{2}{3}$ and hence the suggested decision seems to be relatively insensitive to small changes in the likelihoods assigned to the two possible levels of demand. Accordingly, the meeting is about to break up at 12.45 p.m., having decided to proceed on an overtime basis.

At this stage the managing director intervenes. 'Surely', he says, 'we have simplified rather too much and glossed over too many of the realities and difficulties. Whilst I can accept that the payoff values calculated are probably correct to within 1 or 2 per cent, and that the decision is not particularly sensitive to the probabilities, I feel that we haven't explored some of the other issues fully enough. For example, shouldn't we have looked at a somewhat longer horizon than one year only; or again, shouldn't we have examined a little more critically whether or not EMV is the appropriate criterion for decision?' The others agree that further examination is necessary and decide to hold the decision over and resume discussion after a break for coffee and a club sandwich.

Part II

When the meeting resumes, the accountant and marketing manager are already hard at work on an extended tree diagram. They explain that they are trying to extend the analysis to a more realistic two-year planning period, considering only initial options S_1 (new equipment) and S_2 (overtime), arguing that the earlier analysis effectively ruled out option S_2 (do nothing). The marketing manager feels that, in the second year, he needs three levels of possible sales, rather than two levels, to describe accurately the possible situations that could arise. The tree structure that they reach, without any numbers inserted on it, is shown in Figure 2.2.

The meeting now discusses the structure of the tree. At decision point [1] the choice is between options S_1 and S_2. If S_1 is chosen and sales rise, decision point [2a] is reached, when option S_4 (more new equipment) and S_5 (retain existing equipment but work overtime) are open for choice; similarly along other branches. The general feeling is that, although this tree clearly involves some degree of simplification of the problem, and of the options available, the structure provides a reasonable basis for further analysis and lays bare the essential elements of the problem.

The group now turns to assessing the numerical quantities required. First, they consider the difficult task of probability assessments. Both the marketing manager and the accountant feel that the rev counter has a good long-term sales future. They argue that, if the sales fell over the first year, the probabilities of high, medium and low sales in the second year are 0·4, 0·4 and 0·2 respectively. If the sales rise in the first year, the corresponding probabilities are 0·5, 0·4 and 0·1 respectively. These probability assessments are 'educated guesses' based on the best

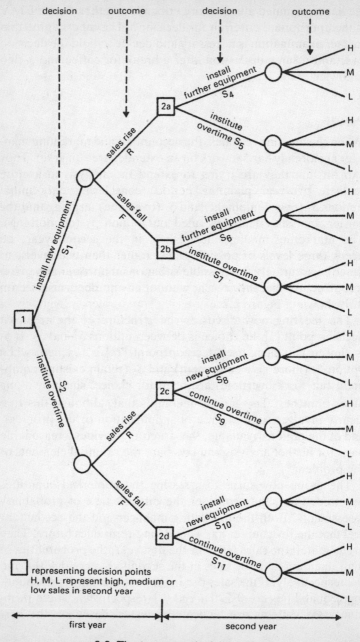

2.2 The two-year decision tree

information currently available, but nevertheless the managers concerned feel that they provide the best summary they can give of their present views.

The next step is to estimate the various payoffs, or net cash flows that will accrue, if the company 'drives' along the many possible routes in the tree. Altogether there are twenty-four possible payoffs to be estimated, each corresponding to an end position on the right-hand side of the tree, the payoff relating to the whole two-year period from the start point, marked [1] on Figure 2.2.

At this stage the managing director comments that the analysis is going to be rather more difficult than for the one-year problem considered that morning. However, the production manager suggests that the principles used earlier could be extended to the two-year problem. He argues that if EMV can be used for the single-stage problem, it can equally well be used for the two-stage problem. The essence of his argument is that, when one of the decision points [2a]–[2d] is reached the decision criterion will still be EMV. Hence the tree should merely be analysed backwards, from right to left, using the EMV criterion for choice, looking at [2a]–[2d] first. The production manager says he believes that this backwards analysis procedure is colloquially called 'rollback'. Decision point [2a] is then considered. The EMV for option S_4 (install further equipment) is:

$$0.5 \times 820 + 0.4 \times 790 + 0.1 \times 760 = 802,$$

whilst the EMV for option S_5 (institute overtime) is:

$$0.5 \times 850 + 0.4 \times 816 + 0.1 \times 790 = 830.4.$$

Hence the better decision is to choose option S_5; accordingly a bar is placed on route S_4 and the value 830.4 placed against decision point [2a], as shown in Figure 2.3 which reproduces only the upper part of the original tree.

A similar calculation for decision point [2b] shows that option S_7 has a higher EMV (660) than option S_6 (632), and hence that S_7 should be preferred. S_6 is accordingly blocked off and the value of 660 placed against decision point [2b]. The two branches leading to the decision points [2a] and [2b] can now be com-

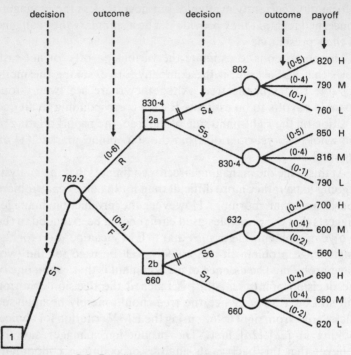

2.3 Detailed analysis of S_1 route

bined. Since the probabilities of a rise or fall in demand in the first year are 0·6 and 0·4 respectively, the overall EMV for the initial option S_1 at decision [1] is:

$$0\cdot6 \times 830\cdot4 + 0\cdot4 \times 660 = 762\cdot2.$$

At this point the managing director asks the others to excuse him whilst he makes a couple of telephone calls, suggesting that meanwhile they deal with the lower part of the tree. On his return about fifteen minutes later, they tell him that the EMV for the initial option S_2 (work overtime) is now 680·8 and that Figure 2.4 gives the outline of the completed tree.

The analysis appears to suggest that the best initial decision now is to install new equipment, a reversal of the morning's decision, and the meeting turns to a discussion as to why this should be so. The reason rapidly emerges, namely that on a one-

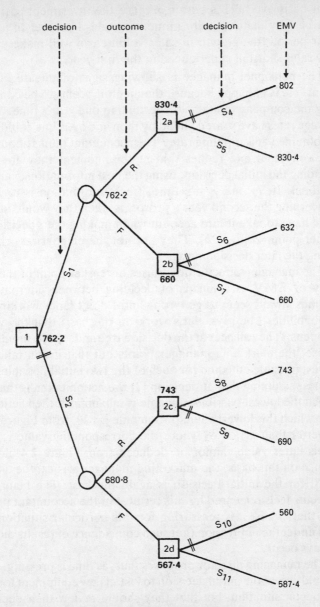

2.4 The two-year tree analysed

year basis overtime is better because the investment cost may not be fully matched with immediate sales increase. In a two-year period, the growth in sales volume can well make up for any sales shortfall experienced in the first year.

The personnel manager is showing signs of unease at this point. He is unhappy because the meeting seems to be committing the company to massive overtime in one year's time. What if wage rates have soared ahead by then and overtime could only be obtained at a crippling rate? The accountant thinks about this for a moment and replies that at this moment they are only deciding the initial decision, using the best information available to them. If, in one year's time, fresh information is to hand concerning the second year's prospects, then they would at that time have to take it into account when making their decision at either point [2a] or [2b]. They are not, he emphasizes, rigidly fixing the later decision now.

The managing director now raises his earlier point of the validity of EMV as a means of deciding between alternatives. 'Things always seem to go wrong and I don't fancy working on probabilities,' he says, 'let's work on the basis that the worst happens.' They all peer at the decision tree and, after a moment's pause, the marketing manager points out that if you take the lowest possible outcome for each of the two initial possible outcomes, assuming that at decision [2] the action taken is that for which the lowest possible outcome is maximized, then action S_1 (for which this lowest value or outcome is 620, from Figure 2.4) is better than action S_2 where the corresponding value is 580. (This latter value cannot be deduced from Figure 2.4 alone.) Hence on this basis, the marketing manager argues, the choice of S_1 for the initial decision is again the best. The managing director feels reassured by this result, but the accountant points out that, whilst it is reassuring for this particular situation, he was under the impression that such coincidence of results did not always occur.

The managing director proposes that, as time is pressing, they should accept the initial decision to install new equipment for this particular situation, but that they should review their decision procedures for future situations in the light of the day's experience. In particular, he proposes that they should later explore not only the question of criteria, but also the need to consider discounted cash flows rather than net payoffs and, finally, the way in which extra information that becomes available, such as further market research results, could be incorporated in a decision. The meeting breaks up at this point with the managing director agreeing to fix a date for the further follow-up session.

Part III

About a month later, in a meeting at Pethow, Mr Chuck Pakin from an associate company which has some experience in using EMV, is present. Pakin suggests that the only reason why EMV is not being accepted automatically as the appropriate logical criterion by Pethow is that the executives are all unconsciously recognizing that in many circumstances their attitude towards money varies according to the capital already possessed. Thus suppose you are personally forced to choose between either

(a) a loss of $100,000 with a probability of 0·001, or
(b) a loss of $150 with probability of 1, i.e. certainty.

'I guess that most of you would choose (b) because you couldn't afford to stand the loss under (a), no matter how unlikely it is. Indeed, you probably already do just this in paying for fire insurance on your house, where the premium is more than the strict expected cost of a fire (because of office expenses, profit, etc.) but you do this with reasonable willingness to avoid the admittedly remote possibility of a loss of $100,000.' For an insurance company the situation is rather different. After paying commission and expenses it is left with the expected cost and its profit (provided it got its sums right). It is happy with this because it has large capital assets, insures a large number of houses and can look forward to adding the appropriate overall expected profit to its assets. Hence the individual (and similarly with a small firm) has an attitude that is conservative towards losses, whilst the insurance company (like many large organizations) is more prepared to operate on an EMV basis. Thus many large firms with a large number of small but separate buildings, offices, etc. may well decide to carry their own insurance rather than pay the excess above expected cost that would be required if it were given over to an insurance company. This line of approach can be summarized by saying that, when considering a proposition where the rewards and costs (or losses) are small in comparison with the total assets, EMV is normally appropriate. Where this is not the case, the approach can still be used if *utility* (or other measure of outcome preference) is substituted for payoff.

The managing director at this point raises again the question of discounting, saying 'it seems to me that we are also ignoring something vital, namely the timing of incoming cash and out-going expenditures'. Chuck Pakin accepts the point immediately suggesting that 'the vital consideration is to get all items on to a common time basis by using an appropriate discount rate: if you commonly use a 10 per cent rate of interest for your appraisal calculations, then use this for each outcome to bring the cash flow to some common base date'. Naturally any such move will only make significant differences when the alternative courses of action have cash flows with very different time profiles. For example, overtime working clearly involves roughly equal additional expenditure over the whole time period concerned. On the other hand, providing extra equipment involves greater expenditure at the beginning of the year concerned. Hence in analysing Figure 2.1 we could expect that, if discounting were incorporated, the value of S_1 would fall relative to that of S_2, and hence S_2 would become even more attractive than it was before. Discounting should, therefore, always be incorporated when the time scale of the entire process is more than a few months.

At this stage, the managing director says, 'I think we are all no doubt gasping for breath, so perhaps we should have a break for a sandwich now, pursue Chuck during the break to elaborate on the points already raised, and return to the outstanding matters afterwards.' The marketing manager interjects to clarify one more point with Pakin. 'What if we consider a planning period of longer than two years, does this affect the analysis?' Pakin states that the analysis would be exactly the same as before except that the structure of the tree would become more complicated. At this point the managing director agrees that they really must have a break.

Part IV

Later, Chuck Pakin and the executives of Pethow resume their discussion by looking into the problem of incorporating fresh information into a decision analysis. To illustrate the argument Pakin suggests that they should look again at the original problem that Pethow considered and suppose that, after the decision tree had been drawn and the various quantities inserted, the marketing manager wants to consider whether to call in the services of a consultant who has worked for the firm on a number of occasions in the past. This consultant is an expert in the field of the marketing of car components and he offers for a fee of $10,000 to sound out in depth, through his various contacts, the possible outlets and come back with a recommendation (or view) as to whether the market for rev counters will rise or fall in the next year. The consultant is by no means infallible, but he has acted as a go-between on a number of deals of this kind and is known to have a reasonable record in these matters. The consultant would provide Pethow with a report that is either favourable (rise) or unfavourable (fall) and the marketing manager summarizes, after some thought, his views of the consultant's reliability in the manner shown by Table 2.2.

Table 2.2 Outcome probabilities

market outcome	consultant's report		
	favourable	unfavourable	totals
rise	0·9	0·1	1·0
fall	0·2	0·8	1·0

This table is read horizontally: thus, should the true market outcome be a rise, there is a 0·9 chance that the consultant will have reported favourably and only a 0·1 chance that he will have reported unfavourably. Conversely, if the market is going to fall, there is a 0·2 chance that the consultant reports favourably and a 0·8 chance that he reports unfavourably. Naturally, Pethow would like the consultant's matrix to read:

$$1·0 \quad 0$$
$$0 \quad 1·0$$

but this is a counsel of perfection that will virtually never be achieved in practice, and account must be taken of the realities of the situation.

The next step, Pakin argues, is for us to see how using the consultant will affect the original probabilities that the marketing manager has assigned to the possible outcomes. These original probabilities are referred to in the literature as *prior* probabilities. Suppose that the consultant is used and he reports favourably. What is now the chance (referred to usually as the *posterior* or *revised* probability) that the market will rise?

The possible combinations of market change and consultant reports that can occur are sketched in Figure 2.5. The four different rectangular areas in the diagram represent the expected proportions with which each type of combination of market–consultant report can occur. In the instance envisaged here, the

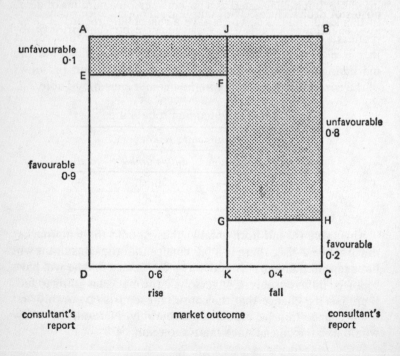

2.5 Revision of probabilities

consultant's report was favourable. Hence only the unshaded area need be considered as the shaded areas correspond to an unfavourable report. Of the unshaded area, the proportionate part corresponding to a rising market is:

$$\frac{\text{Area EFKD}}{\text{Area EFKD}+\text{area GHCK}} = \frac{0\cdot9\times0\cdot6}{0\cdot9\times0\cdot6+0\cdot2\times0\cdot4} = 0\cdot87.$$

In other words, the knowledge that the consultant's report was favourable has lifted the probability of a rising market from a prior probability of $0\cdot6$ to a posterior probability of $0\cdot87$. A similar calculation shows that the revised probability of a falling market would be $0\cdot13$. These two probabilities add up to 1, as they must. If the consultant's report was unfavourable, then the shaded rather than the unshaded area needs to be considered and a similar form of calculation carried out to obtain the appropriate posterior probabilities. The complete set of posterior probabilities is as follows in Table 2.3, with the corresponding prior probabilities shown in parentheses.

Table 2.3 Market discrimination

market expectation	consultant's report	
	favourable	unfavourable
rise	0·87 (0·6)	0·16 (0·6)
fall	0·13 (0·4)	0·84 (0·4)
totals	1·00 (1·0)	1·00 (1·0)

Inspection of this table shows that a far greater discrimination of the two market possibilities has now been obtained than without the consultant's report, and this should in itself serve to refine the decision-making procedure. The production manager asks whether there is any formalized way by which these posterior or revised probabilities can be calculated, particularly when there are rather more categories to consider. Pakin assures him that the calculations are a straightforward application of a probability theorem known as *Bayes's theorem*.

The accountant speaks up at this point. 'I quite see the logic of your approach,' he says, 'but surely, before we go ahead to see if this changes our original decision, we should bear in mind the cost of the information. This information isn't free, and if it costs too much, it could outweigh any advantage there was in deciding to take one action rather than another.' Pakin replies that he did suggest a consultant's fee of $10,000 and perhaps they should see how this, in combination with the accuracy of the report, might affect the original one-year analysis. To understand the revised situation, Pakin sketches Figure 2.6, which is a modification of Figure 2.1, so as to include two distinct levels of decision: first, as to whether or not to retain the consultant, whilst the second is which of the three possible production options should be taken. The appropriate payoffs, together with the revised probabilities just calculated, have been entered, all figures again being expressed in $000.

Some of the tree can be evaluated very simply. The previous analysis corresponded to 'no consultant' and led to an EMV of 372 for a production decision to institute overtime. Hence, if the consultant is to be worth his fee, the EMV of the alternative upper branch of the tree must be at least 372, after taking into account the cost of hiring the consultant. Decision points [2e] and [2f] must now be analysed. Both can be treated in the same way as before. Thus, for point [2e], the three appropriate EMVs are:

$$S_1 \quad 0.87 \times 440 + 0.13 \times 260 = 416.6,$$

$$S_2 \quad 0.87 \times 420 + 0.13 \times 300 = 404.4,$$

$$S_3 \quad 0.87 \times 340 + 0.13 \times 300 = 334.8.$$

Hence S_1 has the highest EMV and both S_2 and S_3 are accordingly barred off on the diagram. Similar calculations made when the consultant's report is unfavourable lead to S_2 (overtime working) having the highest EMV of 319.2. Notice that the two possible consultant reports lead to different actions being recommended – if they did not it would be obvious straight away that the cost of the consultant's service was not worthwhile.

The two best decisions corresponding to points [2e] and [2f] can now be combined, by weighting them according to the likeli-

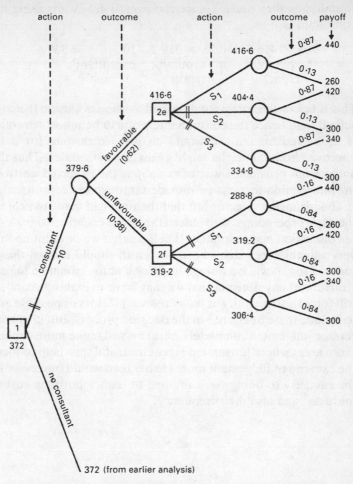

2.6 Further analysis

hood of getting a favourable or an unfavourable result respectively. Consider once again Figure 2.5. The unshaded portion represents the probability of getting a favourable result from the consultant and this area is $0.9 \times 0.6 + 0.4 \times 0.2$ or 0.62. Similarly, an unfavourable result from the consultant corresponds to the shaded area and is equal to 0.38. These two probabilities add to unity, as they must. Hence the overall EMV for using the consultant is

$$0{\cdot}62 \times 416{\cdot}6 + 0{\cdot}38 \times 319{\cdot}2 - 10 \qquad = 369{\cdot}6.$$
   favourable   unfavourable   consultant's
     report   report   cost

This is below the corresponding EMV when not using the consultant, and hence the consultant appears to be not worthwhile. If he halved his fee, he would be just worthwhile (or if he improved his accuracy he might again be worthwhile). Thus the analysis has provided a way of evaluating the expected worth of the information that can be provided through the consultant.

The managing director felt that the time had come to sum up the day's proceedings, and indeed the whole exercise from which the discussion had emanated. 'I believe that we have hit upon a very valuable approach,' he said, 'which should do two things for us. First, it will encourage us to look at the complete logical structure of any decision that we may have to make. Second, it will force us to quantify as many relevant factors as possible and to include these quantities in the decision process. But it will not replace judgement completely, rather it will make more explicit those areas where judgement is required, and thus help to focus the exercise of judgement more clearly than would otherwise be the case. By so doing, we can hope to reduce both the cost of mistakes, and also their frequency.'

3 The Choice of Criterion

Introduction

The 'Rev Counter Decision' case-history in the previous chapter highlights the basic elements of a decision situation, and the way statistical decision analysis can help unravel the company's problems. The internal discussions described were perhaps not so neat, tidy and well organized as they appear to have been when set in print, yet we suspect that many readers who have taken part in such discussions will recognize parts of them and the problems that they raise. In this chapter we use the issues raised by the case to help develop the logic of the decision analysis approach for determining the best strategy to adopt in a given decision problem.

Structure

Decision problems invariably have some definable structure, and the availability of an accepted and analytical approach forces the decision-maker to recognize the existence of certain basic elements in that structure.

First, the decision-maker has a set of *objectives* whose attainment depends upon the decision that he takes. Examples of objectives are profit, return on investment, market share, time for completion, defined level of service, etc. Essentially an objective is a target which a decision-maker is hoping to achieve. For the rev counter situation the objective was to maximize net payoff. In some instances there will only be a single objective, though in many real-life situations there are a number of objectives and conflicts can occur in achieving acceptable levels of each of them. For example, an increase in profits may be achieved at the expense of a reduction in market share, particularly if pricing policy is used as a means of obtaining a short-term gain in profits. Clearly, decision analysis should provide a method for analysing such interdependencies between objectives so that the true cost of taking any particular decision may be seen.

Secondly, the decision-maker must systematically and creatively search for a range of possible *options* from which a set of alternative courses of *action* (or *strategies*) can be determined for consideration in a particular context. This search process is often difficult and may necessitate the decision-maker contemplating various scenarios and strategy paths for the future development of the business. In the rev counter problem, for example, there were three possible strategies in the initial stages. These were labelled $S_i(i = 1, 2 \ldots)$ so that, in this particular instance we have:

S_1 denotes new equipment
S_2 denotes overtime
S_3 denotes existing level.

Thirdly, decision problems normally exist in an uncertain environment. For example, the decision to launch a new product has to be made even though variables – such as the behaviour of competitors, or consumer's reaction to the new product, which affect the firm's situation – are not known with certainty. Sometimes however, the decision-maker has the option of collecting further information, for instance through market research, to throw some light upon the uncertain outcomes which confront him. Information naturally costs money so the decision-maker must judge whether the benefits he gains from the acquisition of the information more than outweigh its cost. This point is taken up more fully in chapter 5.

Again in a product launch situation we may be faced with the immediate possibility of a similar product being launched at a lower price. Such a possibility is one of the set of possible *events* or *outcomes* that may occur if we decide to launch the product. We commonly denote the possible outcomes by $E_j(j = 1, 2 \ldots)$ so that in the rev counter case Chuck Pakin was faced with two outcomes E_1 and E_2 where

E_1 denoted rise in demand ($+15$ per cent)
E_2 denoted fall in demand (-5 per cent).

Fourthly, we need a measure of the *value* or *payoff* of each possible outcome in terms of the decision-maker's objectives. Later we refer to this measure as *utility* but, for the present, refer to it as *money* since in most problems the two concepts are entirely synonymous, although in some problems we may be interested in measures such as time, investment return, market share, etc.

So far, we have identified objectives, strategies, events and payoffs as the basic structural elements present in a decision problem. We can readily identify each of these four elements in the analysis carried out in part I of the rev counter case. Indeed, for a simple one-stage decision problem the payoff matrix used there provides a straightforward way to display the structure of such a decision problem. After structuring the problem the next stage is the analysis and the determination of the best strategy according to the objectives of the decision-maker.

Decision Criteria

Business decision situations are almost invariably analysed in an environment which is uncertain. If the decision-maker knew with certainty the outcomes that would occur, then decision problems would be readily solved. All the decision-maker would have to do would be to choose the strategy for the given outcome which would maximize his gain in terms of his stated objective.

More generally, though, the choice of criterion that the decision-maker should use in selecting an optimal strategy is not so obvious. At this stage we cannot put forward a single best general criterion for selecting a strategy. This is because what is best is often determined by the decision-maker's attitudes, and the norms and policies laid down by the firm which employs him. However, a number of alternative criteria which express different decision-making attitudes have been developed and we can explain the rationale underlying each of them. It should then be clear that the different attitudes of the decision-maker may lead to the selection of different strategies. This situation is one that many find hard to understand but the truth is obvious if the converse is considered, namely that the decision reached is the same whatever the criterion that is used. This is palpably absurd, hence the criterion chosen must influence the decision made.

The various possible criteria are illustrated by considering the managing director's one-year manufacturing problem in part I of the rev counter case. Three alternative strategies have been suggested, namely to purchase some new equipment (S_1), to work overtime (S_2), or to make do with the existing level of plant (S_3). The market demand for the product is uncertain, and two possible levels of demand have been postulated; a 15 per cent rise (E_1) or a 5 per cent fall (E_2). For each combination of strategy and demand the return achievable has been estimated, as shown in Table 3.1. The data will now be used to illustrate the various decision criteria.

Table 3.1. Chuck Pakin's decision payoffs

action	market demand	
	15 per cent rise (E_1)	5 per cent fall (E_2)
S_1 new equipment	440	260
S_2 overtime	420	300
S_3 existing level	340	300

(figures in $000)

Maximin Criterion

Faced with the decision problem, the managing director may take a pessimistic view of the market situation. A natural course of action under these circumstances would be to assume that fate will always act to give him the minimum payoff and he should, therefore, act to ensure that he gets as large a payoff as possible under these circumstances. We call this method of strategy selection the *maximin* approach because it *maxi*mizes the *mini*mum payoff. The calculation is shown in Table 3.2 and leads to selecting the action of working either at the existing level or on an overtime basis. This is because, when the demand is low, the managing director is indifferent between actions S_2 and

S_3. Such an approach is sometimes referred to as a criterion of pessimism in that the worst is assumed.

Table 3.2. Maximin selection of action

action	minimum payoff	maximum of minimum payoffs
S_1 new equipment	260	
S_2 overtime	300	**300**
S_3 existing level	300	**300**

Maximax Criterion

Alternatively, the managing director may be a complete optimist and assume that nature will always be very favourable to him, that is, it will give him the outcome which has the best payoff. He would then choose the *maximax* strategy that maximizes the maximum payoff, demonstrated in Table 3.3, and leading to the selection of S_1, purchasing new equipment.

Note that this is a different choice from that made earlier; this is not surprising in that using a different criterion will often, but not always, lead to a different choice of action. If this were not true, then all criteria would lead to the same action, suggesting that we might as well use a pin to pick our criterion.

Table 3.3. Maximax selection of action

action	maximum payoff	maximum of maximum payoffs
S_1 new equipment	440	**440**
S_2 overtime	420	
S_3 existing level	340	

Because pure attitudes of optimism and pessimism are rare, mixed 'optimistic/pessimistic' strategies have been suggested. For example, if the managing director assigns equal weights to the occurrence of each of the maximum and minimum payoffs, the values for each action would be:

S_1 new equipment $\frac{1}{2} \times 260 + \frac{1}{2} \times 440 = 350$

S_2 overtime $\frac{1}{2} \times 300 + \frac{1}{2} \times 420 = 360$

S_3 existing level $\frac{1}{2} \times 300 + \frac{1}{2} \times 340 = 320.$

The highest value, namely 360, would be selected and hence overtime working would be the best action.

Regret Criterion

It can be argued that it is more natural for decision-makers to think in terms of opportunity costs (or losses) rather than yields (or profits). Suppose that Pakin chose to buy new equipment without the help of any formal decision criterion. If the demand turns out in retrospect to have been high (i.e. a 15 per cent rise) he will have made the correct choice and feel no *opportunity loss* or *regret*. However, if low market demand (i.e. a 5 per cent fall) actually occurs, then Chuck Pakin's decision will have been incorrect. In such a situation, therefore, the decision-maker experiences an opportunity loss (or regret) measured by the difference between the payoff for his chosen action and the payoff for this optimal choice for a low level of demand. In other words, an opportunity loss is the loss incurred because of failure to take the best action available. To illustrate this further, we now turn the original payoff table (Table 3.1) into an opportunity loss (or regret) table. Remember that we define regret formally as the difference between the payoff (or cost) that would have arisen had you chosen the best action for that particular outcome. The results for minimax regret are shown in Table 3.4.

Thus for low demand, either S_2 or S_3 are best and have zero regret, whilst the new equipment option has a regret of 40. It is a matter of convention that regrets (or opportunity losses) are presented as positive. To the table we now apply the minimax principle as before, locating the maximum regret for each row

Table 3.4. Regret (or opportunity loss) matrix

| action | *market demands* | | *maximum regret* | *minimum of maximum regret* |
	15 per cent rise (E_1)	*5 per cent fall (E_2)*		
S_1 new equipment	0	40	40	
S_2 overtime	20	0	20	**20**
S_3 existing level	100	0	100	

and then selecting that action (overtime in this instance) for which the maximum regret is the least.

Probability

The decision criteria so far have not explicitly considered the uncertainties surrounding the occurrence of the possible levels of demand in Pakin's problem. With a series of possible payoffs, the uncertainties pertaining to each element of the series become of importance. To carry our analyses further, we accordingly need to specify the degree of uncertainty concerned. We do this via a scale of *probability* which ranges from 0 to 1. Complete impossibility (e.g. swimming the Atlantic) is represented by 0, and absolute certainty (e.g. that we will die sometime) is represented by 1. We are, however, presented daily with a stream of problems concerning events to which a 0 or 1 answer is inappropriate: will drug X cure your headache, will paint Y prove more durable than your present house paint, will car Z give a better petrol performance. Here the probability value is below 1 in each case as we are slipping away from certainty. To judge how far, think of a spun coin with a probability of ½ of coming down heads, a fair die with a chance of $^1/_6$ of giving a six and so on down the scale. Later, we discuss methods by which probability is measured, meanwhile we will treat it as a formal measure of the degree of uncertainty surrounding some event. The term *likelihood* is sometimes used interchangeably with probability. This is generally acceptable, although we do give a special meaning to likelihood in our discussion in chapter 5. Further reading on the basic concepts of probability is given in the references at the end of this chapter.

Expected Monetary Value

The probabilities of the various outcomes could be readily taken into account by looking, for each action, solely at the outcome having the highest probability and choosing that action for which this highest probability outcome is best. This is, however, limiting in that it ignores completely what happens on either side of the highest probability outcome, e.g. for one action it might be that the payoff is higher if it isn't at that modal or most likely level, in another instance lower. To overcome this defect we consider the *expected monetary value* principle. Under this principle we choose that action which maximizes expected monetary value, where the latter is defined as the sum of the payoffs, weighted by their respective probabilities.

In the rev counter problem, the probabilities assigned to the events 'sales rise' and 'sales fall' are 0·6 and 0·4 respectively, adding to unity as they must if the two levels of sales are the only possible levels. Then, using the payoffs from Table 3.1 the EMVs are:

$$EMV(S_1) = 0·6 \times 440 + 0·4 \times 260 = 368$$
$$EMV(S_2) = 0·6 \times 420 + 0·4 \times 300 = 372$$
$$EMV(S_3) = 0·6 \times 340 + 0·4 \times 300 = 324.$$

The highest EMV is that for S_2 – working the plant on an overtime basis – and this is accordingly the best decision.

Alternatively we could minimize the expected opportunity loss (or EOL). Using the regrets given in Table 3.4, and the probabilities given above, we have

$$EOL(S_1) = 0·6 \times 0 + 0·4 \times 40 = 16$$
$$EOL(S_2) = 0·6 \times 20 + 0·4 \times 0 = 12$$
$$EOL(S_3) = 0·6 \times 100 + 0·4 \times 0 = 60.$$

The minimum EOL is for S_2, and hence the best action is to follow the overtime strategy. This equivalence of action from maximizing EMV or minimizing EOL is always so and the two approaches can be demonstrated to be mathematically equivalent.

EMV provides a systematic way in which all the relevant

information that the decision-maker has about a situation can be brought to bear in a coherent manner. Consistently following EMV as the criterion for choice will lead to the long-run maximization of profit (or appropriate objective). Subsequent discussions here are accordingly based on the EMV principle.

Utility

In the analysis of Pethow Inc.'s decision problem in chapter 2, we obtained the optimal strategy by calculating the EMV criterion. There are some situations in business where EMV is not likely to be a valid criterion. This arises because EMV implicitly assumes that the individual decision-maker is indifferent to the pattern of risk incorporated in the EMV. A simple example using a gambling situation, purely for the purposes of illustration, will reinforce this point.

Suppose that you, the reader, were offered the following gamble: a coin is tossed once, and if it comes up heads you win $250, but if it comes up tails you lose $125. Should you accept the gamble?

Now if your decision criterion were EMV, the logical thing to do would be to accept the gamble. The skeleton calculation is as follows:

(a) probability of head = probability of tail = ½
(b) expected monetary value of accepting gamble is
    ½×$250–½×$125 = $62.5
(c) expected monetary value of refusing gamble is zero.

Following EMV implies that you will expect to get $250 half of the time and lose $125 half of the time, so that on average the net gain is thus $62.5. However, it is fair to ask whether you would accept the offer. The answer to this question is very much dependent upon your financial position. If the $125 loss has minimal effect on your finances you will probably prefer to gamble, particularly if you feel that the option is likely to be offered on further occasions. But if you only have $250 in the bank and you need it for some urgent bills, then you would probably prefer to avoid the gamble as far as possible. In the latter situation the risk of losing means more to you than the chance of winning, whereas the situation is reversed in the former case. Only when the decision-maker is indifferent to individual losses or gains, and is willing to consider just the overall effect, can it be said that EMV is the appropriate decision criterion. Decision-makers will thus sometimes seek to avoid risk, particularly if there is any possibility whatsoever of incurring a loss. There is, therefore, benefit in determining a more generalized measure which describes how the decision-maker values possible outcomes.

In this chapter we have already seen examples of criteria such as maximin which reflect 'pessimistic' or (risk-avoidance) decision-making attitudes. Utility, a measure specified by most decision analysts, ranks the decision-maker's preference for the outcome in the decision problem at issue. In effect the scale on which the outcomes are measured (very often a monetary one) is translated into a utility scale commonly ranging from 0 to 100 utiles, where a utility of 0 utiles corresponds to the worst outcome in the problem and 100 utiles corresponds to the best outcome. The decision criterion used becomes expected utility and EMV is then a special case of the expected utility criterion (see chapter 9). In addition, in the utility section of the book, we analyse the oil wildcatter's decision problem (see chapters 1, 6 and 9) using the expected utility criterion in contrast to the expected monetary value criterion.

Exercises

1. One of the publications carried by a certain store is the *Autodriver* weekly magazine. The dealer pays 60 cents per copy and sells it for 100 cents per copy. Copies unsold at the end of the week cannot be returned and thus have no value. The probability distribution for demand is shown below:

demand (number per week)	probability
10	0·05
12	0·1
14	0·15
16	0·3
18	0·2
20	0·15
22	0·05.

Use each of the following decision criteria to determine the optimal number of magazines to stock:

(i) Maximin criterion,
(ii) Maximax criterion,
(iii) Minimax regret criterion,
(iv) EMV criterion,
(v) EOL criterion.

Which criterion do you consider the most sensible one for the dealer to adopt? Explain why the EMV and EOL criteria lead to the same decision.

2. You have received an offer to participate in a property development venture provided that you put up $100,000. If planning permission is speedily obtained you will receive a net return of $400,000 but if there are significant delays your investment will effectively be a total loss. If you regard EMV as the appropriate decision criterion, what is the minimum probability you would require for speedy planning permission in order for the investment opportunity to be a desirable one?

3. The managing director of a British aircraft company is reviewing his company's policy in the light of various statements by the Government that they may enter the space race. The Government has made it clear that, if it does enter the race, it will either attempt to land spacecraft on the moon (a) without French collaboration; (b) with French collaboration; or (c) attempt landing on some other, as yet unspecified, planet. In the managing director's judgement the probabilities of these three events are 0·5 for (a), 0·1 for (b), and 0·4 for (c).

If either (a) or (b) is attempted the company can use American experience. To reach some other planet, however, a completely new spacecraft would have to be designed and, depending on government action, this may be done with or without French help at company level.

The managing director believes that his company has three possible strategies, viz:

(A) to remain an aircraft company which would provide them with an expected profit of £2m., regardless of any government decision on (a), (b) or (c);

(B) to invest in building spacecraft capable only of reaching the moon;

(C) to invest in designing and building new spacecraft.

The latter two may be undertaken with or without French collaboration and Table 3.5 shows the various payoffs (in £m.) that may occur:

Table 3.5 Payoffs

	(a)	(b)	(c)
(B)	40	40	−30
(C)	−100	20	80

Assuming your decision to be based on the payoffs, what is the appropriate decision using:

(i) Maximin criterion,
(ii) Minimax regret criterion,
(iii) Assumption of equally likely outcomes,
(iv) Expected value criterion?

Which decision would you prefer and why?

4. A delicatessen in Boston stocks fresh lobsters which are brought in daily from the New Hampshire and Maine coast. From past experience the store has assessed the following probabilities for the daily demand for lobsters:

daily demand (number of lobsters)	probability
10	0·1
20	0·1
30	0·3
40	0·3
50	0·2.

The store buys the lobsters for $10 each and sells them for $18 each. Lobsters are a highly perishable item and it has been found that any lobsters not sold by the end of the day will be effectively spoiled and have no value on the next day. If the delicatessen adopts the EMV criterion how many lobsters should it stock each day? Do you consider that EMV is the most appropriate criterion for the delicatessen?

5. John Brown has been employed by an Estate Agent at a salary of $3,000 a month during the past year. Because Brown's work has been good, the manager is considering offering him one of the three alternative salary arrangements for the next year:

(A) $3,750 a month,
(B) $1,500 a month plus $900 per house sold,
(C) No salary, but $1,500 commission per house sold.

Over the past year Brown has made monthly sales as follows:

0 sales 1 month; 1 sale 2 months; 2 sales 1 month; 3 sales 2 months; 4 sales 1 month; 5 sales 3 months and 6 sales 2 months.

What is the appropriate decision using:

 (i) Minimax regret criterion
(ii) Maximin criterion
(iii) EMV criterion (assume Brown's past sales distribution above is typical for monthly sales in the future)?

*6. An old machine in your factory performs a defined operation on a part being manufactured. The cost of labour plus material for the work performed by this machine comes to 92 cents per piece. You have an order for 50,000 pieces. Before commencing production, you consider the possibility of buying a new machine for $17,000 to replace the old machine, whose scrap value is $1,200. Because of increased speed, the new machine can produce pieces at a unit cost of 60 cents.

With the old machine the proportion of defectives is known to be 0·05. Since the defective rate is a function of both the operator and the machine, you cannot specify precisely the defective rate on the new machine. Based on your experience, the following frequency distribution is arrived at for the proportion defective:

| *proportion defective* | 0·05 | 0·07 | 0·09 | 0·11 | 0·13 |
| *relative frequency* | 0·15 | 0·25 | 0·30 | 0·15 | 0·15. |

What decision would you reach about the new machine and what is the expected opportunity loss of the decision? Assume that the entire cost of the new machine would have to be allocated to the 50,000 pieces.

*7. The Ronics Corporation is a medium-sized manufacturer of electromechanical components for the aerospace industry. It frequently develops components for its major customers and subsequently becomes the sole producer of such items. Quality control difficulties have been encountered for some time with an item designed and produced for Gatson Aircraft. Ronics is Gatson's only supplier for this item, which is sold at $240 per unit.

Gatson uses the item as a component of a major sub-assembly of a missile guidance control system. If the sub-assembly fails a particular test, Gatson knows that the fault lies in the Ronics component. It is then necessary to strip it, regrind the mating surfaces of the Ronics component and reassemble it. By the terms of the contract, there is a $130 penalty charge to Ronics whenever this occurs.

Over the period since Ronics began producing this component for Gatson, it has paid this penalty charge on 30 per cent of the items produced and Ronic's quality control engineer is concerned since there seems to be no improvement in the manufacturing process. Further, no means of identifying the faults before shipment has been found.

One of the engineers suggests that the fault could be rectified if an additional grinding process were introduced at the end of the assembly line at a cost of $30 per unit. The defective rate would then be negligible. At the same time, a new quality control device has come on the market which, when applied to a number of known good and bad units, gives the proportions of positive and negative results shown in Table 3.6.

Table 3.6 Instrument discrimination

	state of component	
instrument reading	good	bad
positive	0·75	0·20
negative	0·25	0·80
totals	1·00	1·00

The cost of using the device is $8 per unit tested, and it is assumed that the nature of the quality control device is such that, for each component, the same result is obtained no matter how many times the particular component is tested.

(i) Should Ronics use the testing device assuming that, in their opinion, there is no loss of goodwill in shipping defective components to Gatson?

(ii) If loss of goodwill is a factor, how might it be taken into account in making the decision as to whether to use the testing device?

Further Reading

B. F. BAIRD, *Introduction to Decision Analysis*, Duxbury, Mass., 1978.

R. V. BROWN, A. S. KAHR and C. PETERSON, *Decision Analysis for the Manager*, Holt, Rinehart & Winston, 1974.

D. V. LINDLEY, *Making Decisions*, Wiley, 1985.

P. G. MOORE, 'The Managers' Struggles with Uncertainty', *Journal of the Royal Statistical Society*, 1977, Series A, vol. 140, pp. 129–65.

H. RAIFFA, *Decision Analysis: Choice Under Uncertainty*, Addison-Wesley, 1974.

4 Decision Trees

Introduction

A businessman contemplating a problem often sees a vista of possible decisions spread over a long period of time and not just one immediate decision. Such a situation is particularly suitable for structuring in terms of a tree diagram. For example, although the initial decision facing an oil executive may involve the location of a new refinery, later decisions might involve whether or not he should increase its capacity, or perhaps build another one. By generalizing our notions about the nature of decision problems we can cope with this situation, and the use of *decision trees* becomes more meaningful and relevant.

A decision tree allows us to break down a big decision problem into a series of smaller problems which can be tackled separately and then combined to provide a solution to the larger problem. The device is especially useful where a more complex situation can be broken down into a sequence of simpler problems which follow one another in some natural order. Many decision problems are sequential in character. For example, an engineer designing and building a plant would probably not have to make one overall decision and then adhere to it completely. He could perhaps make a few initial decisions, leaving others until later in the design and construction process when he has more information available. The entire plant construction operation would then consist of a sequence of interconnected decision problems.

Suppose, as an illustration, that we must initially decide between two actions (call them a_1 and a_2). If we select a_1, then after two years the possible outcomes are b_1, b_2 and b_3. Suppose that outcome b_1 occurs. Then we are faced with a choice of, say, three new actions labelled a'_1, a'_2 and a'_3 respectively, and each of these could lead to one of a number of possible outcomes.

The process of choice of decision followed by outcome could be repeated many times. A similar situation would arise had we decided on action a_2 at the start, rather than action a_1. The whole array of possible sequences of actions and outcomes can be very conveniently represented by the branching diagram shown in Figure 4.1, which is a generalized form of decision tree.

In such a tree the branches split into other branches; these points of split are referred to as *nodes*. The nodes are of two distinct types which can be described by reference to Figure 4.1. The point marked 'start' is a node that gives rise to two branches representing alternative actions or decisions that are at the decision-maker's choice. Consequently, this form of node is referred to as a *decision node* and is commonly represented by a square box. Following branch a_1, we reach a second node from which three branches b_1, b_2 and b_3 emanate. The decision-maker at this node normally has no direct control over which branch is followed (in most cases there is some probabilistic mechanism

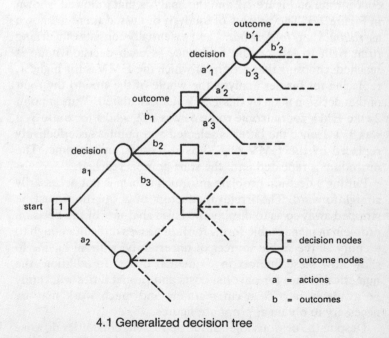

4.1 Generalized decision tree

behind the outcome occurring). The situation is therefore different from a decision node and is referred to as an *outcome or chance event node*, commonly represented by a circle. A typical decision tree therefore consists of a series of branches stemming from nodes of two types, decision and outcome. Moving along the branches from left to right the two types of node alternate, beginning with a decision node and ending with an outcome one. Each branch is labelled: all those springing from a decision node with an action; the others from outcome nodes being described by uncertain outcomes. Such trees can be written down for any decision problem, being particularly useful where the problem can be broken down into a sequence of inter-related sub-problems.

Rev Counter

Reference back to Figures 2.1 and 2.2 in the rev counter case shows two decision trees constructed for that problem. We will concentrate on Figure 2.2 and the analysis that followed, shown in Figure 2.3. The process of analysis discussed there is known as '*rollback*' or '*folding back*' and essentially consists of working from right to left on the tree and, as each decision node is reached, choosing that action for which the EMV is the highest, replacing for further analysis the whole of the tree to the right of that decision node by this EMV just calculated. Thus at point 2a the EMV for outcome route S_4 was 802, whilst for route S_5 it was 830. Hence the latter is selected and point 2a is effectively replaced by the EMV of 830 as if it were an outcome. The procedure is repeated until the start point is reached.

Putting a decision problem into such a form is not necessarily straightforward. The irrelevant factors of a situation must be stripped away so as to display the basic anatomy of the decision problem in manageable form. It often proves difficult enough to identify all the viable sources of uncertainty, without having to show how these interact in sequential order. In addition, the numerical values for payoffs, costs and probabilities will rarely be available in a clear-cut manner, and much work may be necessary to obtain appropriate figures.

Despite the obvious logic of the approach, difficulties do arise in practice. These are of two types: the assessment of values (which is discussed later in chapters 7 to 10), and the structure of the tree itself. In most business problems the decision-maker has quite a range of alternatives and uncertainties to consider. If he is not careful the tree can quickly become a 'bushy mess' with an over-emphasis on the need to take account of every possible eventuality. How should a decision-maker *decompose* the problem, i.e. how should he arrive at a trade-off between the feasibility of analysis and the need to model reality and complexity as far as possible? There is no simple answer to this question. Effective and meaningful description of a problem in the form of a decision tree really depends upon the decision-maker's ability to see the 'wood for the trees' and concentrate upon the essentials of the problem. Though decomposition is more art than science, the decision tree concept can help to reduce the decision-maker's initial confusion. If he sets out all the possible occurrences and choices over the planning horizon, he can try out the feasibility of each of the possible strategies by making rough assessments for probabilities and payoffs. Certain strategies may turn out to be clearly dominated by others and, in this way, several strategy paths and other branches can be pruned out of the tree before a formal analysis is carried out. Also, by testing the sensitivity of his informal analysis to changes in his rough assessments of probabilities and payoffs, he can check again on the feasibility of some of the branches.

Though the task of preparing a decision tree is a difficult one, decision-makers tend to draw more realistic trees once they have had experience and practice with them. Improvement in the diagramming of decision trees, therefore, will be achieved by encouraging decision-makers to use them in all their decision problems. The next section discusses the issues involved in formulating a decision tree for a new plant decision, and illustrates the compromises which must be made in arriving at a final decomposition of the problem in decision tree terms. This is followed by a further example concerned with the analysis of a decision tree relating to an R and D decision.

The Dissolving Chemical Company

The manager of this company has to decide whether to manufacture a new product with an expected market life of ten years and, if so, whether to build a small plant or a large one to manufacture it. The decision hinges partly on the size of the market the company can obtain for the product.

Demand may possibly be high during the first two years but, if many of the initial users find the product unsatisfactory, the demand could then fall to a low level thereafter. High initial demand might alternatively indicate the possibility of a sustained high-volume market. If the demand is initially high, and remains so, and the company finds itself with insufficient capacity within the first two years, competitive products will certainly be introduced by other manufacturers.

If the company initially builds a big plant, it must live with it for the whole ten years, whatever the size of the market demand. If it builds a small plant, there is the option of expanding the plant in two years' time, an option that it would only take up if demand were high during the introductory period. If a small plant is built initially and demand is low during the introductory period, the company will maintain operations in the small plant and make a good profit on the low-volume throughput.

The manager is uncertain as to the action he should take. The company grew rapidly during the early 1970s, keeping pace with the chemical industry generally. The new product, if the market turns out to be large, offers the company a chance to move into a new period of extremely profitable growth. The development department, particularly the development project engineer, is anxious to build the large-scale plant in order to exploit the first major product development the department has had in some years.

The chairman, a principal stockholder, is wary of the possibility of having a large amount of plant capacity lying idle. He favours a smaller initial plant commitment, but recognizes that possible later expansion to meet high-volume demand would, overall, require more investment and be less efficient to operate. The chairman also recognizes that, unless the company moves promptly to fill the demand which develops once the product is on the market, competitors will be tempted to move in with equivalent products.

Various items of information have been obtained, or estimated, by the appropriate managers within the company. This information is summarized as follows:

Marketing Information

The marketing manager suggests a 60 per cent chance of a high demand in the long run and a 40 per cent chance of a low demand, developing initially as follows:

initially high, sustained high demand	60%	
initially high, long-term low demand	10%	} Low 40%
initially low, continuing low demand	30%	
initially low, subsequently high demand	0%	

Annual Income

The management accounting section have put forward the following financial estimates:

(i) A large plant with high market volume would yield $2 m. annually in cash flow (for ten years).

(ii) A large plant with low market volume would yield only $0·2 m. annually because of high fixed costs and inefficiencies.

(iii) A small plant with low market demand would be economical and would yield annual cash income of $0·8 m. per annum.

(iv) A small plant, during an initial period of high demand, would yield $0·9 m. per annum, but this would drop to $0·5 m. per annum in the long run if high demand continued, because of competition from other manufacturers.

(v) If an initial small plant were expanded after two years to meet sustained high demand, it would yield $1·4 m. annually for the remaining eight years and so would be less efficient than a large plant built initially.

(vi) If the small plant were expanded after two years, but high demand were not sustained, the estimated annual cash flow for the remaining eight years would be $0·1 m.

Capital Costs

Estimates obtained from construction companies indicate that a large plant would cost $6 m. to build and put into operation, a small plant would cost $2·6 m. initially, and an additional $4·4 m. if expanded after two years.

The manager must decide now upon his initial action. Should he recommend the company to build or not, and if it is to build, should it build big or small? It will be assumed that the company uses expected monetary value as its criterion for decision. Further, for purposes of simplicity, discounting of the cash flows will be ignored at this stage (equivalent to assuming an interest rate of zero). This does not affect the principles behind the analysis, but reduces the arithmetic involved.

The Analysis of the Problem

If no building is carried out at all, it is clear that the EMV will be zero; no expenditure, no income. Hence the problem is reduced to a consideration of the other courses of action to see whether the best of them gives an EMV which exceeds zero. As a first step, a decision tree is constructed to illustrate the structure of the decision which has to be made. Figure 4.2 gives this. Each path through the tree from the start to the finish (left to right) represents a separate logical possibility. Thus the path AD represents the initial decision 'build big' which is then followed by the outcome of low demand for all ten years. The path AL represents 'abandon project'. The path AEH represents the initial action 'build small', then the outcome of high demand for the first two years, followed by action 'to expand the plant', resulting in the outcome of low demand for the remaining eight years. Similarly for the other paths. A cursory examination of the original data shows that there would be no point in expanding a small initial plant if the demand in the first two years were low. This possibility has accordingly been omitted from path AF.

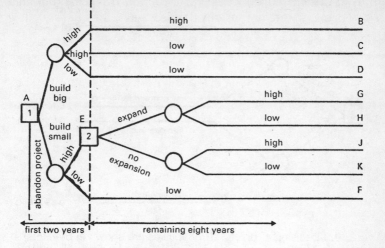

4.2 Basic decision tree

The power of the decision tree diagram lies in the opportunity it affords for the logical analysis of the various alternatives to be studied before making a decision. To analyse the diagram, various quantities are required, but notice first that there are basically two decision points, labelled 1 and 2. If the decision at point 1 is to be examined, it is necessary to know the values to be placed upon the two alternatives that are then open; the value of building a small plant can be assessed only if it is known what value can be expected if decision point 2 is reached. Hence it is necessary to evaluate decision point 2 first, i.e. the diagram is examined from right to left using the rollback principle.

Decision point 2 is shown in more detail in Figure 4.3. The initial data given earlier enable the following deductions to be made for the last eight years if there has been high demand in the first two years:

$$\text{probability of high demand} = \frac{0\cdot6}{0\cdot6+0\cdot1} = 0\cdot86$$

$$\text{probability of low demand} = \frac{0\cdot1}{0\cdot6+0\cdot1} = 0\cdot14.$$

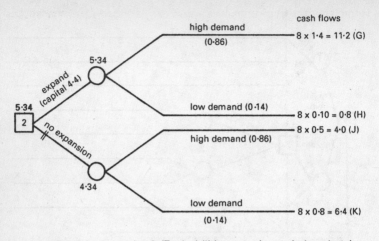

4.3 Decision at point 2 (Probabilities are shown in brackets)

The cash flows for the last eight years of production are entered on Figure 4.3 at the right-hand side. These are calculated from the data given, remembering that the first two years must have given rise to high demand. Thus, if the plant is expanded and there is high demand, the annual cash flow will be $1·4 m., from paragraph (v) giving a total cash flow of $8 \times 1·4$, or $11·2 m. Similarly for the other possibilities.

Hence the expected monetary value (EMV) of expansion at point 2 will be:

$$\text{EMV (expansion)} = 0·86 \times 11·2 + 0·14 \times 0·8 - 4·4$$

$$\begin{array}{ccc} \text{(high} & \text{(low} & \text{(capital} \\ \text{demand)} & \text{demand)} & \text{cost)} \end{array}$$

$$= 9·63 + 0·11 - 4·4 = 5·34.$$

(Note that since 4·4 represents an outlay as opposed to a gain, it is shown as a negative gain. All money is expressed as $m.)

Similarly, for no expansion the financial situation is:

$$\text{EMV (no expansion)} = 0·86 \times 4·0 + 0·14 \times 6·4$$

$$\begin{array}{cc} \text{(high} & \text{(low} \\ \text{demand)} & \text{demand)} \end{array}$$

$$= 3·44 + 0·90 = 4·34.$$

(Note that there is no extra capital expenditure incurred by this action.)

As the former EMV exceeds the latter (5·34 versus 4·34) the decision, if point 2 were reached, would be to expand the plant, on the grounds that expansion gives rise to a higher EMV. The expected value of the decision at that moment of time would be 5·34.

Using this analysis for decision point 2 the original decision tree can now be modified to give the tree shown in Figure 4.4. In this revised figure, decision point 2 has effectively been replaced by an expected monetary value equivalent. The com-

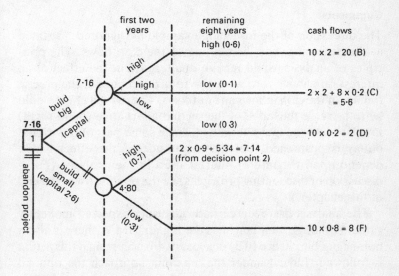

4.4 Decision at point 1 (Probabilities are shown in brackets)

plete tree can now be evaluated on similar lines to those used above. For the decision to build big this gives:

$$\text{EMV (build big)} = \underset{\substack{\text{(high} \\ \text{demand)}}}{0\cdot6\times20} + \underset{\substack{\text{(high/low} \\ \text{demand)}}}{0\cdot1\times5\cdot6} + \underset{\substack{\text{(low} \\ \text{demand)}}}{0\cdot3\times2} - \underset{\substack{\text{(capital} \\ \text{cost)}}}{6}$$

$$= 12 + 0\cdot56 + 0\cdot6 - 6$$

$$= 7\cdot16.$$

Similarly, for the decision to build small:

$$\text{EMV (build small)} = 0.7 \times 7.14 + 0.3 \times 8 - 2.6$$

	(decision	(low	(capital
	point 2)	demand)	cost)

$$= 5.00 + 2.4 - 2.6$$
$$= 4.80.$$

Since the EMV for 'build big' exceeds that for 'build small' (7·16 versus 4·80), the decision would be to build big initially. The expected monetary value of such a decision would be 7·16.

Comments

The discussion of the foregoing example has ignored, as stated at the beginning, any discounting of the cash flows. The principles of analysis would remain unaltered, but the effect of an interest rate above zero would be to take account of the precise timings of the cash inflows and outflows. The overall effect would be to increase the value of the second alternative (build small) in relation to the first alternative, since some part of the capital outlay is postponed, but the magnitude of the effect would depend upon the rate of interest used in the analysis. (For a discussion of discounting principles see the reading list at the end of this chapter.)

The analysis has been carried out using expected monetary value. Although 'build big' has the higher EMV, there is also a non-negligible chance (0·3) of a loss of 4·0 occurring if this action is followed. Indeed under the maximin approach the optimal action is to 'build small' and never expand under any circumstances, giving a profit of at least 3·2. Any other could lead to a loss under certain circumstances. Hence a play-safe policy gives a rather different result from EMV, but such a decision process ignores possibilities such as a gain of 14·0 which could occur under a 'build big' action. For a small firm to whom a possible loss of 4·0 would be disastrous, the maximin approach is probably relevant; for others, the EMV approach would be more appropriate. Moreover, the decision tree concept is valuable for illustrating the structure of problems such as investment decisions and can assist in the evaluation of many commercial opportunities.

Since decision trees, by definition, tackle problems that are sequential in character and have a substantial time span, care must be taken to ensure that, when subsequent decision points on the tree are reached, the conditions have not changed. For example, suppose that the analysis of the Dissolving Chemical Company suggested that a small plant be built initially and expanded after two years if there had been high demand. When this point has been reached, the situation should be re-examined to see that all the conditions are maintained and that meaningful changes have not occurred, e.g. in terms of the options available, or the values to be placed upon the various options. What has happened to date is a sunk cost; what is now at stake is optimizing the future, given the past. The next example raises a number of these further issues in the construction and analysis of a decision tree.

An R and D Decision

The executives of High Precision Electronics (HPE) face an R and D decision about a project to develop a series of sophisticated electronic measurement instruments. Although the measurement instruments will give the firm a competitive edge, the R and D manager has doubts about the firm's technical capability in this new area of electronic measurement. The marketing and sales engineers are pushing him hard, however, because they feel there will be a huge market demand for the instrument if it can be developed and launched within two years. Under the circumstances the R and D manager believes the firm has a 50:50 chance of completing the development within the two-year period. If the two-year period has to be exceeded, the firm will lose money because of incurring extra development costs and forgoing the opportunity of establishing a strong initial market hold. The R and D manager sets down a rough draft of the decision tree, shown in Figure 4.5.

Certain features of this draft need elaboration. First, the decision-maker (R and D manager) has assumed a five-year sales life for the product and a two-year development period. This is

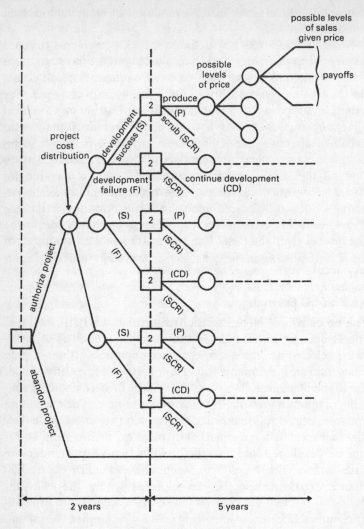

4.5 Initial decision tree

thought to be in line with the views of the marketing staff, though different diagrams could be drawn for other product life-cycle patterns. Second, the whole of the diagram has not been drawn out because the decision-maker quickly realized that the simple decision tree he was hoping to draw was becoming a 'bushy mess' in need of some immediate remedial pruning. The number of chance events considered (i.e. uncertainties in the project's investment cost, final price and sales levels), quite apart from the number of possible strategies, required the assessment of too many probabilities and the valuation of too many end-points in the decision tree. The R and D manager decided to consult with his project engineers and after some discussion he came up with an amended and simpler version of the decision tree (Figure 4.6).

This revised decision tree assumes that project cost and price can be estimated with reasonable certainty. The R and D manager feels that he can put forward a strong case to justify the firm's accurate price estimate for the product because the number of competitors is small, i.e. the market is oligopolistic (has few suppliers). Although cost estimation in this firm is not always very accurate, the project engineers have assured the R and D manager that the cost figure given is the maximum conceivable figure. If the project looks good on this cost basis then it should be undertaken because we are looking at the largest possible cost that the engineers feel will happen, i.e. the extreme point on the probability distribution for cost.

At this stage the R and D manager sits down with his project engineers to estimate the probabilities and monetary valuations necessary for the analysis of the decision tree. Working outwards from the initial decision they estimate the maximum cost for the research as $400,000. Despite protests from a few project engineers, the R and D manager obtains a consensus view that there is a 50:50 chance of completing the development successfully in two years. If the development is a failure, they feel that they might be able to authorize a further sum of $200,000 (in present-value terms) to enable the research team to complete the development work within the next year. The chances of successfully completing the development work in that further year are assessed as a 30:70 chance, on the group view that technical uncertainties uncovered in the first two years would make the task of the research team in 'tying up loose ends' that much more difficult in the third year of development.

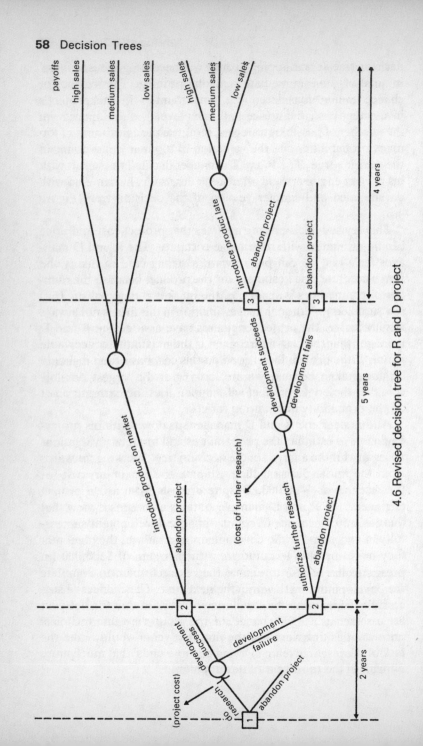

4.6 Revised decision tree for R and D project

It is felt that the project should be abandoned if the development work does not turn out a viable working instrument in three years. Competitive instruments would be nearing market launch by that time, and would reduce the market share which HPE could expect. On the other hand, if they had a product ready to launch at the end of three years the group assess a 1 in 10 chance of getting a discounted payoff (in terms of contribution – net of all taxes and operating costs) of $1·2 m., a 5 in 10 chance of getting a discounted payoff of $600,000 and a 4 in 10 chance of getting a discounted payoff of $300,000.

Further, the payoff prospects would be much better if they could get the product on to the market in two years. In those circumstances, they assess a 2 in 10 chance of a discounted payoff of $1·6 m., a 5 in 10 chance of a discounted payoff of $800,000 and a 3 in 10 chance of a discounted payoff of $400,000.

Finally, if the project had to be abandoned at any time, they would not count as losses any inroads that competitors might make through the introduction of a similar product.

With this information they draw the final decision tree and work out whether or not they should proceed with the development work on the instrument. The decision tree, together with the associated analysis, is presented in Figure 4.7.

The optimal strategy, in terms of the EMV criterion, is to carry out the research and introduce the product, if the development is successful after two years, but to abandon the project if the development work fails in the initial two-year period. The EMV of the optimal strategy in present-value payoff terms is $20,000. This value should be compared with the EMVs of other possible projects before research is authorized and commenced.

Of course, the EMV figure is an expected figure and in practical terms it only gives a guideline for the actual gain that may accrue to the firm. Indeed in any particular situation the actual outcome is unlikely to be exactly equal to the EMV; in the long run, however, consistent application of the EMV principle to a wide range of situations will maximize total expectation, with the actual and expected values coalescing.

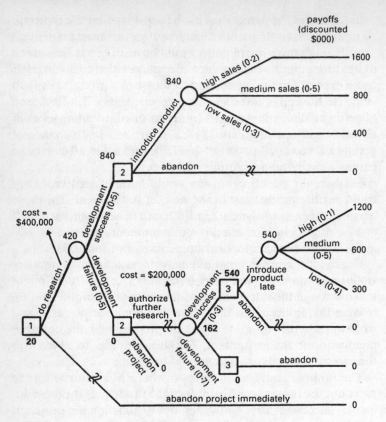

payoffs
(discounted
$000)

high sales (0·2) — 1600

840

medium sales (0·5) — 800

low sales (0·3) — 400

840

introduce product

2 abandon — 0

cost = $400,000

420 development success (0·5)

high (0·1) — 1200

540

medium (0·5) — 600

low (0·4) — 300

do research

development failure (0·5)

cost = $200,000

540

3 introduce product late

abandon — 0

authorize further research

development success (0·3)

162

162

1
20

abandon project — 0

development failure (0·7)

3 abandon — 0
0

abandon project immediately — 0

4.7 Decision tree analysis for HPE

Exercises

1. The United States Atomic Energy Commission (AEC) is undertaking a programme of research and development on advanced reactor projects with the aim of developing second generation nuclear power reactors that consume fuel (uranium ore) more efficiently and have lower generating costs than present nuclear reactors. The main focus of the present AEC programme is on a breeder reactor – the liquid metal cooled, fast-breeder reactor (LMFBR). The LMFBR has the lowest generating costs theoretically possible of present AEC research

efforts. Several projects less costly to research (and less promising in performance) are being developed simultaneously, primarily as backups in the event that the main effort should fail. The Government has, however, already decided to invest in the LMFBR, regardless of the number of backups.

The Bureau of the Budget is faced with a very tight budget in 1988 and would like to know exactly how many backup concepts should be developed as of February 1988. The decision-maker is told that by 1996 it will be possible to ascertain with certainty the success or failure of any of the backup concepts on which research and development is begun immediately. Furthermore, it is considered undesirable to invest in any additional concepts until 1996 when further information will be available.

The decision-maker can invest in not more than three backups now. He also has the option of investing in further backups in 1996, but the total number of backups developed in 1988 and 1996 combined must not exceed three.

How should the decision-maker structure his problem in the form of a decision tree?

2. A young student is deciding whether or not to replace his rather old car with a newer second-hand one. The decision has been prompted by the offer of a car, which has just passed its annual state vehicle inspection test, for $800; while his car has yet to be submitted for the test. However, the offer would be withdrawn in two weeks. If he submits his car for the test he feels that the probability of passing the test is ⅜. Failure on the test can occur through one, and only one, of the following four causes being identified: either the superstructure or the front brakes might be considered unsafe, the two rear tyres might not satisfy the thickness requirement and, finally, the clutch and gearbox may need replacement. Given failure, the relative chances of these four faults occurring are assessed at 40 per cent, 20 per cent, 15 per cent and 25 per cent respectively. Although the cost of such a test is only $3, he feels that within the time available he would only be able to obtain one repeat test if the car fails on the first attempt.

If he decides to repair the fault causing the car's failure at the first test, he estimates the chances for a successful second attempt at the test would be increased by that fault's probability of occurrence. (E.g. if the failure occurred on superstructure, the revised probability of passing is $0.375+0.4 = 0.775$.) The cost of repairs are: $50 for welding the superstructure; $60 for the front brakes; $120 for a new clutch and gearbox and $30 for each new tyre. As a measure of the 'worth' of his car he could sell it for $180 less an allowance of the cost of the repairs identified to date.

Construct a decision tree and use the minimum expected cost as a criterion to suggest a strategy.

3. The purchasing manager of Transatlantic Fruit Ltd (TF) in London has to decide what to do about forward dealings in grapefruit. TF knows of only two cargoes of grapefruit due to be landed in London in January next year, one of 1,000 tons and one of 700 tons. The purchasing manager can purchase either at £200 a ton, but he cannot afford to buy both, and he must sign a contract of purchase immediately. Smaller quantities of up to 400 tons can usually be purchased at any time for immediate delivery, at a price of £220 a ton.

The two big customers for grapefruit are British Produce (BP) and National Fruit (NF). Their requirements for January are 1,000 tons and 600 tons respectively, and they are usually prepared to pay £260 a ton. They will place contracts for the whole of their requirements with a single supplier next month, and TF feels that it stands a good chance of winning these contracts. If TF fails to win either, it can sell small quantities (up to say 100 tons) at £240 a ton, but larger quantities would all have to be sold at clearance prices, probably £200 a ton. TF does not have any space to store grapefruit.

TF's sales manager has been thinking about the chances of winning either the BP or NF contracts. He cannot bid for both because the two companies insist on more than one supplier. If TF purchases the 1,000 ton cargo, the sales manager feels he has a 50:50 chance of winning the BP contract – competition in this market is rarely in terms of price, and great emphasis is placed on security of supply. So if TF buys the large cargo, and bids for the smaller NF contract, the sales manager feels that he has an

80 per cent chance of winning, whereas if he buys the smaller cargo, he has only a 70 per cent chance of winning. It would be possible to buy the small cargo and then bid for the BP contract, relying on day-to-day purchases to make up the difference. But he feels that BP would be rather wary of his ability to supply, and his chance of winning would fall to 40 per cent.

Use a decision tree to show TF's alternative decisions, and to select the optimal strategy.†

4. A builder is offered two plots of land for house building at £40,000 each. If the land does not suffer from subsidence, he would expect to make a net profit of £20,000 on each plot when a house is built on it. However, if there is subsidence, the land is only worth £4,000 so he would make a loss of £36,000 on each plot.

The builder believes that the chance that both plots will suffer from subsidence is 0·2, that one and only one will suffer from subsidence is 0·3, and that neither will suffer is 0·5. He has to decide whether to buy the two plots or not. Alternatively, he could buy one, test it for subsidence, and then decide whether to buy the other plot.

Assuming that the subsidence test is a perfect predictor of subsidence, and that it costs £400 for the test, what action should the builder take?

*5. In 1975 a US manufacturing company, Holgate Inc., was considering the possibility of establishing future markets for their products in another country. Only two countries, Singapore and South Africa, were left for the final selection; other contenders had been rejected as unsuitable on the basis of their performance judged against a set of constraining criteria. Holgate now wished to look at the remaining countries against two further criteria, namely the political stability and remittance laws of the countries concerned. Once committed to a country, Holgate's possible alternatives were the establishment of a manufacturing plant or an agency. The establishment of a plant was a risky project; the

† This exercise is based upon material provided by Mr P. Morris.

granting of export rights to an agency less so, but correspondingly less profitable.

The company's political advisers assessed the probabilities of three levels of political stability – secure, stable and less than stable – as 75 per cent, 20 per cent and 5 per cent for Singapore and 20 per cent, 50 per cent and 30 per cent for South Africa.

In the event of a less than stable political climate Holgate's policy was to reject the establishment of a manufacturing plant as a non-viable alternative. The total cash flows (in $10,000s) for the estimated payoffs of the possible options were discounted at Holgate's 1975 cost of capital to give net present values as shown in Table 4.1.

Table 4.1 Discounted payoffs

| | political climate | | | | | |
| | Singapore | | | South Africa | | |
	secure	stable	less than stable	secure	stable	less than stable
manufacturing:						
favourable laws	540	240	N/A	600	320	N/A
unfavourable laws	280	−36	N/A	280	−120	N/A
agency:						
favourable laws	200	200	200	240	240	240
unfavourable laws	180	180	180	200	200	200

(N/A = not applicable)

The probabilities of the remittance laws proving to be favourable or unfavourable, once Holgate has established a plant or an agency, depends on the country and its political climate and were assessed as follows:

Table 4.2 Remittance probabilities

	political climate					
	Singapore			South Africa		
remittance laws	secure	stable	less than stable	secure	stable	less than stable
favourable	0·7	0·65	0·5	0·5	0·5	0·35
unfavourable	0·3	0·35	0·5	0·5	0·5	0·65

(each column sums to unity)

Draw a decision tree for the problem facing Holgate, and use EMV to analyse the tree.

Further Reading

R. A. BREALEY and S. C. MYERS, *Principles of Corporate Finance*, 2nd edn., McGraw-Hill, 1984.

B. H. P. RIVETT, *Model Building for Decision Analysis*, Wiley, 1980.

J. W. ULVILA and R. V. BROWN, 'Decision Analysis Comes of Age', *Harvard Business Review*, 1982, vol. 60, no. 5, pp. 130–41.

G. E. WELLS, 'The Use of Decision Analysis in Imperial Group', *Journal of the Operational Research Society*, 1982, vol. 33, pp. 313–18.

5 The Synthesis of Information

Introduction

A procedure was developed in part IV of the rev counter case (chapter 2) whereby *prior probabilities* formulated by the marketing manager and his staff, were reviewed and revised in the light of additional information to form revised or *posterior probabilities*. The latter were then incorporated in the analysis of the decision process under study. This illustrates a general principle involving Bayes's theorem by which additional information can be incorporated formally into the decision analysis approach.

For example, in weather forecasting the forecaster concerned makes an initial assessment of tomorrow's weather early in the morning of the preceding day. During the day further information becomes available from weather stations, ships, aircraft etc., which is then used to revise the forecast. The consequence is that the forecast of Saturday's weather made at 6 p.m. on Friday will often be different from that made at 6 a.m. on Friday. Both may differ from what actually happens, but we would expect that the proportion of correct forecasts over a long period would be higher for those made at 6 p.m. than for those made at 6 a.m. The latest forecasts in turn will be more useful for those who have to make decisions on the forecasts – we have all heard of the agonizing conferences that General Eisenhower held with his meteorologists prior to D-Day in 1944.

The natural reaction of most of us when faced with making a decision with uncertainty present is to try to remove those elements of uncertainty by attempting to find out something about the true state of affairs. Knowledge is, in general, assumed to be beneficial to the making of a decision. Complete knowledge is certainly a way out of all difficulties, provided we are clear as to the criteria we would use for decisions, but it is rarely practicable where decisions involve consideration of the future. Thus a Stock Market investor trying to decide whether or not to invest in a particular stock or share would not know for certain whether the stock was going to appreciate or not. Again, cost may be a powerful deterrent to the removal of uncertainty; it may simply be too expensive to find out the complete truth. An engineer designing a plant will not often be able to build a trial plant, but may think it useful to build a prototype to resolve some of the uncertainties in the design problem. A prototype will, however, sometimes cost so much that it is better to build the plant in a fairly flexible manner and learn the form of any required modifications through experience.

Thus while it is usually desirable to seek the removal of all uncertainty from a problem, it is commonly not a practicable aim. There is often, however, a partial solution available to us in attempting to remove part of the uncertainty, namely to obtain some relevant additional information about the problem. Thus, the investor may consult his investment analyst, who is presumably more knowledgeable than the investor, as to expectations concerning the particular stock in question. The engineer, thwarted of his prototype, may obtain some information from calculations of the likely behaviour of the system, or from visits of inspection to similar plants. The business executive considering the launch of a modified and improved product may conduct some market research to determine the likely sales volume that will be achieved. In these situations we will still not be able to determine the true situation, but at least in general we will be more knowledgeable than we would have been without the information. Combining this extra information with the prior probabilities to form revised probabilities, the latter are then referred to as posterior probabilities, and provide us with a revised basis on which to make our decision.

Posterior Probabilities

Assume that we have available to us the prior probabilities of occurrence of certain alternative outcomes. Some relevant experiment is now performed, or sample investigation carried out, and the resultant information is known to us. What are now

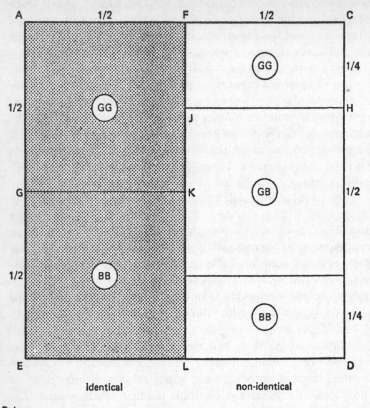

B=boy
G=girl

5.1 Composition of twin population

the posterior probabilities corresponding to the original prior probabilities of the various outcomes? A simple illustration concerned with the sex of twins will help to make the position clear.

First, we are asked to accept that twins are of two types, identical (I) and non-identical (N), and that in the population as a whole there are 50 per cent of each type. Second, it is known that identical twins are always of the same sex, with a 50 per cent chance of each sex occurring, while for non-identical twins the sex of each child has an independent 50:50 chance of being male or female. The mix that would result from these suppositions is shown pictorially in Figure 5.1. Identical twins, half of the total, occupy the left-hand shaded portion, non-identical twins the right-hand unshaded portion. Each of these two blocks is further sub-divided by the various sex combinations of the twins concerned. For example, the prior probability that a pair of twins chosen at random are both girls is given by the area ACHJKG or $\frac{1}{2} \times \frac{1}{2} + \frac{1}{2} \times \frac{1}{4} = \frac{3}{8}$. Again, the chance that a randomly chosen pair of twins are identical is given by the area AFLE, or $\frac{1}{2}$. Such probabilities are referred to as prior probabilities.

Imagine that, having selected a pair of twins at random from the population, you are given the additional information that both of the twins are known to be girls. What is now the revised (or posterior) probability that the twins form an identical pair? It seems unlikely that you would still assign equal probabilities to the twins being identical or non-identical, since more identical sets of twins have two girls than do non-identical sets of twins. The argument, therefore, proceeds as follows:

Of all the twins in the population, the proportions that were both girls can be categorized into subsets as follows in Table 5.1:

Table 5.1 Probabilities of twin girls

both girls and non-identical	Area FCHJ	$\frac{1}{2} \times \frac{1}{4} = \frac{1}{8}$
both girls and identical	Area AFKG	$\frac{1}{2} \times \frac{1}{2} = \frac{1}{4}$
both girls and either non-identical or identical	Area ACHJKG	$\frac{1}{2} \times \frac{1}{4} + \frac{1}{2} \times \frac{1}{2} = \frac{3}{8}$

Hence, the probability that the twins were identical, given that we know they are both girls, is the ratio of the two areas AFKG and ACHJKG shown in Figure 5.1, or $\frac{1}{4} / \frac{3}{8} = \frac{2}{3}$.

The calculations can also be laid out in the tabular form shown in Table 5.2. The outcomes on which interest is concentrated, namely identical or non-identical, are listed in column (1), their original prior probabilities being given in column (2). The prior probabilities in this column sum to unity, indicating that the events in column 1 are mutually exclusive and the only ones possible. Column (3) shows, first, the probability (or likelihood) of two girls, given that they were identical twins, and, second, the corresponding probability (or likelihood) given that they were non-identical twins. The values can be taken directly from Figure 5.1

Table 5.2 Calculation of posterior probabilities

	prior probabilities		revised probabilities	
event of interest (1)	*probability of event in (1)* (2)	*probability of two girls given (1)* (3)	*joint probability of two girls with event in (1)* (4) = (2)×(3)	*probability of event in (1) given two girls* (5) = (4)÷Σ(4)
identical	½	½	¼	⅔
non-identical	½	¼	⅛	⅓
totals	1	—	⅜	1

The basic theory of probability can now be used to compute revised probabilities from the two sets of basic probabilities, given in columns (2) and (3), the work being shown in the last two columns of Table 5.2.

First, the multiplication rule of probability is used to compute the joint probabilities of 'two girls and identical' and 'two girls and non-identical', shown in column (4). The addition rule of probability is similarly used to sum column (4) to give the overall prior probability of two girls; this is the ⅜ total given at the foot of column (4). Finally, column (5) uses the definition of conditional probability to compute the revised or posterior probabilities as the ratio of the appropriate probability in column (4) to the total of column (4). The two posterior probabilities sum to unity. Note that the probabilities in column (3) do not necessarily sum to unity and the total has no significance in the present context.

Bayes's Theorem

The preceding deductions regarding the probabilities of twins provide a special case of the application of Bayes's theorem, named after Thomas Bayes, a Fellow of the Royal Society of

London, who first formulated it in about 1760. The general form of the theorem, which is not proved here, is as follows:

If $E_i(i = 1, 2 \ldots r)$ are r mutually exclusive and the only possible results, such that an event F can occur only if one of these r events happens, then the probability that E_j happens when F is known to have occurred is:

$$P(E_j|F) = P(E_j)P(F|E_j) \bigg/ \sum_{i=1}^{r} P(E_i)P(F|E_i)$$

where

$P(E_i)$ represents the prior probability of event E_i.

$P(F/E_i)$ represents the conditional probability that outcome F occurs, given that event E_i has occurred.

$P(E_i/F)$ represents the posterior probability of event E_i, given that event F has occurred.

Three examples, of differing complexity, of the application of this theorem are given.

Example 1

The Whizzer Company is launching a new car. The marketing executive assigns a subjective probability of 0·9 to the event 'car is superior to its immediate competitor'. However, he is not sure if his assessment is correct because of his total commitment to, and enthusiasm for, the new car. He engages a reputable market research company to carry out a quick survey to confirm or reject his initial assessment. The market research executive tells his client that the survey will only be 80 per cent reliable because of the potential extent of measurement and sampling errors. In operational terms, 80 per cent reliability means that the survey will indicate either superiority or inferiority of the new car so that, if the new car is really superior, the survey will indicate superiority with probability of 0·8 and, similarly, if the car is really inferior the survey will indicate inferiority with probability 0·8. The marketing executive wants the market research firm to tell him what his revised probability assessment for the event 'car is superior to its immediate competitor' should be after completion of the survey.

In terms of Bayes's theorem we define E_1 as event 'new car is superior to its immediate competitor' and the event E_2 to denote 'new car is inferior to its immediate competitor'. Then we have:

$$P(E_1) = 0.9, \qquad P(E_2) = 0.1.$$

Let F denote the event 'market research indicates new car is superior to its immediate competitor'. Then the conditional probabilities are:

$$P(F|E_1) = 0.8, \qquad P(F|E_2) = 0.2,$$

and Bayes's theorem gives us

$$P(E_1|F) = \frac{P(E_1)P(F|E_1)}{P(E_1)P(F|E_1) + P(E_2)P(F|E_2)}$$

$$= \frac{0.9 \times 0.8}{0.9 \times 0.8 + 0.1 \times 0.2} = 0.97.$$

From this final figure of 0.97 we can say that, if the market research findings indicate that the new car is superior, the marketing director's posterior assessment for the probability of the new car being superior should be 0.97, i.e. very close to certainty.

The reader is left to work out that the posterior probability of the new car being superior, if the market research suggests it is not superior, is equal to 0.69, i.e. somewhat lower than the original 0.9.

Example 2

A dealer has purchased a batch of machine parts from a manufacturer. He knows that the parts are produced by either machine A or machine B, but he does not know which machine has manufactured the particular batch he has purchased. From past experience, he believes that if machine A produced the parts 15 per cent will be defective, while if machine B produced them 25 per cent will be defective. The manufacturer has reported to him that 60 per cent of batches come from machine A and 40 per cent from machine B. If the dealer selects a random sample of three parts from the batch and finds none defective, what is the (posterior) probability that the batch was produced by machine A?

Let E_1 and E_2 represent manufacture on each of the two machines and F the event that, with a random sample of three parts, no defectives are found. From the data given, the following probabilities can be directly deduced:

(i) The prior probabilities that the two particular machines would give rise to the batch purchased are

$$P(E_1) = 0 \cdot 6, \qquad P(E_2) = 0 \cdot 4.$$

(ii) The probabilities, for each machine in turn, that in a random sample of three items drawn from a batch produced by that machine, none will be found defective are

$$P(F|E_1) = (1 - 0 \cdot 15)^3 = 0 \cdot 85^3,$$
$$P(F|E_2) = (1 - 0 \cdot 25)^3 = 0 \cdot 75^3.$$

Hence

$$P(E_1|F) = \frac{P(E_1)P(F|E_1)}{P(E_1)P(F|E_1) + P(E_2)P(F|E_2)}$$
$$= \frac{0 \cdot 6 \times 0 \cdot 85^3}{0 \cdot 6 \times 0 \cdot 85^3 + 0 \cdot 4 \times 0 \cdot 75^3} = 0 \cdot 686.$$

Note that the incorporation of the sample information has lifted the initial prior probability for machine A of $0 \cdot 6$ to a posterior probability of $0 \cdot 686$. This is clearly in the right direction, since the sample result is more suggestive of machine A than of machine B.

The reader is left to verify that the posterior probability that the batch was produced by machine B is $0 \cdot 314$ and hence that the two posterior probabilities sum to unity.

Example 3

A bookclub sells paperback reprints of hardback scientific books by mail order to its registered members. The bookclub has been offered the paperback rights to a hardback book, *Analogue Business Controls* (ABC), and will make a profit provided that it sells copies at the normal bookclub price to more than 4,000 of its 100,000 members. Past experience suggests that (in a simplified form) the sales of this kind of book are likely to fall into one of three categories with the prior probabilities shown in Table 5.3.

Table 5.3 Bookclub selling probabilities

category (event)		proportion of members purchasing (p_1)	prior probability
low sales	E_1	0·01	0·04
medium sales	E_2	0·03	0·30
high sales	E_3	0·05	0·66

Event E_3 would lead to financial success, while events E_1 and E_2 would lead to financial loss. The publisher, not entirely satisfied with his prior chance of 0·66 of financial success, decides to test the market. He does this by sending out an advance card to 100 of his members, randomly selected from his membership list, asking them if they wish to place an order for the book. (Any orders received can be met, even if the publisher does not go ahead with the paperback edition, by supplying hardback copies at a small loss.) Of the 100 cards sent out, six result in an order being placed for ABC. What is now the revised posterior probability of E_3 (the only financially rewarding event)?

Clearly, we cannot rule out E_1 and E_2 on the grounds that, although the observed result is most consistent with E_3, there is still some chance that it could have arisen from an E_1 or E_2 situation. But the result will, nevertheless, affect the prior probabilities originally established.

The prior probabilities are:

$$P(E_1) = 0·04, \qquad P(E_2) = 0·30, \qquad P(E_3) = 0·66,$$

which sum to unity. The probabilities of obtaining the sample information for each of the three events can be found from the binomial theorem in probability as follows (readers unfamiliar with this theorem should pass to the results):

$$P(F|E_1) = \binom{100}{6}(0{\cdot}01)^6(0{\cdot}99)^{94} \qquad \text{since } p_1 = 0{\cdot}01;$$

$$P(F|E_2) = \binom{100}{6}(0{\cdot}03)^6(0{\cdot}97)^{94} \qquad \text{since } p_2 = 0{\cdot}03;$$

$$P(F|E_3) = \binom{100}{6}(0{\cdot}05)^6(0{\cdot}95)^{94} \qquad \text{since } p_3 = 0{\cdot}05.$$

Hence,

$$P(E_3|F) = \frac{P(E_3)P(F|E_3)}{P(E_1)P(F|E_1)+P(E_2)P(F|E_2)+P(E_3)P(F|E_3)}$$

$$= \frac{0{\cdot}66\binom{100}{6}(0{\cdot}05)^6(0{\cdot}95)^{94}}{0{\cdot}04\binom{100}{6}(0{\cdot}01)^6(0{\cdot}99)^{94}+0{\cdot}30\binom{100}{6}(0{\cdot}03)^6(0{\cdot}97)^{94}+0{\cdot}66\binom{100}{6}(0{\cdot}05)^6(0{\cdot}95)^{94}}$$

$$= 0{\cdot}868.$$

This is considerably higher than the original prior probability of 0·66, and would incline the publisher more firmly in favour of undertaking the paperback venture. By a similar calculation $P(E_1|F) = 0{\cdot}000$ (to three decimal places) and $P(E_2|F) = 0{\cdot}132$. These three posterior probabilities sum to unity.

It is worthwhile exploring this example further to illustrate the value of yet more information in terms of the effect it would have on the posterior probabilities. Suppose that the publisher had sent out 200 cards and twelve came back placing an order for ABC. The percentage of successful response is the same as before, namely 6 per cent, but the number of members sampled is doubled, at 200 in place of 100. How would this sample investigation have affected the posterior probabilities? We carry out the calculations as before, using the same prior probabilities, only in this instance the probabilities $P(F|E_i)$ will represent the probability that in a sample of 200 members, each of whom has a probability p_1 of ordering, there are exactly twelve orders.

Calculation gives:

$$P(F|E_1) = 0\cdot0000;$$
$$P(F|E_2) = 0\cdot0113;$$
$$P(F|E_3) = 0\cdot0948;$$

and then, using Bayes's theorem again, the corresponding posterior probabilities are:

$$P(E_1|F) = 0\cdot000;$$
$$P(E_2|F) = 0\cdot051;$$
$$P(E_3|F) = 0\cdot949.$$

Thus, the posterior probability of E_3, the profitable category, has risen still further. This is surely to be expected, since there is now even more sample information pointing to the veracity of E_3. Indeed, as the amount of sample information available grows, the prior probabilities become of less and less importance and the sample information becomes dominant.

Value of Information

The kind of analysis that was carried out in part IV of the rev counter case in chapter 2 has wide applicability. As demonstrated in example 3 above, the quantity of information processed is very relevant and, since quantity is generally linked to cost, we have given ourselves a very powerful tool with which to examine the amount of money worth spending on gathering extra information. Generally speaking one would spend $M on gathering information provided that the difference in the expected monetary value of the optimal decision with the $M spent exceeds the expected monetary value of the optimal decision without spending the $M, by more than $M. Now it is well recognized that the relative value of information is not linear, greater proportionate value accruing from the earlier

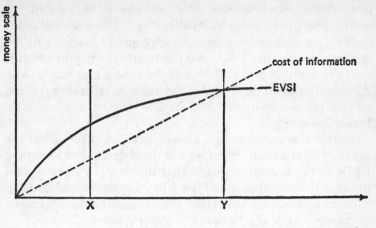

5.2 Optimum value of information

increments of expenditure on information. Figure 5.2 shows a typical situation where the unbroken line represents the value of the information in terms of the extra expected gain achieved from adopting the optimal decision, and the broken line represents the cost of obtaining that information. The difference between the two lines represents the net expected gain from the information. This difference rises at first to some maximum at around point X and then decreases until finally it becomes zero, at point Y, and then negative. Hence, for any additional information obtained beyond point X, the marginal gain in expected value from the optimal decision falls short of the marginal extra cost of the information. It is only by the use of Bayes's theorem that such an analysis can be made and point X located.

Return for a moment to review the analysis in part IV of the rev counter case in chapter 2. In that situation Pethow is evaluating the worth of hiring a consultant at a cost of 10 (or $10,000) in order to obtain additional information about the eventual market outcome, rise or fall. Using the graphical analysis of Figure

2.5 revised probabilities for the outcomes, rise or fall, are calculated conditional upon the indication about the state of the market likely to be given by the consultant. These revised probabilities are then entered into the appropriate branches of the decision tree and the EMV that results from hiring the consultant is analysed in Figure 2.6 using the rollback principle. The numerical value of the EMV of the 'consultant' branch is 379·6 and this must be compared with the EMV of the 'no consultant' branch, namely 372.

At this stage we can use certain basic concepts about the worth of information. First, we call the difference between the EMV of the optimal decision after information gathering (in this case the consultant) and the EMV of the optimal decision without information collection the *expected value of sample information* (EVSI). In the rev counter situation:

$$EVSI = 379·6 - 372 = 7·6.$$

Thus 7·6 is the expected benefit which results from the process of acquiring information. Clearly, this expected benefit has to be traded-off against the cost of the information in order to obtain the *expected net gain from sample information* (ENGSI). Formally, ENGSI = EVSI−cost of information, so that

$$ENGSI = 7·6 - 10·0 = -2·4.$$

This is a negative quantity in this instance which means that the information is not worthwhile in cost-benefit terms, and that we are beyond point Y in terms of the graph shown in Figure 5.2.

Summarizing, the consultant is nearly always an imperfect forecaster who provides us with partial information about the eventual market outcome. Perfect information is rarely obtainable but, as a theoretical concept, the principle of perfect information helps us to set upper limits to the amount that might be worth spending on information collection.

Consider again the one-year decision problem of Pethow examined extensively in parts I and IV of the rev counter case. The optimum EMV for the decision problem without the consultant was obtained as 372 for strategy S_2, using the payoff matrix given again in Table 5.4.

Table 5.4 Payoff matrix for rev counter

	demands	
	E_1	E_2
	5 per cent fall	
	(probability)	15 per cent rise
actions	(0·4)	(0·6)
S_1	260	440
S_2	300	420
S_3	300	340

We now introduce the concept of the EMV under certainty (EMVUC). If the decision-maker at Pethow knew with certainty that the market outcome was going to be a 5 per cent fall situation, then he would go for either S_2 or S_3 with a payoff of 300. On the other hand, if it was known with certainty that a 15 per cent sales rise was going to occur, then he would opt for S_1 with a payoff of 440. The best information we currently have about the outcomes rise (15 per cent) or fall (5 per cent) are given by the prior probabilities, 0·6 and 0·4 respectively.

In these circumstances $EMVUC = 0·6 \times 440 + 0·4 \times 300$
$$= 264 + 120$$
$$= 384,$$

since on 60 per cent of occasions he would obtain 440 and on 40 per cent of occasions 300. Finally, we define the *expected value of perfect information* (EVPI) as being equal to the difference between EMVUC and the EMV of the optimal decision without further information. Thus $EVPI = EMVUC - EMV$ (optimal current decision), i.e.

$$EVPI = 384 - 372 = 12.$$

This quantity can be interpreted as the maximum that it would be worth paying under any circumstances for further information on the sales level. The next example gives another illustration of the value of information concept.

A Product Launch

This problem relates to the possible launch of a new product. Simplifications have been made to reduce the length of the discussion, but they do not affect the general principles concerned. A company has developed a new product and, after some preliminary consumer studies, the marketing executive reviews the situation by making some estimates of profit and loss resulting from the achievement of differing market share levels of 10 per cent or 2 per cent respectively. The costs involved in dropping the product are put at zero, on the argument that development costs for the new product are sunk and are not relevant for current decision-making. Table 5.5 gives the marketing executive's prior estimates of the chances of achieving the various levels of market share, at the price proposed.

Table 5.5 Payoffs for initial decision ($000)

	market share levels	
decisions	10 per cent (0·7 chance)	2 per cent (0·3 chance)
launch product	500	−250
drop product	0	0

An immediate prior analysis of the decision problem gives:

$$\text{EMV (launch)} = 500 \times 0\cdot7 - 250 \times 0\cdot3 = 275$$

whilst

$$\text{EMV (drop)} = 0.$$

Hence, on the basis of selecting the action with the higher EMV, the decision would be to launch the product. Notice, however, that there is still a 30 per cent chance that launch will, with hindsight, turn out to have been the wrong decision. An important question to ask after such analysis, commonly referred to as a *prior analysis*, is whether it is worthwhile to collect some additional market research information that will throw further light upon the probability assessments for market share before taking the final decision. To determine the benefits of such research we compare the expected monetary value of what appears to be the optimum decision after research, less the cost of the research, with the expected monetary value of the apparently best act before research. If the first expected net gain after research is greater than the latter (and positive), then the market research information is economically worthwhile.

To set limits on the value of the research, it is useful to consider first of all what would happen with 'perfect information'. The expected profit under conditions of certainty is that which would be realized if the best decision is taken for each market share that actually materializes. Thus, if a market share of 10 per cent is forecast, the optimum decision would be to introduce the new product; if a 2 per cent market share is forecast, the optimum decision would be to drop the product. So, if you always made the best decision on perfect information, you would launch 70 per cent of the time; the expected monetary value of the optimum decision under these conditions of perfect certainty would therefore be:

$$EMVUC = 0.7 \times 500 + 0.3 \times 0 = 350.$$

The difference of 350−275 or 75, that is between the expected value of the optimum decision under conditions of perfect certainty and the EMV for the optimum decision before any research (based on the subjective probabilities), is the expected value of perfect information, EVPI. The result immediately rules out the spending of more than 75, even for a research project which would predict the subsequent market share perfectly.

Suppose now that a specific market research proposal at a cost of 10 is offered to the marketing manager. The proposal offers the option of either test marketing the product or collecting information from consumer panels. After some discussion, the test marketing option seems more favourable, because it can be done extremely quickly. The manager sets out to evaluate the worth of this particular proposal. The basic rule is that the gain in expected monetary value of the optimum decision after the research, over that prevailing before the research, must at least be equal to the cost of that research if it is to be worthwhile.

The research company says that the market test it is going to

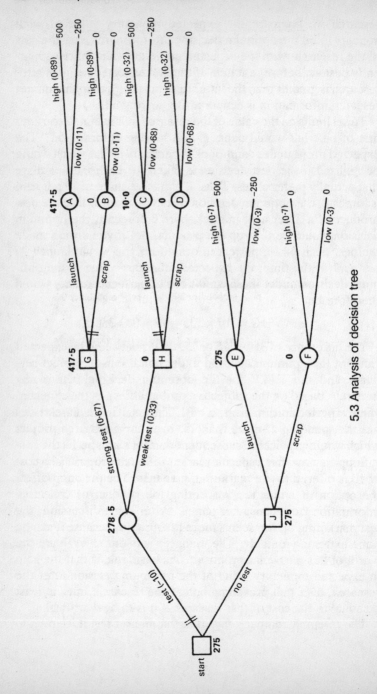

5.3 Analysis of decision tree

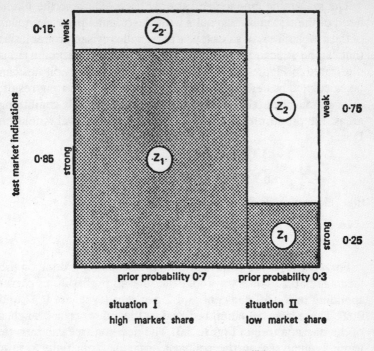

5.4 Combinations of probabilities

carry out will indicate either a high market share (high test) or a low market share (low test). This indication will not, however, be completely reliable in its linkage to 10 per cent and 2 per cent market shares. This is shown in Table 5.6, which should be read horizontally. Figure 5.3 shows the structure of the appropriate decision tree, with the payoffs shown together with the probabilities for the 'no test' branch.

Table 5.6 Effect of market research information

| | test market indication | | |
sales level	strong	weak	totals
high (10 per cent)	0·85	0·15	1·00
low (2 per cent)	0·25	0·75	1·00

The marketing manager must now try to combine the likelihood of the test market results with the original prior estimates of the probabilities of sales levels to provide revised probabilities that can be attached to the two sales levels. The method used is illustrated in Figure 5.4. The required revised probabilities can be calculated as before. If the test market gives a strong result, then we must be in the shaded areas of Figure 5.4. By combining areas, the proportion relating to the 10 per cent level (situation I) is:

$$\frac{0\cdot7\times0\cdot85}{0\cdot7\times0\cdot85+0\cdot25\times0\cdot3}=0\cdot89;$$

that relating to the 2 per cent level (situation II) will be:

$$\frac{0\cdot25\times0\cdot3}{0\cdot7\times0\cdot85+0\cdot25\times0\cdot3}=0\cdot11.$$

For weak research results, a similar calculation is done on the unshaded area. This shows that the revised probabilities corresponding to the 10 per cent and 2 per cent levels are $0\cdot32$ and $0\cdot68$. These have been entered against the appropriate branches of the decision tree in Figure 5.3. The decision tree can now be formally analysed on the rollback principle from right to left. This indicates that the $EVSI = 278\cdot5-275 = 3\cdot5$. Thus, $ENGSI = 3\cdot5-10 = -6\cdot5$ and demonstrates that the research proposal is not worthwhile. Of course this result does not imply that no test market survey is worthwhile. If a survey was a better predictor of the situation it might be worth doing, depending upon the precise relationship between the accuracy expected from the market research and the cost involved.

Exercises

1. You have an opportunity to buy a copper mine for \$C. As a first step in deciding whether or not to make the purchase, the problem is considered in the following simplified manner.

Calculations show that, if the proportion of copper (P) in the ore is greater than P_0, there will be a clear profit of \$A. On the other hand, if it is not above P_0, the purchase money will be lost. To help you decide whether to purchase or not, a test on samples of the ore is to be made. It is known from past experience that, if the proportion of copper is above P_0, then the test will indicate that it is with probability 0·95 and, if the proportion of copper is not above P_0, the test will indicate that it is not with probability 0·9.

(i) Define the possible actions, the possible outcomes and the loss as a function of P.

(ii) Determine the optimum decision using (a) maximin gain and (b) minimax regret as the appropriate criteria. Comment on the suitability of these principles of choice for this problem.

(iii) Find an appropriate decision rule where $C = A$, and the prior probability that the proportion of copper in the ore is above P_0 is assessed at 0·2.

2. A complex airborne navigating system incorporates a sub-assembly which unrolls a map of the flight plan synchronously with the movement of the aeroplane. This sub-assembly is bought on very good terms from a subcontractor, but is not always in perfect adjustment on delivery. The sub-assemblies can be readjusted on delivery to guarantee accuracy at a cost of $220 per sub-assembly. It is not, however, possible to distinguish visually those assemblies that need adjustment.

Alternatively, the sub-assemblies can each be tested electronically to see if they need adjustment at a cost of $48 per sub-assembly tested. Past experience shows that about 40 per cent of those supplied are defective; the probability of the test indicating a bad adjustment when the sub-assembly is faulty is 0·7, while the probability that the test indicates a good adjustment when the sub-assembly is properly adjusted is 0·8. If the adjustment is not made and the sub-assembly is found to be faulty when the system has its final check, the cost of subsequent rectification will be $600.

Draw up a decision tree to show the alternatives open to the purchaser and use it to determine his appropriate course of action.

3. The buyer of a liquor store is given the choice of three barrels of wine – A, B or C – when making a purchase of a single barrel.

He wishes to choose the barrel of best quality for subsequent bottling on his premises. If the barrels are ranked in true order of quality, his loss function will be

$$\text{loss} = (\text{rank of chosen barrel}) - 1.$$

The buyer employs two expert wine-tasters who independently sample the barrels and rank them in order of quality. It can be assumed that each taster gives the correct order with probability $\frac{2}{5}$, with probability $\frac{1}{5}$ giving each of the two orderings, which differ from the true order by the interchange of a single neighbouring pair, and giving with probability $\frac{1}{15}$ each of the three remaining erroneous orderings. (Thus, for example, if the true order is BCA, this is chosen with probability $\frac{2}{5}$, CBA and BAC are each chosen with probability $\frac{1}{5}$, while CAB, ACB and ABC are each chosen with probability $\frac{1}{15}$.)

The expert tasters nominate the orders BAC and ACB. Using a prior distribution which gives probability $\frac{1}{6}$ to each of the six possible orders of quality, find the posterior distribution of the true order. Hence, find an appropriate rule which indicates the barrel the buyer should choose.

4. An insurance company in Hartford, Connecticut, classifies drivers in class A (good risks), class B (medium risks) and class C (poor risks). The company believes that class A risks constitute 30 per cent of the drivers who apply for insurance, class B 50 per cent and class C 20 per cent. The probability that a class A driver has an accident in any twelve-month period is 0·01; for a class B driver the probability is 0·03; and for a class C driver it is 0·1. Assume that the probability of more than one accident in a year is negligible.

(i) Mr David Jones takes out an insurance policy and within 12 months he has an accident. What is the probability that he is a class C risk?

(ii) If a policyholder goes five years without an accident, and we assume years to be statistically independent, what is the probability that he belongs to class A?

5. The Great European Hotel Association is about to poll its members whether or not the association should accept a certain credit card. The secretary of the association attaches the probabilities shown in Table 5.7 below to various percentages of members in favour. (The continuous distribution here is approximated by four discrete values.)

Table 5.7 Probabilities in favour

percentage of member hotels in favour	prior probability of exactly that percentage in favour
30	0·1
40	0·3
50	0·4
60	0·2

(i) On this information, would you as secretary expect a vote for the credit card to be carried?

(ii) Suppose a random sample of fifteen hotels were drawn and eight were in favour and seven opposed. What probabilities would you now assign to the various percentage of hotels in favour?

(iii) After the sample in (ii) has been taken, what is the expected proportion of hotels in favour?

6. A simplified version of the way a law relating to drunken driving operates in a number of countries is as follows. A motorist can be stopped by a policeman and asked to take a breath test. If this is negative, no further action ensues. If the test is positive the motorist is taken to a police station where a second test based on a blood test is given. If this second test is negative the motorist is released, if positive the motorist is automatically charged and convicted of drunken driving.

The two tests concerned are not entirely precise in their operation and their accuracy has been investigated with a large-scale controlled trial on a probabilistic basis with the results shown in Table 5.8 below.

Table 5.8 Probabilities of test results

| test | motorist's true state | | test result |
	drunk	sober	
first test	0·8 ⎫ ⎬ 1·0 0·2 ⎭	0·2 ⎫ ⎬ 1·0 0·8 ⎭	+ —
second test	0·9 ⎫ ⎬ 1·0 0·1 ⎭	0·05 ⎫ ⎬ 1·0 0·95 ⎭	+ —

(i) What is the probability that a motorist stopped who is in reality drunk will be convicted under this law? Conversely, what is the probability that a motorist who is stopped and is in reality sober will be convicted?

(ii) Past information suggests that the proportion, P, of those stopped for the first test who are in reality drunk is 0·6. A motorist is stopped for testing and subsequently convicted. What is the probability that he was actually drunk? What is the probability that he was sober? Comment on how the latter probability varies with changes in P.

7. Candida Foods must determine whether or not to market a new cake mix. The manager concerned must also decide whether to conduct a consumer test marketing programme that would cost $50,000. If the mix is successful, Candida's profits will increase by $2m.; if the mix fails, the company will lose $500,000. To abandon marketing the product will not affect profits. The cake mix is considered to have a 60 per cent chance of success without testing. The assumed probability for a favourable test marketing result is 50 per cent. Given a favourable test result, the chance of product success is judged to be 85 per cent. However, if the test results are unfavourable, the probability for the product's success is judged to be only 35 per cent.

Construct an appropriate decision tree and determine the optimal course of action under the EMV principle.

*8. Two out of three prisoners, A, B and C, are to be executed. C does not know which two will be chosen, and hence evaluates his own probability of remaining alive as ⅓. He subsequently reasons that, since it is common knowledge that at least one of A and B must die, the jailer would not be giving away any information were he to divulge the name of one of them. The jailer accepts this argument, and tells C that A is to be executed. C now feels much happier, since either he or B remains alive, and hence his own probability of doing so is ½ and not ⅓ as he thought originally.

Discuss this 'paradox' using subjective probabilities and Bayes's theorem.

*9. A company prospecting for minerals divides its exploration area into ten plots, intending to drill to a depth of 300 feet near the centre of each plot. Geological data suggest that the ten plots are either wholly within a large mineral field discovered in a neighbouring area or wholly outside the field, and that there is a 50:50 chance of either. Drilling to 300 feet within the field would give a 50 per cent chance of a strike, whereas outside the field there would be virtually no chance of a strike.

On striking minerals the total operating profit can be expected to be $50 million, excluding the cost of exploratory drilling, the cost of which is $100,000 per hole.

After each hole has been drilled a decision is made whether or not to continue drilling with the next hole. The criterion used for this decision is whether the expected drilling cost, not including the holes already drilled, exceeds the expected operating profit.

(i) What is the probability that the plots lie within the field, given that no successful holes have been drilled?

(ii) How many unsuccessful holes will the company drill before abandoning the search, and what is the expected drilling cost before the operation starts?

State any assumptions you make.

Further Reading

R. L. WINKLER, *An Introduction to Bayesian Inference and Decision,* Holt Rinehart & Winston, New York, 1972.

6 More Decision Trees

Introduction

Chapter 3 discussed, through single-stage decision examples, a number of possible decision criteria, dwelling in particular on the use of expected monetary value as an appropriate criterion for choice between alternative courses of action. Chapter 4 considered multi-stage decision problems showing how, in these circumstances, the payoff table or matrix could be replaced by the decision tree. The tree could then be analysed, continuing to use EMV as a consistent criterion of choice throughout, starting with the later decisions first, and folding back the tree until ultimately the optimal initial decision was selected. In the examples given in those chapters it was assumed that the information currently available was all that could be obtained.

Obviously, in many situations, extra information can be bought before the initial decision is made. In chapter 5 we considered in some detail how such extra information could, if of a probabilistic nature, be combined with the original, or prior, probabilities of various outcomes to give the revised or posterior probabilities of these same outcomes. The appropriate decision tree could then be analysed. In this chapter, three further examples of a more complex nature than hitherto are analysed in depth, but no new concepts are introduced.

Metal Broker's Problem

A metal broker has an option to buy a bulk shipment of 1,000 tons of copper ore from an African government at $1,200 per ton, a price that is well below the world price of approximately $1,650 per ton. The broker believes that he can obtain $1,575 per ton for this ore, but he is also a trifle worried as to whether he will obtain the requisite import licence for the copper. Should he contract to buy the copper and subsequently fail to obtain the licence, the contract could be annulled at a penalty to the broker of $120 per ton. The broker estimates, from experience of related contracts, that his chance of getting the licence is 0·6. He realizes that he could delay his decision on the option while he gathers some additional information. The first way this could be done is to apply for government permission before he actually commits himself to purchasing the ore. However, he fears that by the time he gets an answer, the option may no longer be available to him. On reflection, the broker thinks that the chance that the option will still be open by the time he finds out the government's answer is 0·5. A second way in which he could gather further information is to consult an expert, who offers, for a fee of $15,000, to sound out in depth, through his various contacts, the government position on importing copper from the particular African country concerned. The consultant is by no means infallible, but he has acted as a go-between on a number of deals of this kind and has a reasonable record in these matters. The consultant will provide a report that is either favourable or unfavourable as regards obtaining approval and the broker summarizes his views of the consultant's reliability as shown in Table 6.1. This table is read horizontally. Thus, should the government be going to give approval, there is a 0·9 chance that the consultant reports favourably and only a 0·1 chance that he reports unfavourably. Conversely, if the government is not going to give its approval, there is a 0·2 chance that the consultant reports favourably and a 0·8 chance that he reports unfavourably. Any delay through using the consultant will not, in the broker's opinion, lead to any risk of the option being removed

Table 6.1 The consultant's reliability

government outcome	consultant's report		
	favourable (F)	not favourable ($\bar{F}$)	total
approval (A)	0·9	0·1	1·0
non-approval ($\bar{A}$)	0·2	0·8	1·0

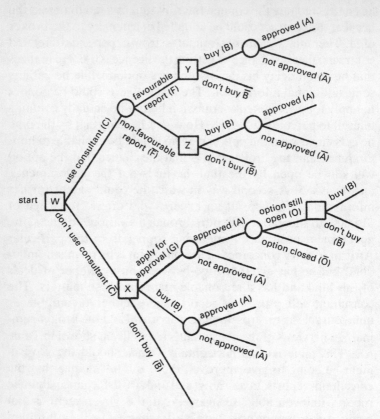

6.1 Metal broker's decision tree

before receiving the consultant's report. The problem that now faces the broker is: what should be his immediate decision?

The various alternatives are shown in Figure 6.1, with the decision points marked with bold squares as before, and the various actions and outcomes labelled as indicated. Figure 6.2 gives the consequential net cash flows for each branch of the tree. Thus, the net yield for the sequence 'use consultant' – 'favourable report' – 'buy' – 'approved' is

$$1,000 \times (1,575 - 1,200) - 15,000 \quad \text{or} \quad +360,000.$$

For the sequence 'use consultant' – 'non-favourable report' – 'buy' – 'not approved' it is

$$1,000 \times (-120) - 15,000 \quad \text{or} -135,000.$$

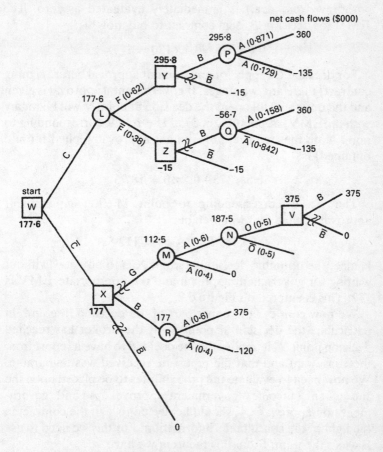

6.2 Metal broker's analysis

Similarly for the other branch networks. All monetary quantities given on the tree are expressed in $000s and the $ symbol is dropped when it does not cause confusion. There are four key decision points, labelled W, X, Y and Z respectively. There is also a fifth decision point labelled V, but the decision here, namely, to buy, is self-evident without formal analysis.

We will evaluate point X on the lower branch first. There are three alternatives here, of which $\bar{B}$ (do not purchase option, withdraw from deal) is immediately evaluated as zero. The EMV for decision B (sign contract to buy now) is:

$$0.6 \times 375 - 0.4 \times 120 = 177.$$

For decision G (apply for government approval before signing contract) there are two stages. If governmental approval is given and the option is still open, the decision at point V will be to buy with an EMV, at point V, of 375. The EMV corresponding to point N on the tree (i.e. government approval applied for and obtained) is:

$$0.5 \times 375 + 0.5 \times 0 = 187.5.$$

The EMV corresponding to point M (i.e. government approval applied for) will then be:

$$0.6 \times 187.5 + 0.4 \times 0 = 112.5.$$

Hence, the optimum decision at point X is to buy now without waiting for government approval and the appropriate EMV is 177. This is entered on Figure 6.2.

We now consider the upper part of the decision tree and, in particular, the decision at point Y. If the broker has reached decision point Y, it implies that he decided to have a report from the consultant and that the report he received was favourable. We now need to evaluate the probabilities to be placed upon the subsequent outcomes 'government approval', A, and 'government non-approval', $\bar{A}$, should he decide to sign the contract in the light of the consultant's information. For this we need to use Bayes's theorem. From this theorem we have:

$$P(A|F) = \frac{P(A)P(F|A)}{P(A)P(F|A) + P(\bar{A})P(F|\bar{A})}$$

Now, from the data given:

$$P(A) = 0.6 \qquad P(F|A) = 0.9 \qquad P(F|\bar{A}) = 0.2$$
$$P(\bar{A}) = 0.4 \qquad P(\bar{F}|A) = 0.1 \qquad P(\bar{F}|\bar{A}) = 0.8,$$

and these are the quantities required for insertion in the Bayes expression for $P(A|F)$. Hence:

$$P(AF) = \frac{0 \cdot 6 \times 0 \cdot 9}{0 \cdot 6 \times 0 \cdot 9 + 0 \cdot 4 \times 0 \cdot 2} = 0 \cdot 871,$$

and, similarly, $P(\bar{A}|F) = 0 \cdot 129$, so that:

$$P(A|F) + P(\bar{A}|F) = 1 \cdot 000.$$

We can now evaluate the decision B (contract to buy) and $\bar{B}$ (do not contract to buy) at point Y. For decision B we have:

$$EMV = 0 \cdot 871 \times 360 - 0 \cdot 129 \times 135$$

$$= 295 \cdot 8.$$

For decision $\bar{B}$ the value is $EMV = -15$. Hence, the optimum decision at point Y is, not surprisingly, to go ahead with the contract to buy and the appropriate EMV is then $295 \cdot 8$.

We can now evaluate, in a similar fashion, the decision at point Z. We find from Bayes's theorem that:

$$P(A|\bar{F}) = \frac{P(A)P(\bar{F}|A)}{P(A)P(\bar{F}|A) + P(\bar{A})P(\bar{F}|\bar{A})}$$

$$= \frac{0 \cdot 6 \times 0 \cdot 1}{0 \cdot 6 \times 0 \cdot 1 + 0 \cdot 4 \times 0 \cdot 8} = 0 \cdot 158$$

and similarly $P(\bar{A}|\bar{F}) = 0 \cdot 842$, giving: $P(A|\bar{F}) + P(\bar{A}|\bar{F}) = 1$.

Hence the appropriate EMVs for the decision of whether to contract to buy or not are:

$$EMV(B) = 0 \cdot 158 \times 360 - 0 \cdot 842 \times 135$$

$$= -56 \cdot 7,$$

while

$$EMV(\bar{B}) = -15.$$

The decision $\bar{B}$, not to contract to buy, has the higher EMV and hence is, again not surprisingly, the better decision to make.

This result is now entered on Figure 6.2. The next step is to compute for the decision tree the probabilities corresponding to the two branches F and $\bar{F}$, so that the two EMVs for points Y and Z can be appropriately weighted to get an overall EMV at point L for the decision to call in the consultant.

The original prior probabilities given to the two outcomes A and $\bar{A}$ by the broker were 0·6 and 0·4 respectively. Hence, the probability that the consultant, if called in, will give a favourable (F) reply is:

$$P(F) = P(A)P(F|A) + P(\bar{A})P(F|\bar{A})$$

$$= 0·6 \times 0·9 + 0·4 \times 0·2 = 0·62,$$

and, similarly:

$$P(\bar{F}) = P(A)P(\bar{F}|A) + P(\bar{A})P(\bar{F}|\bar{A})$$

$$= 0·6 \times 0·1 + 0·4 \times 0·8 = 0·38.$$

These two probabilities add to unity as they must do. The EMV for the decision to hire the consultant is thus:

$P(F) \times$ EMV for optimum decision at point Y plus $P(\bar{F}) \times$ EMV for optimum decision at point Z

$$\text{or} \quad 0·62 \times 295·8 - 0·38 \times 15 = 177·6.$$

Hence, the initial choice is now between:

hire consultant   EMV = 177·6
don't hire consultant   EMV = 177·0.

On the basis of choosing that decision which has the higher EMV, the broker should hire the consultant, giving himself an overall EMV of 177·6.

Notice that the two EMVs for the initial decision are extremely close, with a difference of only 0·6. If the consultant proposed to charge 18, then the EMV for the decision 'hire consultant' would fall to 174·6, and the optimum initial decision would change to 'contract to buy'. Indeed, one could say from this analysis that the maximum amount that it is worth paying for the consultant's advice is 15·6 because at that level the EMVs of the two decisions 'hire consultant' and 'don't hire consultant' become equal, and our decision-maker (the broker) should, on the basis of EMV, become indifferent between the two decisions.

Finally, as shown in Table 6.2, it is instructive to put down for the two initial decisions the possible net cash flows that can occur and the probabilities associated with each, assuming that we select the optimum actions subsequent to the initial decision. These results show that, although the decision to hire the consultant is only marginally better on an EMV basis than the alternative decision not to hire him, calling in the consultant has an added merit. This arises because the probability of a large loss is very considerably reduced, there being a loss of 135 with a probability of only 0·08, compared with a loss of 120 with the much higher probability of 0·4 should the broker contract to buy right from the start without calling in the consultant. On a strict minimax approach, the broker would do nothing. But if that option were eliminated he would contract to buy without hiring the consultant, as the maximum possible loss is only 120 compared with 135 for the situation when he hires the consultant.

Table 6.2 The probabilities of gains and losses

decision	possible cash flows		probability	
hire consultant	(i)	360	0·62×0·871 = 0·54	⎫
	(ii)	−135	0·62×0·129 = 0·08	⎬ 1·00
	(iii)	−15	0·38	⎭
don't hire consultant	(iv)	375	0·6	⎫ 1·00
	(v)	−120	0·4	⎭

The Oil Wildcatter

The next example concerns a situation that is commonly referred to as the oil wildcatter's decision problem that was outlined in chapter 1. It will be recalled that the basis of the problem is that an oil wildcatter must decide whether or not to drill for oil at a given site before his option on the site expires. He is uncertain about many things: the cost of drilling, the extent of the oil deposits at the site, the cost of raising the oil if there is any, and so forth. He has available the objective records of similar and not quite so similar drillings in the same area, and he has already discussed the features peculiar to this particular option with his geologist, his geophysicist and his land agent. He could gain further relevant information (but still not necessarily perfect information) about the underlying geophysical structure at this particular site by arranging for seismic soundings to be taken. Such information, however, is quite costly and not of a stratigraphical nature (i.e. it does not indicate the kind of rock, sandstone, limestone, etc.) Only drilling can determine this, and the wildcatter has to decide whether or not to purchase this information before he makes his basic decision whether or not to drill.

To put the problem in a more formal framework, suppose that any well sunk can be either dry (w_1) or wet (w_2) or soaking (w_3). The former is bad and would lead to a net loss of \$1m. Outcome w_2 is so-so and would give a net profit of \$1m., while outcome w_3 is very good and would lead to a net profit of \$5m. Net profit or loss here is the difference between sales revenue and all costs of production, including the sinking of the well. After appropriate discussions, but without taking any seismic soundings, the oil wildcatter estimates that the probabilities of the three possible outcomes are 0·5 for w_1, 0·25 for w_2 and 0·25 for w_3. The seismic soundings, which could help him to determine more precisely the nature of the underlying geological structure, would cost \$300,000. They will give a result in the form of a good or not so good indication. A good indication (G) is linked to the presence of oil (i.e. to outcomes w_2 and w_3), while a not so good indication ($\bar{G}$) is linked to the absence of oil (i.e. to outcome w_1). However, these are not precise deterministic relationships, but probabilistic ones. Past experience of seismic soundings, in this and other areas, shows that the probabilities given in Table 6.3 are a reasonable summary of the relationship between the results of seismic soundings and subsequent drilled well results.

Table 6.3 Seismic results

drilled well	seismic sounding		
	G	$\bar{G}$	total
w_1 dry	0·2	0·8	1
w_2 wet	0·6	0·4	1
w_3 soaking	0·8	0·2	1

Thus, if a drilled well at a site were wet (w_2), then a seismic survey carried out at the site would have a probability of 0·6 of giving a positive result and a probability of 0·4 of giving a negative result. Similarly, the corresponding probabilities are given

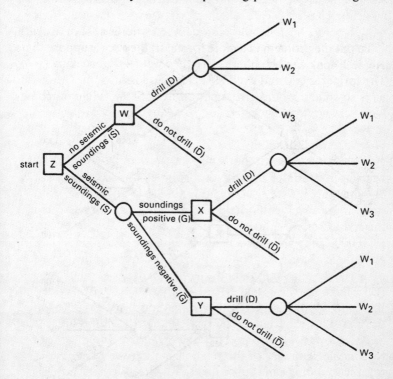

6.3 Oil wildcatter's decision tree

for the other two possible drilling outcomes. Note that the seismic sounding results are very much linked to the drilling outcomes, and that such soundings discriminate, albeit not precisely, between good and bad situations. The whole situation and the alternatives open to the oil wildcatter are summarized in the decision tree shown in Figure 6.3.

We can now proceed to the analysis, the details of which are displayed in Figure 6.4. The first thing we do is to place against each possible branch of the tree the total payoff or net gain. This is done on the right-hand side in Figure 6.4. All net gains are expressed in $000s and the $ symbol is dropped when it cannot cause confusion. There are four decision points, which have been labelled W, X, Y and Z.

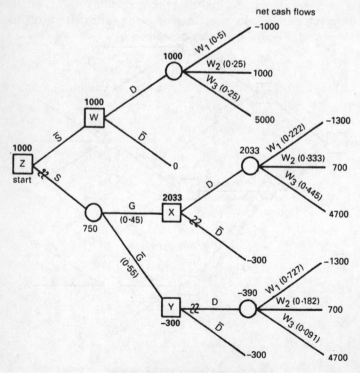

6.4 Oil wildcatter's analysis

We will analyse first of all the upper portion of the decision tree, namely the decision not to take seismic soundings. The EMV at decision point W for the decision 'drill' will be:

$$0.5 \times (-1,000) + 0.25 \times 1,000 + 0.25 \times 5,000 = 1,000.$$

The EMV for the decision not to drill is clearly zero. Hence, the decision at point W will be to drill (D), since this has the higher EMV. The value of 1,000 is accordingly inserted on the decision tree at point W and branch $\bar{D}$ is barred.

We next turn to the decision at decision point X. This point is only reached if seismic soundings are taken and they give a positive response (G). To evaluate the EMV for a decision to drill, we need the posterior probabilities of the three possible outcomes w_1, w_2 and w_3, given both the original prior probabilities and the seismic sounding evidence of a good response. From the data given earlier, we have the following information on the prior probabilities of the three outcomes:

$$P(w_1) = 0.5; \qquad P(w_2) = 0.25; \qquad P(w_3) = 0.25.$$

Conditional probabilities of the seismic sounding outcomes, given the drilling outcome, are:

$$P(G|w_1) = 0.2 \qquad P(\bar{G}|w_1) = 0.8$$
$$P(G|w_2) = 0.6 \qquad P(\bar{G}|w_2) = 0.4$$
$$P(G|w_3) = 0.8 \qquad P(\bar{G}|w_3) = 0.2.$$

Using Bayes's theorem, we have:

$$P(w_1|G) = \frac{P(w_1)P(G|w_1)}{P(w_1)P(G|w_1) + P(w_2)P(G|w_2) + P(w_3)P(G|w_3)}$$

$$= \frac{0.5 \times 0.2}{0.5 \times 0.2 + 0.25 \times 0.6 + 0.25 \times 0.8}$$

$$= \frac{0.10}{0.10 + 0.15 + 0.20} = \frac{2}{9} = 0.222.$$

Similarly,

$$P(w_2|G) = \frac{0.15}{0.45} = \frac{3}{9} = 0.333,$$

and

$$P(w_3|G) = \frac{0.20}{0.45} = \frac{4}{9} = 0.445.$$

These three probabilities add up to unity, and are now entered on the appropriate branches of the decision tree. The EMV for the decision to drill at decision point X is now given by:

$$\tfrac{2}{9} \times (-1{,}300) + \tfrac{3}{9} \times 700 + \tfrac{4}{9} \times 4{,}700 = 2{,}033.$$

The decision not to drill ($\bar{D}$) has an EMV of -300, and so the better decision, on an EMV basis, is to drill. The EMV of 2,033 is now entered at point X and the decision $\bar{D}$ is barred.

At decision point Y a similar line of reasoning is followed. Here the result of the seismic sounding has been a not so good response. Using the same basic probabilities given above, Bayes's theorem can again be used to give the appropriate posterior probabilities.

Thus we have:

$$P(w_1|\bar{G}) = \frac{P(w_1)P(\bar{G}|w_1)}{P(w_1)P(\bar{G}|w_1) + P(w_2)P(\bar{G}|w_2) + P(w_3)P(\bar{G}|w_3)}$$

$$= \frac{0.5 \times 0.8}{0.5 \times 0.8 + 0.25 \times 0.4 + 0.25 \times 0.2} = 0.727.$$

Similarly,

$$P(w_2|\bar{G}) = 0.182 \qquad P(w_3|\bar{G}) = 0.091,$$

and the three probabilities again add up to unity as they should.

Hence, the EMV for the decision to drill at decision point Y is:

$$0.727 \times (-1{,}300) + 0.182 \times 700 + 0.091 \times 4{,}700 = -390.$$

Comparison of this EMV with that of the decision not to drill shows the latter to be the better, as the EMV of the latter is only -300 in comparison with -390. Hence, we insert -300 at point Y and bar the decision to drill (D).

The next step is to combine the two branches, G and $\bar{G}$, weighting them according to the prior probabilities of obtaining G or $\bar{G}$ results, should we decide to take seismic soundings. These marginal probabilities can be computed as follows:

$$P(G) = P(w_1)P(G|w_1) + P(w_2)P(G|w_2) + P(w_3)P(G|w_3)$$

$$= 0\cdot5 \times 0\cdot2 + 0\cdot25 \times 0\cdot6 + 0\cdot25 \times 0\cdot8$$

$$= 0\cdot45.$$

Hence $P(\bar{G})$ is equal to $1-0\cdot45$ or $0\cdot55$, although this result could be calculated from the basic data in precisely the same manner as was done for $P(G)$. These probabilities are entered on the decision tree. The combined EMV for the decision to take seismic soundings can now be evaluated as:

$$0\cdot45 \times 2{,}033 + 0\cdot55 \times (-300) = 749\cdot8.$$

We can now, finally, look at the starting position denoted as decision point Z. The EMV for the decision to have a seismic sounding (S) is 750, while that for the decision not to have a seismic sounding ($\bar{S}$) is 1,000. The latter is the higher EMV, and, hence, the oil wildcatter should go ahead without a survey and drill: his EMV thereby will be 1,000.

The seismic survey, on these data, would have to be reduced in cost to 50 if it were to become a viable proposition on an EMV decision basis. It is, however, worth pointing out once again that the probabilities of a loss (any loss) under the two initial decisions are very different. Under the decision to take the seismic survey, the probabilities of losses are as follows:

loss of 1,300   probability $0\cdot45 \times {}^2\!/_9$ or $0\cdot1$
loss of 300   probability of $0\cdot55$.

Under the decision to drill straight away without a seismic survey at all, the probability is:

loss of 1,000   probability of $0\cdot5$.

Hence, if a loss of 1,000 (i.e. $1m.) or more is serious to the oil wildcatter, but losses of less than that amount are not so serious, the decision to drill straight away carries with it certain important implications and the wildcatter might prefer to take the survey. If any form of loss is of importance to the oil wildcatter, then the two decisions do not differ very materially in this respect.

Choice of Level of Information – a Marketing Example

The two examples discussed so far in this chapter have incorporated as one possible initial decision the purchasing of additional information of a fixed quantity and defined quality at a predetermined price. In some instances, not only the question of purchasing further information is open to the decision-maker but also, if he decides to obtain information, he can choose the amount he purchases. The next example involves a situation where such a double choice exists.

The marketing executive of Midway Foods Inc.† is concerned with the sales appeal of the company's present label for one of its products. Marketing research indicates that supermarket consumers find little eye appeal in the drab, somewhat cluttered appearance of the label. The company has hired a design artist who has produced some prototype labels, all of which have been evaluated by the company's marketing executives. One label design has consistently come out on top in all preference tests which have been conducted among these executives. Nevertheless, the marketing executive is still in some doubt as to whether the new label would appreciably benefit sales. He accordingly decides to make a more exhaustive quantitative analysis of the consequences of a decision to switch to the new label.

First, he considers the costs associated with converting his company's machinery, inventory, point of purchase displays, etc., to the new label, and estimates that an out-of-pocket, once and for all, cost of $250,000 would be involved. If the new label were really superior to the old, the marketing executive estimates that the present value of all net cash flows over and above

† The example is partially based on a problem discussed by P. E. GREEN and R. E. FRANK in *Applied Statistics*, Vol. 15, p. 175.

this cost related to increased sales generated over the next three years by the more attractive label will be \$400,000. (For purposes of simplicity the analysis is kept to a three-year planning horizon only.) But, based on his prior experience and the discussions he had held with his colleagues, he is willing to assign only a 0·5 probability to the outcome 'new label superior to old'. Rather than make his decision on these data alone, however, he could delay it and obtain further market research information. Again, the market research can be done in various ways. After discussions the manager confines his attention to three possible forms, the cost and reliability varying from one form to another. The possible forms of market research are:

Market research type M_1	A 'perfect' survey at a cost of \$150,000.
Market research type M_2	A survey that is 80 per cent reliable at a cost of \$50,000.
Market research type M_3	A survey that is in two stages. The first stage is 70 per cent reliable, but the survey can be taken to the second stage when the reliability increases to 80 per cent. Cost of the first stage sample is \$35,000 and the second stage, if needed, costs an extra \$40,000.

The appropriate decision tree can now be drawn to show the various alternatives open to the marketing manager and is given in Figures 6.5(a) and 6.5(b). The decision to change to the new label is denoted by D_1 and to keep the old by D_2. The outcome 'new label superior to old' is denoted by B_1 and the outcome 'new label not superior to old' by B_2. The information from the market research surveys is shown as either positive (R) or negative ($\bar{R}$) in favour of the new label. Subscripts are used to denote the two-part sampling for market research of type M_3. All monetary quantities are inserted as \$000s and the \$ sign is omitted where there is no likelihood of confusion. The net cash flows at the end of each branch include the costs of the surveys, where relevant.

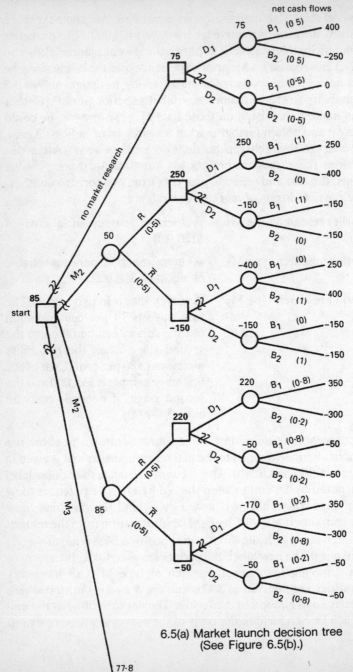

6.5(a) Market launch decision tree
(See Figure 6.5(b).)

net cash flows

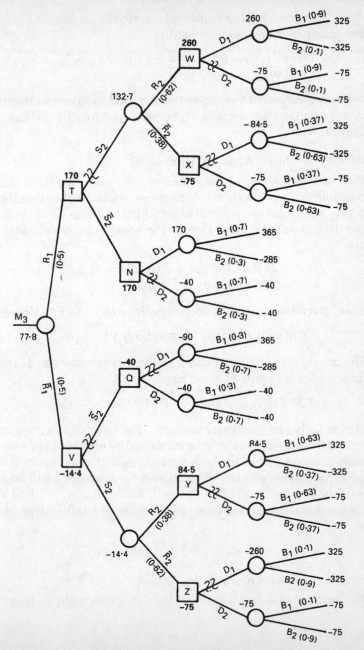

6.5(b) Market launch decision tree

Analysis of No Market Research Branch

We can evaluate the top branch relating to the decision 'no market research' very straightforwardly:

$$\text{EMV}(D_1) = 0.5 \times 400 + 0.5 \times (-250) = 75.$$
$$\text{EMV}(D_2) = 0.$$

Hence, decision D_1 is the better decision to take and this is entered on the tree, decision D_2 being barred for this particular branch.

Analysis of Market Research M_1 Branch

We next tackle the branch labelled M_1. Here we have the possibility of a perfectly reliable survey, which implies that the survey would disclose without error which outcome, B_1 or B_2, is the 'true state' of nature. Hence, the conditional probabilities are:

$$P(B_1|R) = 1; \quad P(B_2|R) = 0;$$
$$P(B_1|\bar{R}) = 0; \quad P(B_2|\bar{R}) = 1.$$

Thus, given that the information is positive (R), the EMVs are:

$$\text{EMV}(D_1) = 250; \quad \text{EMV}(D_2) = -150.$$

Hence, D_1 is the better decision in these circumstances. If the information is negative $(\bar{R})$ we have:

$$\text{EMV}(D_1) = -400; \quad \text{EMV}(D_2) = -150.$$

Hence D_2 is now the better decision. The two possible market research outcomes must now be combined by weighting the optimum decision EMVs for each market research outcome by the prior probability of each of them and by summarizing. These probabilities are clearly both 0.5 and, hence, the overall EMV for the initial decision to undertake market research of type M_1 is:

$$0.5 \times 250 + 0.5 \times (-150) = 50.$$

Analysis of Market Research M_3 Branch

The next branch which will be tackled is that relating to the initial decision to undertake market research of type M_3. Here we indicate in Figure 6.5(b) the first survey results by R_1 and $\bar{R}_1$, and the second survey results, if taken, by R_2 and $\bar{R}_2$. The decision to take the second survey is indicated by S_2, while the decision not to take it is indicated by $\bar{S}_2$. The key decision points are labelled N, Q, T, V, W, X, Y and Z. We must now interpret formally the original statements made concerning the reliability of the surveys. For the first survey we take the statement to imply that:

$$P(R_1|B_1) = 0\cdot7; \qquad P(\bar{R}_1|B_1) = 0\cdot3;$$
$$P(R_1|B_2) = 0\cdot3; \qquad P(\bar{R}_1|B_2) = 0\cdot7.$$

Hence we have $P(B_1|R_1) = 0\cdot7$ and $P(B_2|R_1) = 0\cdot3$ since both $P(B_1)$ and $P(B_2)$ are equal to $0\cdot5$.

Assuming that we decide not to take the further part of the survey, the EMVs for the two alternative decisions D_1 and D_2 will depend upon whether the initial survey is positive (R_1) or negative ($\bar{R}_1$) and will be as follows:

For R_1 (and $\bar{S}_2$) at point N

$$\mathrm{EMV}(D_1) = 0\cdot7 \times 365 + 0\cdot3 \times (-285)$$
$$= 170.$$
$$\mathrm{EMV}(D_2) = 0\cdot7 \times (-40) + 0\cdot3 \times (-40)$$
$$= -40.$$

Hence, the decision at decision point N in this instance would be to accept the new label (D_1), giving an EMV of 170. When the initial survey results are negative ($\bar{R}_1$) we have:

For $\bar{R}_1$ (and $\bar{S}_2$)

$$\mathrm{EMV}(D_1) = 0\cdot3 \times 365 + 0\cdot7 \times (-285)$$
$$= -90.$$
$$\mathrm{EMV}(D_2) = -40.$$

Hence, the decision at decision point Q in this instance would be not to accept the new label (D_2), giving an EMV of -40.

These two results can be entered on the decision tree and the non-optimum routes barred.

Next we need to consider the consequences of deciding to take the second survey. Initially we consider the situation where both parts of the survey give positive results. The information given earlier concerning the accuracy of results in the second part of the survey can be summarized as follows:

$$P(R_2|B_1) = 0\cdot8; \qquad P(\bar{R}_2|B_1) = 0\cdot2;$$
$$P(R_2|B_2) = 0\cdot2; \qquad P(\bar{R}_2|B_2) = 0\cdot8.$$

The probabilities associated with B_1 and B_2 can now be found from Bayes's theorem:

$$P(B_1|R_1, R_2)$$

$$= \frac{P(B_1)P(R_1|B_1)P(R_2|B_1)}{P(B_1)P(R_1|B_1)P(R_2|B_1) + P(B_2)P(R_1|B_2)P(R_2|B_2)}$$

$$= \frac{0\cdot5 \times 0\cdot7 \times 0\cdot8}{0\cdot5 \times 0\cdot7 \times 0\cdot8 + 0\cdot5 \times 0\cdot3 \times 0\cdot2}$$

$$= 0\cdot9.$$

Similarly,

$$P(B_2|R_1, R_2)$$

$$= \frac{P(B_2)P(R_1|B_2)P(R_2|B_2)}{P(B_1)P(R_1|B_1)P(R_2|B_1) + P(B_2)P(R_1|B_2)P(R_2|B_2)}$$

$$= \frac{0\cdot5 \times 0\cdot3 \times 0\cdot2}{0\cdot5 \times 0\cdot7 \times 0\cdot8 + 0\cdot5 \times 0\cdot3 \times 0\cdot2}$$

$$= 0\cdot1.$$

By similar calculations we can obtain the appropriate probabilities for the other three possible combinations of survey results as follows:

$$\bar{R}_1 \text{ with } R_2 \quad \begin{cases} P(B_1|\bar{R}_1, R_2) = 0.63 \\ P(B_2|\bar{R}_1, R_2) = 0.37. \end{cases}$$

$$R_1 \text{ with } \bar{R}_2 \quad \begin{cases} P(B_1|R_1, \bar{R}_2) = 0.37 \\ P(B_2|R_1, \bar{R}_2) = 0.63. \end{cases}$$

$$\bar{R}_1 \text{ with } \bar{R}_2 \quad \begin{cases} P(B_1|\bar{R}_1, \bar{R}_2) = 0.1 \\ P(B_2|\bar{R}_1, \bar{R}_2) = 0.9. \end{cases}$$

We can now evaluate the EMVs associated with the point marked W.

These will be:

$$\text{EMV}(D_1) = 0.9 \times 325 + 0.1 \times (-325) = 260.$$
$$\text{EMV}(D_2) = 0.9 \times (-75) + 0.1 \times (-75) = -75.$$

Hence, the best decision at point W will be D_1 with an EMV of 260.

At point X the EMVs will be:

$$\text{EMV}(D_1) = 0.37 \times 325 + 0.63 \times (-325) = -84.5.$$
$$\text{EMV}(D_2) = 0.37 \times (-75) + 0.63 \times (-75) = -75.$$

Hence, the best decision at point X will be D_2 with an EMV of -75.

At point Y, the EMVs will be:

$$\text{EMV}(D_1) = 0.63 \times 325 + 0.37 \times (-325) = 84.5.$$
$$\text{EMV}(D_2) = 0.63 \times (-75) + 0.37 \times (-75) = -75.$$

Hence, the optimum decision at point Y will be D_1 with an EMV of 84.5.

Finally, at point Z, we have:

$$\text{EMV}(D_1) = 0.1 \times 325 + 0.9 \times (-325) = -260.$$
$$\text{EMV}(D_2) = 0.1 \times (-75) + 0.9 \times (-75) = -75.$$

Hence the optimum decision at point Z will be D_2, not to change, with an EMV of -75.

We can now merge the decisions at points W and X, in that the probability of R_2 occurring on that branch is:

$$P(R_2|R_1) = P(R_1R_2)/P(R_1)$$

$$= \frac{P(R_1, R_2|B_1)P(B_1) + P(R_1, R_2|B_2)P(B_2)}{P(R_1|B_1)P(B_1) + P(R_1|B_2)P(B_2)}$$

or

$$\frac{0.7 \times 0.8 + 0.3 \times 0.2}{0.7 + 0.3} = 0.62.$$

Similarly, the probability of $\bar{R}_2$ occurring on that branch is:

$$P(\bar{R}_2|R_1) = \frac{P(R_1, \bar{R}_2|B_1)P(B_1) + P(R_1, \bar{R}_2|B_2)P(B_2)}{P(R_1|B_1)P(B_1) + P(R_1|B_2)P(B_2)}$$

or

$$\frac{0.7 \times 0.2 + 0.3 \times 0.8}{0.7 + 0.3} = 0.38.$$

This gives an overall EMV for this upper branch of:

$$0.62 \times 260 + 0.38 \times (-75) = 132.7.$$

Hence the optimum decision at point T will be not to take the second survey, as the EMV of 170 for $\bar{S}_2$ is higher than the EMV of 132.7 for S_2. In a similar way we can merge the decisions at points Y and Z. A computation, analogous to that just made, gives the probabilities of R_2 and $\bar{R}_2$ on this branch as 0.38 and 0.62 respectively. This gives an overall EMV for this branch of:

$$0.38 \times 84.5 + 0.62 \times (-75) = -14.39.$$

Hence, the optimum decision at point V is to carry out the second survey, when the overall EMV will be -14.4, in preference to not carrying it out when the EMV is -40. Note that this EMV is negative, but it is still worth taking the second survey, as we would already have expended 35 on the first survey and we would, therefore, have a positive expectation of $35 - 14 \cdot 4$ or $20 \cdot 6$ in going on to the next stage.

The final step in the evaluation of the M_3 branch of the overall tree is to combine the EMVs at the two decision points T and V. Since the prior probability of result R_1 is $0 \cdot 5 \times 0 \cdot 7 + 0 \cdot 5 \times 0 \cdot 3 = 0 \cdot 5$, and similarly for $\bar{R}_1$, we have an overall EMV for decision M_3 of:

$$0 \cdot 5 \times 170 + 0 \cdot 5 \times (-14 \cdot 4) = 77 \cdot 8.$$

Analysis of Market Research M_2 Branch

The reader is now left to carry through the similar, but somewhat less protracted, calculations appropriate for initial decision M_2. The key figures obtained are shown in Figure 6.5(a) and the overall EMV obtained is 85. From Figure 6.5(a) the highest EMV of 85 corresponds to decision M_2, and hence this, under the EMV principle, is the optimal initial decision. Under this decision, a market research survey of 80 per cent reliability is taken and, if the survey is favourable, the change is made, but not otherwise. Of course if, by the time the survey has been carried out, extra information concerning markets or costs has come to hand, this must be included in the assessment made at that stage.

Summary of Procedure

In this and the preceding chapter we have been concerned with the use of posterior probability concepts to examine the value of differing quantities of information in order to reach optimal decisions. The basic steps necessary for the analysis of such problems are:

(i) A decision tree is drawn to display the alternative actions and outcomes, including the purchase of various levels of information (if relevant).

(ii) The net cash flows are calculated and placed on the extremities of the appropriate branches.

(iii) The relevant probabilities are placed on the tree, using Bayes's theorem to convert prior probabilities to posterior probabilities when sample information is being obtained.

(iv) The tree is analysed on the rollback principle, working from the extremities back to the main trunk.

(v) Expected monetary value is used as a means of deciding between alternative decisions at each node or decision point.

Using this approach, complex problems can be broken down into a number of simpler problems, each of which can be analysed through such an approach. At each node on the appropriate decision tree, the choice between alternatives is made following the expected monetary value principle. This is illustrated in schematic form in Figure 6.6 where θ refers to the outcome, u the associated payoffs, x the extra information made available and a the possible actions. The dotted line indicates the principle followed if no extra information is available from which to form posterior probabilities – which was the situation for the problems discussed in chapter 4. The unbroken lines indicate the procedure to be followed when extra information is available, as in this chapter, for incorporation with the prior probabilities in the decision analysis.

In the examples studied, the optimal policy for a series of sequential decisions has been found by considering the final decision first and working backwards to the initial decision. To do so, all the circumstances in which the final decision might be made had to be envisaged. It is not necessary to consider how each outcome arises, or what previous decisions were. As a result this enables the various decisions to be considered one at a time. The structure of analysis adopted is formally referred to as dynamic programming and, whilst many problems of this form can be tackled by dynamic programming, this is not universally the case. For example, it is necessary to assume that the payoffs from each decision are additive, and that no matter how an outcome arose, the consequences for the future are the same.

The methods and the illustrative examples used in the last four chapters of this book have all made extensive use of probabilistic data. This has involved the estimation of probabilities, and their interpretation, in ways that are not as neat and tidy as the way in which probability is commonly conceived. Chapters 7 and 8 are accordingly devoted to a discussion of the assessment of probabilities, and are placed at this point in the development of the material since the reader is by now familiar with the kind of problem whose analysis concerns us.

So far in this book we have made the tacit assumption that the attractiveness of various alternative results is directly reflected in the monetary payoff associated with each of these alternatives. By such means, gains and losses can be satisfactorily measured in terms of money. Two problems arise here; first, it is sometimes difficult to attach such a monetary scale to many outcomes. For example, somebody's arrival at a business meeting on time is not something to which we can readily attach a monetary payoff. Hence, we are necessarily restricted in the range of problems for which we may directly use our means of analysis.

Second, we are inherently assuming that the decision-maker's attitude towards the gain or loss of money is linear and that EMV is thus the relevant criterion. By this we mean, for example, that his attitude towards acquiring or losing an extra $500 when he already possesses $25,000 capital is precisely the same as his attitude would be should his capital only be $2,500. Although such an attitude might well be true of two business firms, one with a capital of $10 million and the other with a capital of, say, $12 million, each concerned with a project that could gain or lose them $50,000, it is demonstrably not true in many other situations. These difficulties can be surmounted by using, in place of money, a numerical scale of utility, which is discussed in more depth in chapters 9 and 10.

Exercises

1. M. Borel, the owner of a French cargo shipping line, is offered two ships of a European line that is going out of business, in exchange for an ongoing interest in M. Borel's line. M. Borel proposes either to accept the European line's offer or to reject it outright. The condition of the two ships (i.e. whether or not they require a major overhaul) is a key determinant of the payoff that M. Borel will receive if he accepts the offer. If he rejects the offer, his payoff is zero in any case.

M. Borel decides to base his decisions on an EMV approach. He has no precise information on the condition of the two ships, but is able to assign the prior probabilities shown in Table 6.4 as to

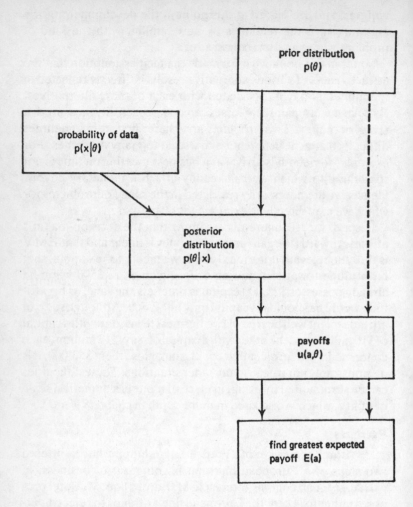

6.6 Schematic form of Bayesian analysis

the conditions of the ships as a set on the basis of judgement and experience. (He does not attempt to apply probabilities to the individual ships.) Also shown are M. Borel's specific estimates of the total discounted payoffs that he would receive if he accepts the offer under the different possible outcomes (in millions of French francs).

Table 6.4 Foreign line ship data

no. of ships requiring major overhaul	prior probability	payoff if accepted
0	0·30	60
1	0·10	10
2	0·60	−40

 (i) Suppose M. Borel must make his decision between accepting and rejecting the offer without obtaining further information on the condition of the two ships. Which decision should he make?

 (ii) M. Borel has the option of having one or both ships taken to a reliable inspection station in a second foreign country before he makes his decision. The cost (to be paid by M. Borel) is 0·6 million francs per ship so inspected. What is M. Borel's best strategy? Give the number of ships he should inspect (i.e. 0, 1 or 2) together with the action he should take in each eventuality (e.g. inspect two, one fails and he accepts the offer, etc.) and the EMV of following your proposed strategy.

(iii) Are there conditions under which M. Borel might not be willing to take the action proposed under (ii)?

2. A manufacturer's agent receives, periodically, railroad shipments of four large machines from one of the companies he represents. The machines have to be moved from the railyard on arrival and installed in good working order in the customers' plants. The representative must either accept or reject the shipment on arrival at the yard. If the agent accepts responsibility he receives a fee of $800 from the manufacturer but must then reset, at his own cost, any machines that may have been jarred out of alignment while being shipped. The cost of resetting each machine found to be out of alignment is about $300. If the agent rejects responsibility for a given shipment, he receives no fee but is reim-

bursed by the manufacturer for any direct costs incurred in resetting of damaged machines in that shipment. Shipping costs are paid by the purchaser and do not concern the agent.

The agent has collected extensive data on the number of machines that have had to be reset in past shipments of similar machines. The relevant frequency distribution that he has compiled from this information is as follows:

no. of damaged machines	0	1	2	3	4
relative frequency	0·4	0·2	0·1	0·1	0·2

Time just permits the agent to examine two of the machines in the shipment before making his final decision, should he desire to do so. This would cost him $100 in time and labour, but he would be able to determine precisely for the two machines examined whether they did or did not need resetting. The machines to be examined would be chosen at random. What is the agent's optimal strategy, assuming that he uses EMV as his decision criterion?

3. A government official wishes to determine the most effective way to control tree damage from the gypsy moth. There are three methods for attacking the pest:

(1) spray with a pesticide; (2) use a scent to lure and trap males, so that the remaining males must compete for mating with a much larger number of males that have been sterilized in a laboratory and then released; and (3) to spray with a juvenile hormone that prevents the larvae from developing into adult moths.

The net improvement in current and future tree losses using the pesticide is zero, because it is assumed that the pesticide will never completely eradicate the moth.

If the scent-lure programme is instituted, the probability that it will leave a low number of native males is 0·5, with an 0·5 chance that it will leave a high number. Once the scent-lure results are known, a later choice must then be made either to spray with the pesticide or to release sterile males. The cost of the scent lures is $5m. If this two-phase programme is successful, the worth of present and future trees saved will be $30m. If scent lures leave a small native male population, there is a 90 per cent chance of success using sterile males; otherwise there is only a 10 per cent chance of success using sterile males. A failure results in no savings.

The juvenile hormone must be synthesized at a cost of $3m. There is only a 0·2 probability that the resulting produce will work. If it does, the worth of trees saved would be $50m., because the gypsy moth would become extinct. If the hormone does not work, the savings would be zero.

Construct a decision tree and determine the course of action that maximizes expected payoff.

4. A company sells welding supplies to industrial customers and maintains an extensive distribution network throughout the United States with its 250 salesmen. The company has been in existence for about twenty-five years and sells only the most traditional types of welding supplies. In recent years a fairly new welding method, Tungsten inert gas welding (TIG) has been making some inroads into the sales of this company. There is, however, still a vast untapped market of potential customers estimated to be equivalent to at least 100,000 units.†

Recently, the company has been given an opportunity to market a new, inexpensive and very flexible TIG torch which could be used as an adaptor for a traditional arc welder. The marketing of this product would involve a fixed investment of approximately $50,000, consisting mostly of sales literature and advertising. Net profit, that is the sales price less the manufacturer's royalties and salesmen's commissions, was conservatively estimated to be $25 per sale. The management of the company has to decide whether or not to market the product.

The product planning committee has met in emergency session and agreed that an appropriate prior distribution for π, the proportion of the potential market who would buy the torch, was given by an exponential distribution with a mean of 0·025, i.e. $p(\pi) = 40e^{-40\pi}$.

There is just time to carry out a small test marketing of the prod-

---

† Based in part on a problem discussed by L. HARRIS in *Applied Statistics*, vol. 17, p. 39.

uct. This could be done by selecting a simple random sample of 100 potential customers at a cost of $4,000, including the purchase of the torches likely to be sold on such a test marketing.

What should be the company's choice of initial strategy – accept the offer, carry out a test market, or reject the offer? If you recommend a test market, state the decision rule for acceptance or rejection of the offer that would be followed. (Note that the suggested prior distribution actually allows π to be greater than 1, but the probability of such a value is effectively zero.)

5. In early March 1980, Mr Sparrow, the president and sole owner of the Sparrow Drilling Company, was about to reach a final decision concerning a lease that Sparrow held on a plot of land in an oil-bearing region in Central Kansas. The lease gave the lessee (Sparrow) the right to drill for oil at any time up to a final date of 31 March 1982; the right would automatically lapse if drilling had not begun by that date. If drilling began before the final date, it could be continued until either oil was struck or the driller decided to give up; if oil were struck, the lessee was obliged to pay the lessor (the owner of the land) royalties equal to one-sixth of the gross revenues received from all oil raised.†

The Sparrow Drilling Company had been founded in 1974 by Mr Sparrow, until then operations vice-president of a large petroleum company, in an effort to 'make money for myself instead of for others'. Until 1979 the company's business had consisted entirely of drilling exploratory wells for the major oil producers, but in that year Sparrow decided to try exploratory drilling on Sparrow's own account. A large bank loan payable in instalments over three years had been obtained to finance the drilling, with Sparrow's drilling rigs being pledged as security. Leases had been negotiated for drilling rights on five widely scattered sites in 1979, and drilling had taken place on four of the sites, leaving Central Kansas untouched by the spring of 1980. All these holes had turned out to be dry, and unexpected delays in redeploying Sparrow's four drilling rigs from these private ventures back to paid

---

† Based in part on a problem described in the case of the Acme Drilling Company, Harvard Business School and reproduced by permission of the President and Fellows.

work for the major oil producers had put Sparrow in a precarious financial position in the spring of 1980. Working capital had been reduced practically to zero, and Sparrow had been compelled to obtain the bank's consent to a delay in the first scheduled payment on the instalment loan.

From April 1980 to March 1982, Sparrow's four rigs had been kept busy more than 90 per cent of the time drilling exploratory wells on a contract basis; profits on these contract operations had been sufficient to permit Sparrow not only to meet all payments on the bank loan as they fell due, but also to build its working capital back to about $80,000. Drilling contracts already in hand were expected, in the absence of bad luck, to generate the funds needed to make the last $100,000 loan payment when it fell due in November 1983.

In these circumstances Sparrow was financially able in March 1982 to drill the last of its five sites. Although it was true that drilling a dry hole would again put Sparrow in a difficult financial position, success would mean that, for the first time since Sparrow was founded, it would be in the pleasant situation of having a really substantial amount of cash in the bank. Mr Sparrow had already decided that, if he did drill and strike oil, he would sell the site immediately to a major company rather than tie up his capital in lifting the oil himself and thus risk very serious embarrassment should his drilling contracts not yield enough cash to pay off the bank loan. The sale would be very straightforward from Sparrow's point of view, since the buyer would be responsible for all costs incurred in 'completing' the well and for the payments to the lessor called for under the lease. Sparrow would receive a single, immediate cash payment proportional to the ultimate recoverable reserves as estimated immediately after oil was struck. At the going prices for new wells in this region, the payment would yield Sparrow $1.50 per barrel net after taxes.

Sparrow did not propose to carry out the drilling with his own rigs, however, since these were completely tied up in contract work for several months ahead. Accordingly, Mr Sparrow had asked his treasurer, Mr Russell, to obtain bids for the drilling from other contract drillers who had rigs in the vicinity of the plot on which Sparrow held the drilling lease. In seeking these bids Sparrow had asked bidders to quote a single total price for drilling until either oil was struck, or a depth of 6,000 feet was reached (at which point the well would be abandoned), whichever occurred first. This was not the usual form of contract, which specified a fixed price per foot and left the person paying for the drilling free to stop at any depth he chose. Mr Sparrow had, however, decided after consultation with his geologist, Mr Heffern, that the unusual form of contract would almost certainly be advantageous to Sparrow under the special circumstances of this particular case. Experience with wells that had been drilled in the general area surrounding Sparrow's site, together with knowledge of the geological formations in this area, had convinced Mr Heffern that if there was any oil at all under the site, it almost certainly lay somewhere between 5,500 and 6,000 feet below the surface. Under the usual system of pricing by the foot, drilling contractors usually quoted a price high enough to cover their fixed costs – particularly the cost of bringing the rig to the site – even if the drilling were to stop at a depth of 2,000 or 3,000 feet. Mr Sparrow believed that by guaranteeing, in effect, payment for 6,000 feet he would almost certainly get a lower effective price per foot, even if oil was actually struck at a depth of only 5,000 feet.

Mr Sparrow's reasoning was confirmed when the bids came in, several of them corresponding to per-foot prices appreciably less than those usually quoted in this area of the country. The most favourable bid was from Klimm Drillers, Inc., who made their price contingent on the depth at which a lime-shale formation was encountered. If such a formation was not encountered, or was encountered at a depth greater than 4,000 feet, the net cost to Sparrow after adjustment for tax effects would be only $64,000. If a lime-shale formation was encountered above 4,000 feet, the net cost after taxes would be $72,000. This offer was only open, however, for two weeks, since the reason Klimm was able to bid so low was that they currently had a rig in the immediate vicinity of the Sparrow plot. Since even the $72,000 cost was lower than that proposed by any other bidder, Mr Sparrow felt that he should reach some definite decision immediately.

The indefiniteness about drilling costs that resulted from uncertainty about the depth at which a lime-shale formation would be encountered bothered Mr Sparrow very little in thinking about his decision problem, but this same uncertainty about the lime-shale formation also entered the problem in two other, much more important ways. The lime-shale formation in the general region of the plot leased by Sparrow was known with near certainty to lie nearly horizontally at a depth of about 5,000 feet except where it rose abruptly to a depth of about 2,500 feet in so-called 'flat domes', and both the chances of finding oil at all, and the amount of these reserves if oil was found, depended on whether the well penetrated one of these domes. Mr Heffern told Mr Sparrow that, considering both the general geology of the region and the available information concerning other wells drilled in the region, he thought there was about one chance in three of finding oil beneath a dome, but only about one chance in ten elsewhere; as to the size of the reserves in case oil was struck, he thought the most probable figure was 600,000 barrels, if the oil was found under a dome, but only 400,000 barrels if it was found elsewhere.

When Mr Sparrow questioned Mr Heffern concerning the chances that a dome would actually be found beneath the Sparrow site, Mr Heffern replied that, on the basis of the same kind of evidence that underlay his other opinions, the chances were about two in five; but on this point much better evidence could be obtained by having a seismic sounding made. Seismic soundings indicated the depth of the lime-shale formation and hence could be used to predict the existence or non-existence of a dome. A sounding would cost Sparrow only $10,000 net after tax and could be made within a week or ten days, the time being required to engage a specialist in seismic work and get his crew and apparatus to the site.

The idea of a seismic sounding appealed to Mr Sparrow as a relatively inexpensive way of reducing the risk of drilling a dry hole, the loss on which would again virtually wipe out Sparrow's working capital. He was, however, far from certain that it reduced the risk enough, since even if a sounding revealed the presence of a dome, the chances of drilling a dry hole would still be higher than 50 per cent.

Mr Sparrow called a meeting with Mr Russell and Mr Heffern to discuss their course of action. Just as the meeting opened, a telephone call was received from Klimm Drillers who said that their contract prices were incorrect; they should be $100,000 if a lime-shale formation was not encountered or was encountered at a depth greater than 4,000 feet; $108,000 otherwise.

The meeting started to discuss the effect of this change in costs, when Mr Heffern pointed out that the assumption that a seismic sounding would tell for sure whether or not there was a dome beneath the Sparrow leasehold was not really true. 'Well, just what are the chances?' asked Sparrow.

'There isn't really any clear answer to that question,' Mr Heffern replied, 'because it depends on what else you know about the place where the sounding is made. If you have a site in a region where you know to start with that there are a lot of domes, and then a sounding indicates a dome, it might make sense to bet 9 to 1 or better that you've actually got a dome. But if you're in a basin where you know that domes are few and far between, you won't feel at all sure that you've got a dome even though a sounding does seem to say you have – you'll think it more likely that the sounding was misinterpreted.'

'That makes sense,' Mr Sparrow remarked, 'but how about this region and our site? If we have a sounding made and it seems to say there's a dome, what are the chances that we'll actually strike a dome if we drill?'

'I don't know,' Mr Heffern answered. 'There isn't a single instance I know of in this region where somebody has taken a sounding and then drilled and actually found out what was under the surface.'

'But you said the reliability studies carried out were encouraging,' Mr Sparrow rejoined somewhat impatiently. 'What do they tell you, if they don't tell you what the chances are that there's really a dome when the sounding says there is?'

Mr Heffern then explained that the studies did not deal with the dome question directly at all. What they did was to consider a large number of cases where the known depth of a geological formation or stratum could be compared with an estimate of that same depth based on a seismic sounding, and their conclusions concerned the chances that seismic depth estimates would be incorrect by various amounts. Since the nature of the sounding and estimating process was such that errors of any given type were no more likely in one region than in any other, these results could be applied to a seismic made on the Sparrow leasehold even though the underlying data came from other regions. What the seismic expert would do if a sounding were made on the Sparrow site would be simply to look at the seismic trace and decide whether it looked more like what he would expect from a lime-shale formation at a 2,500 foot depth, or more like what he would expect from a lime-shale formation about 5,000 feet down. In the former case, they would interpret the seismic as indicating a dome, in the latter, as indicating no dome; and the findings of the studies were such as to lead Heffern to conclude that there was only about one chance in five that the seismic would indicate a dome if no dome existed and about the same chance that the seismic would indicate no dome if a dome did exist.

At this point Mr Sparrow decided to get down on paper all the relevant pieces of information in order to assess the relative values of the alternatives open to him. Assume that you are being retained by Mr Sparrow as adviser.

(i) Make an analysis of Mr Sparrow's decision problem that will be valid if Mr Sparrow accepts EMV as a complete guide to action, i.e. if Mr Sparrow wants to choose the immediate act that has the greatest EMV.

(ii) Assuming that Mr Sparrow understands the logic underlying the use of EMV, do you think that he would accept it as a complete guide in this problem?

(iii) Even if Mr Sparrow does not accept EMV as a complete guide in this problem, does any part of the EMV analysis lead to useful conclusions concerning any parts of the complete decision problem?

(In answering these questions, assume that, if oil is struck, the ultimate recoverable reserves will be equal to Mr Heffern's 'most probable' estimate thereof.)

Further Reading

A. ARBEL and R. M. TONG, 'On the generation of alternatives in decision analysis problems', *Journal of the Operational Research Society*, 1982, vol. 33, pp. 377–87.

H. BEIRMAN and W. H. HAUSMAN, 'The Credit Granting Decision', *Management Science*, April 1970, pp. B519–32.

D. W. BUNN and H. THOMAS, 'Decision analysis and strategic policy formulation', *Long Range Planning*, vol. 10, pp. 23–30.

R. D. BUZZELL and C. C. SLATTER, 'Decision theory and marketing management', *Journal of Marketing*, 1962, vol. 26, no. 3, pp. 7–16.

G. M. KAUFMAN, *Statistical decision and related techniques in oil and gas exploration*, Prentice-Hall, New Jersey, 1963.

C. W. KIRKWOOD, 'A Case History of Nuclear Power Site Selection', *Journal of the Operational Research Society*, 1982, vol. 33, pp. 353–63.

L. R. PHILLIPS, 'Requisite Decision Modelling: A Case Study', *Journal of the Operational Research Society*, 1982, vol. 33, pp. 303–11.

7 Assessing Uncertain Events

Introduction

In the decision-making problems discussed in earlier chapters, uncertainty about the outcomes of various situations is an important element of the analysis of the alternative strategies from which we must choose. For example, in new-product decisions, uncertainty exists about the likely sales of the product, and this must be resolved satisfactorily before a decision to launch it is irrevocably made. Many decision-makers find, however, that they are unused to the notion of assessing and expressing uncertainty on any formal scale of measurement.

The Language of Uncertainty

The uncertainty in a business situation is often expressed verbally in terms such as 'it is likely', 'it is probable', 'the chances are', 'probably', 'possibly' and so on. This approach is usually unsatisfactory because words are only useful to convey meaning when both the writer and the reader (or speaker and listener) agree on the meanings to be ascribed to the words. When we enter the realms of describing uncertainty, this is found to be untrue. As an illustration, the following list of ten expressions was culled from the same article which was discussing, in a literary rather than numerate style, some forecasts that had been made in the consumer durables field: 1 *probable*, 2 *quite certain*, 3 *unlikely*, 4 *hoped*, 5 *possible*, 6 *not unreasonable that*, 7 *expected*, 8 *doubtful*, 9 *not certain* and 10 *likely*.

Some 250 executives on middle and senior general management programmes at a Business School were asked to rank these ten words or phrases in decreasing order of uncertainty, and Table 7.1 gives the results for a typical group of forty executives, the expressions being re-ordered in descending order of average rank. The final column shows the range of ranks given to each of the ten expressions, illustrating the considerable overlapping of ranks that occurs for many of the expressions and thus the inconsistency between the respondents. Indeed, only three of the respondents produced precisely the same rankings. A further experiment where the ranking was repeated after an interval of about a month, showed that respondents were not even consistent over time in their ranking of the same expressions.

Table 7.1 Ranking of uncertainty expressions

expression	average rank	range of ranks
2 quite certain	1·10	1–3
7 expected	2·95	1–6
10 likely	3·85	2–7
1 probable	4·25	2–9
6 not unreasonable that	4·65	3–7
5 possible	6·10	3–9
4 hoped	7·15	3–10
9 not certain	7·80	3–10
8 doubtful	8·60	7–10
3 unlikely	8·75	3–10

There are, of course, innumerable other words and phrases used in ordinary communications to convey uncertainty, and the present experiment covered only a small selection. Nevertheless, there is little reason to doubt that another list of words would produce similar results. If executives are inconsistent in their use of words the treatment of uncertainty is promptly downgraded in importance from the consideration of other items, such as costs, that are thought capable, at least on the surface, of being measured and communicated more precisely.

The Nature of Probability

The evidence given in Table 7.1 indicates clearly that verbal expressions are imprecise descriptions of an individual's level of uncertainty and, more importantly, that considerable disagreement can occur between individuals about the meanings of words describing the nature of uncertainty. The vagueness and imprecision that results from the use of verbal expressions to describe uncertainty does not mean that an individual's feelings about uncertainty cannot be made precise. Rather, it gives impetus to the view that a quantitative language of uncertainty is preferable to a qualitative one. It is for this reason that we use probability as a suitable language for the communication of uncertainty and its incorporation into the analysis of decision problems.

Whilst the mathematical results of probability theory are seldom in dispute, the same cannot be said about the interpretation of the probability concept. There are two main interpretations of probability. The first considers the estimation of the probability of an event in terms of the *relative frequency* with which the event in question has occurred under similar conditions in the past. This is commonly referred to as *objective* probability. The second views probability as being the extent of an individual's *belief* in the occurrence of an event. This is commonly referred to as *personal* or *subjective probability*. These two terms polarize the methods of approach. Nevertheless, it is our contention that no estimation of a probability in practice is entirely objective or entirely subjective. All probability estimates are a mixture, but the precise balance between objective and subjective inputs will vary greatly from one situation to another.

Objective Probability

Objective probability uses statistical data provided by past events in order to predict (or place probabilities upon) the recurrence of future events. It employs two forms of extrapolation, one based on the frequency of past occurrences of the event itself and the other based on an aggregation of frequencies for a whole set of antecedent happenings that are thought to determine the event.

Illustrations of the former occur in the field of insurance. For example, the determination of the premium to be charged on a life assurance policy will be computed using a life table that is based upon the mortality experience of recent cohorts of men (or women). The probabilities obtained from the table are used, possibly with some modification to allow for trends in the mortality rates, to predict the appropriate probability for a new assurance policy. Again, for motor insurance, similar tables of accident rates in the past can be compiled for drivers of different age, sex, location, type of car and then used in a predictive sense to provide a quotation. Similar situations arise in many industrial situations; for example if past experience shows that 1·5 per cent of components mass-produced on a machine are defective, this figure can be used for predictive purposes when dealing with complaints policies or allowing for wastage.

The more complex form of objective probability arises when there are no 'long-run' relevant data and the situation has to be simulated from past data. Examples would be the probability of a core meltdown in a reactor, or a collision between two Boeing 747 aircraft, or the possibility of collapse of a dam. Appropriate probabilities can be derived from objective data, but one is commonly dealing with very low levels of risk and verification is therefore the more difficult.

More commercial situations than are commonly recognized do have available substantive amounts of objective data on which to base probability estimates, and these data should not be ignored merely because there are other non-objective elements involved. Sales forecasting of an established product is a case in point; past data should have priority over subjective 'guesses', at any rate in the first analysis.

Subjective Probability

There are, however, many events which can be thought of in probabilistic terms, but cannot be given a relative frequency interpretation. Consider the situation facing a firm launching a completely new product. It cannot observe the process of launching this product twenty times, or even twice, neither can it usually argue that previous new product launches by the firm will enable it to assess objectively and precisely the chances of success of the current new product launch. But, whilst the firm's marketing manager cannot get an objective measure of the probability of success of the launch, he nevertheless has his own views about the product and its likely success. These introspective feelings and judgements can be quantified in probabilistic terms as degrees of belief using the subjective probability concept.

The subjective interpretation of probability is fundamental to the analysis of many decision problems in business and government, particularly those in which the events are unique in the sense that the situations cannot be duplicated. For example, consider each of the following non-repeatable events and note that for each one, a subjective probability (but not a relative-frequency) could be assessed:

  (i) The chance of the price of gold moving by more than 10 per cent either way in the next six months.
 (ii) The chance of a black President of the United States within the next fifty years.
(iii) The chance of the United Kingdom being a net exporter of oil in the year 2000.
 (iv) The chance of there being a non-Italian Pope within the next fifty years.

The reader might himself be able to make an assessment of the probability of each of these events occurring. However, it is likely he would wish to consult experts on politics, economics, religion and natural resources, using their expert judgement to reach appropriate subjective probabilities.

The concept of *subjective* (or personal) *probability* is based on the premise that everyone has a degree of belief concerning the likely occurrence of some event relevant to them and their environment. The value of the concept is that it allows the decision-maker or expert to describe his feelings about the effects of uncertainty in defined and understood numerical terms, and thus incorporate his judgement explicitly into the decision process. The resulting numbers do not imply objectivity or authority; they are an understood way of putting subjective views into a more precise form providing, in turn, a basis for comparison when relating one decision-maker's evaluation with another. Thus, as judgements differ, so may subjective assessments. This in no way invalidates the theoretical basis for subjective probability. Subjective assessments are based on the information available to the assessor at the time of assessment; as the same information becomes available to all the assessors, their differing assessments should reasonably converge to a common figure.

Probabilities and Betting Odds – A Numerical Scale for Probability

We have stressed the need to quantify uncertainty in numerical terms, using the language of probabilities. However, some assessors feel more comfortable making *odds* rather than *probability* assessments, even though, in theoretical terms at least, they are merely different ways of expressing uncertainty. This is because individuals commonly, in their day-to-day lives, talk in betting terms. Sometimes these are expressed in terms of money, e.g. betting on horses in a horse-race, or on the outcomes of soccer matches, but they commonly have no monetary basis. The essential difference between the two measures is that *odds* express the *relative chance of occurence* of some event, whilst probabilities reflect the *absolute chance* of that event occurring. Consider the following example. Suppose that the probability of rain tomorrow (R) is assessed as

$$P(R) = 0.8.$$

Then the probability of no rain tomorrow ($\bar{R}$) must be

$$P(\bar{R}) = 0.2.$$

The relative chance of the occurrence of rain is

$$\frac{P(R)}{P(\bar{R})} = \frac{0.8}{0.2} = \frac{4}{1}.$$

This ratio is expressed as 'the odds on rain tomorrow are 4 to 1' meaning that it is four times as likely for rain to occur as not to occur tomorrow. Alternatively, we could say that the 'odds against rain tomorrow are 1 to 4'.

Because odds can easily be interpreted in terms of bets, and individuals find the language of odds an effective means of expressing uncertainty, decision analysts sometimes use odds assessments to check a direct probability assessment of some event. Consider again the assessment of rain tomorrow (R), i.e. $P(R) = 0.8$, that is to say, 'odds of 4 to 1 on rain tomorrow, or 4 to 1 against no rain tomorrow', made by an individual. This individual should, if he has made an internally consistent assessment, be indifferent as between either of the two bets itemized below:

> Bet A   You win $10 with odds 4 to 1 on
> You win $0 with odds 4 to 1 against
> Bet B   You win $10 if it rains tomorrow
> You win $0 if it does not rain tomorrow.

If you prefer Bet A, then your odds on rain tomorrow are not as favourable as 4 to 1 on, i.e. the probability of rain is less than 0.80. If you prefer Bet B, then the opposite applies.

Placing the assessment task in a betting context allows the decision-maker to view this assessment from a different psychological viewpoint. This is because the bet specifies a particular act implied by his uncertainty assessment, and the decision analyst can thus check the accuracy of the decision-maker's assessment by getting him to judge whether he would be willing to act in the manner specified by his assessment.

Odds are additionally useful because they allow a decision-maker to compare multiple probabilities. For example, consider the following probability assessments made by an economist about the state of the economy during next year:

$P(M) = 0.1$, where M is the event that economic conditions will improve;
$P(S) = 0.4$, where S is the event that economic conditions stay the same;
$P(D) = 0.5$, where D is the event that economic conditions deteriorate.

This implies the following ratios:

$$P(M):P(S):P(D) = 1:4:5.$$

An analyst could check these assessments by asking the economist if he believes it is five times more likely for economic conditions to deteriorate as to improve, or whether it is four times as likely for conditions to stagnate as improve. If he remains satisfied with these ratios, then he can be sure that his probability assessments accurately reflect his degree of uncertainty.

In the next section we alert the reader to some of the difficulties which arise in the process of probability assessment, thus demonstrating that probability assessment requires considerable patience and care if it is to be undertaken successfully.

The Process of Probability Assessment

Probability assessment consists of a number of distinct phases, which together form a logical structure (see Figure 7.1). Initially, the individual assessor must be taken through a pre-assessment phase in which he is trained in the meaning and relevance of probability concepts, and is made aware of potential behavioural and motivational biases which can occur when he assesses probabilities in practice. The encoding phase in probability assessment which follows relates to the actual quantification of the decision-maker's judgement in probabilistic terms. The most suitable methods here are those which the assessor finds he can

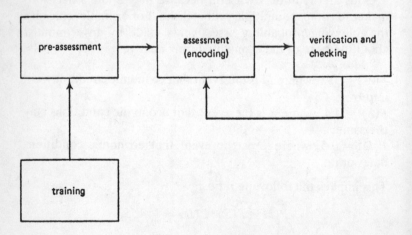

7.1 Phases in probability assessment

understand and use in a consistent and coherent manner. However, there is no guarantee that any particular probability assessment will be meaningful and a subsequent verification and checking phase is needed in which the responses obtained in the encoding phase are checked for consistency.

We concentrate here primarily on the encoding phase, in which an appropriate assessment method is chosen and applied. The result is a probability distribution either for discrete events (e.g. attributes of the either 'does' or 'does not' occur variety) or for a continuous event or quantity, x (e.g. the proportion of defective units from some new production process). Often the latter is not assessed directly. Instead a cumulative probability distribution is determined, whereby the quantity assessed is the probability of a proportion x or less defectives occurring.

No attempt is made here to cover all the possible approaches for assessing probability that have been suggested in decision analysis. Instead we present a discussion of the more common approaches – considering the discrete case of a single event or series of events in this chapter and the case of continuous uncertain quantities in the next chapter.

Practical Guidelines

The following checklist gives the preparatory steps to be taken for obtaining meaningful assessments from managers.

(i) An essential prerequisite is that the decision problem is meaningfully decomposed into its logical structure and the influence of uncertainty on the structure clearly delineated.

(ii) Probability assessments should be conducted by the analyst with the manager alone, to remove him or her from the influence of group pressures.

(iii) The events or uncertain quantities to be assessed should be relevant and important to the manager, so that he has the incentive to allocate time and effort to the task.

(iv) The terms in which the events or uncertain quantities are described should be at the discretion of the manager. For example, in assessing the likely market for a product, the manager might think of the percentage share, overall size, volume etc., and should assess the uncertainty in relation to the variable which, for him, most closely describes the likely market.

(v) The assessor should not be forced to worry about inconsistencies in his assessments. The task of the analyst is to design further tasks in the process of assessment so that he can feed them back and remove inconsistencies.

Fundamentally a decision-maker must feel involved in the solution of the decision problem at issue, and have reached the point at which a basic decision tree structure has been agreed with the analyst. At the same time, a crude sensitivity analysis of the tree is usually performed to identify those uncertain factors which are crucial or extremely sensitive in relation to the analysis of the problem. The aim is then to proceed to a careful assessment of the probabilities for the events and uncertain quantities which finally appear on the decision tree.

Assessment of Probabilities for Discrete Events

It is useful to classify the methods for assessing probability as being either *direct* or *indirect*. A direct assessment implies that the analyst asks the assessor questions about the uncertain events that require odds or probability statements as answers. On the other hand, indirect methods of assessment require that the assessor's degrees of belief be inferred from his choice behaviour when he is asked to discriminate between two or more bets or alternatives.

We also assume that there is an identifiable individual to whom decision-making is delegated, and from whom we need to extract meaningful assessments. We return in the next chapter to discuss the problem of how we obtain a *consensus* probability assessment from a number of managers who form the decision-making group.

In the discrete case, the prior distribution consists of a set of possible and exclusive events, together with their probabilities of occurrence. The only constraints are that the probabilities are each non-negative and sum to unity. Given these restrictions, the assessor determines his prior probability distribution. For example, the marketing manager may want to assess the number of units of a particular product which will be sold next year. One way of approaching this problem is to ask him to specify the possible range of the number of units sold, say 0 to 1,000 units, and then translate this range into sales events or sub-ranges as follows:

event	range
R_1	0–249 units sold
R_2	250–499 units sold
R_3	500–749 units sold
R_4	750–999 units sold.

Each of these sub-ranges represents a discrete event, and probabilities can be assessed by the marketing manager for each of these discrete events along the lines discussed below. Numerous techniques are available for this purpose and we discuss some of the most useful ones in the following sections.

A Direct Method

Obviously the easiest way in which to obtain a person's probability assessment for some event is to ask him. An individual may express his beliefs, if he has adequate knowledge of probability concepts, by stating either a probability value between 0 and 1, or by giving an equivalent odds statement about that event. Such a direct method is quick and easy but the disadvantage is that the assessor may make an ill-considered judgement. The only way to overcome this is to confront the assessor with consistency checks. For example, if he assigns a probability of 0·8 to some event, then he should be asked if he is willing to bet $4 to win back $5 – the original stake plus $1. If he says no, then his judgements should be explored and reconsidered until he behaves in accordance with his assessed probability. When there are more than two values of an uncertain quantity, it is often sensible to determine a prior distribution by considering the *relative chances* of the various values of the uncertain quantity occurring. Suppose you are interested in the change in price of ITT stock when the New York Stock Exchange opens for trading tomorrow. The stock can either go up (G), stay the same (S) or fall in price (*F*). You feel, after consideration, that the stock is three times as likely to fall as to remain at today's level, and twice as likely to stay the same as to go up. This implies that:

$$\frac{P(F)}{P(S)} = 3 \quad \text{and} \quad \frac{P(S)}{P(G)} = 2.$$

Now,

$$P(G) + P(S) + P(F) = 1,$$

and, by substitution,

$$\tfrac{1}{2}P(S) + P(S) + 3P(S) = 1.$$

Hence

$$P(G) = \tfrac{1}{9}, \; P(S) = \tfrac{2}{9}, \; P(F) = \tfrac{2}{3}.$$

The complete prior distribution has been evaluated. Note that it was not necessary to consider all possible event outcomes at once. Instead, odds were found for the outcomes in pairs, and probabilities derived from those odds assessments.

Indirect Methods

Indirect methods of assessment require the individual's degrees of belief to be inferred from his behaviour. Instead of asking directly for an assessment, the decision-maker's behaviour is observed in relation to certain situations, e.g. lotteries, betting odds, insurance premiums, and so on, and his degrees of belief are inferred from his behaviour in the situations specified.

The Equivalent Urn. A very simple indirect method employs a standard reference device, an equivalent urn, as the means for assessing a probability. To see how this is used in a practical contest suppose that you, as a research manager, want to determine the probability of success, within a specified time period, of a particular R and D project. You are asked to consider two bets, A involving the event whose probability you wish to assess,

B involving the equivalent urn (standard device). The first bet is drawn up as follows:

Bet A   If the R and D project is a success within a given time
period, you win $1,000.
If the project fails you win nothing.

The tree diagram of Figure 7.2(a) represents this bet.

Imagine next that an urn has been filled with 1,000 identically shaped balls – each ball being identified with a number from 1 to 1,000. Suppose that balls 1 to 500 in the standard urn have been coloured red, while the remaining 500 balls have been coloured blue. The balls are thoroughly mixed, and one is to be drawn by a blindfold observer. The second bet is drawn up as follows:

Bet B   If the ball drawn is red, you win $1,000.
If the ball is blue, you win nothing.

This bet is displayed in tree diagram form in Figure 7.2(b) where the probabilities of drawing either a red or a blue ball are clearly both 0·5.

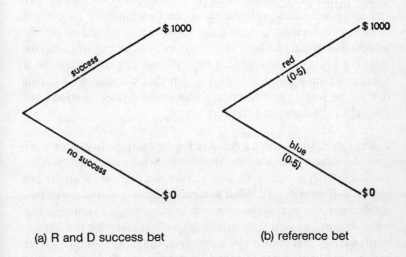

(a) R and D success bet   (b) reference bet

7.2 Tree diagrams for alternative bets

As research manager, you are now asked which bet do you prefer, A or B? Suppose that you prefer B. Then there must be a better chance for you to win $1,000 with bet B than with bet A. Thus, the probability of success, in your judgement, is clearly less than 0·5.

By changing the proportion of red balls in the urn, a mix of red and blue balls can eventually be found for which you are indifferent between the two bets. When this point is reached, we are justified in assigning the same probability to the event 'red ball is drawn' as we are to the event 'success of the R and D project'. At no time in this process is it necessary to ask a question more complex than 'Do you prefer this bet or that one, or are you indifferent between them?' From answers to these questions concerning preferences between bets, we obtain a numerical measure of the individual's degrees of belief.

The Pie Diagram Device. Other standard devices can be used to elicit probability assessments. An alternative is to use a pie diagram device, called a probability wheel, as a reference process for probability assessment (see Figure 7.3).

The probability wheel is a circle divided into two sectors, say red and blue, whose relative sizes can be adjusted. To use the device, you must imagine that the spinner rotates and randomly selects one of the two sectors. You then ask the expert to bet on either a fixed event, e.g. that 'the R and D project will be a success within a given time period', or that the spinner will rest in the blue sector. The amount of blue in the wheel is varied until the expert becomes indifferent.

Lottery or Choice among Bets. A further alternative is to infer an individual's probabilities from his choices amongst bets or gambles. Imagine that once again you are presented with the bet shown in Figure 7.2(a). What amount of money would make you indifferent between playing the bet or accepting the money? Put another way, what is your minimum selling price for the bet or, equivalently, if someone else owned the bet, what would be your maximum buying price? Let the amount of money be designated as Y. The assumption is that you have specified the expected monetary value (EMV) of the bet, so that Y = EMV. Now let p stand for the probability of 'R and D success within a given time period'.

If Y = expected monetary value of Bet A
then $Y = p \times \$1,000 + (1-p) \times \$0$.

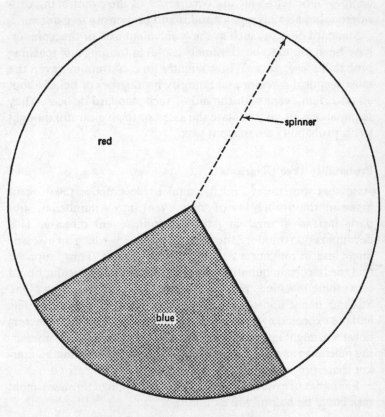

7.3 Probability wheel or spinner

Solving for p gives

$$p = \frac{Y}{1,000}$$

The main criticism of methods based on betting frameworks is the introduction of gambling terminology, particularly in regard to the sizes of the stakes involved in the bets. It is possible that the probability assessor may exhibit 'special' gambling behaviour in betting situation, implying that the probability assessment for a particular event might reflect, not only the decision-maker's degrees of belief about the occurrence of the event being considered, but also his risk attitudes and propensity to gamble.

Standard devices, such as the 'equivalent urn' or the 'spinner' have been found to be extremely useful in training and teaching probability assessors. Whilst slightly time-consuming, even the most sceptical assessor can quantify his degrees of belief about an uncertain event with the aid of such standard devices. They seem, above all, to stimulate the assessor to give careful thought to his probability assessment task.

Probability Tree Diagrams

Assessors sometimes find it useful to decompose the task of assessing the probability of some event into a number of sub-parts instead of analysing the uncertain event directly. This decomposition 'models' the thought processes which an assessor might use in making a probability assessment. Thus, suppose that the uncertain quantity was the number of a particular brand of washing machines that would be sold in the next year. One assessor might approach this by considering the retail outlets and the expected average sales in each outlet. Another assessor, however, might approach it by considering the market for washing machines as a whole, combining this with an estimated market share proportion for the particular brand concerned.

Examples of events for which decomposition of the assessment task could be helpful are as follows:

(i) The chance that a nuclear reactor used for electricity generation explodes within the next year.

(ii) The chance of an earthquake occurring in Los Angeles County in the USA during the next year.

(iii) The amount of money (in $ million) which IBM will spend on research into computer software in 1990.

(iv) The chance that the Dow Jones Index will increase by 200 points at some stage within the next year.

Consider for illustration item (iv), which is an event that is dependent upon various possible factors such as the general state of the economy, the incidence of short-run strikes, the political situation and the level of business expectations. This situation can be handled by decomposing the problem in probability tree form. This is shown in Figure 7.4 where the expert has conditioned the movement of the Dow Jones Index on three factors: cost of living, rate of strikes, and the level of wage claims. In order to determine the overall probability of a rise of 200 points in the Dow Jones Index, it would first be necessary to assess probabilities for each chance event on the tree, noting that most of the assessments after the initial node are in terms of conditional probabilities. Subsequently, the overall probability of a rise can be obtained by folding the diagram back and by summing the path probabilities for each of the eight end outcomes corresponding to the situation of a 200 points rise.

Figure 7.5, on the other hand, demonstrates that the expert could first choose to prune the tree and then make his probability assessment based on the amended tree. This amended tree omits the factor of wage claims as it could be argued that the level of wage claims and the rate of strikes are highly correlated and, in effect, measure the same thing. In addition, a two-branch fork indicating the possibility of either a rise (R) or a fall ($\bar{R}$) in the Dow Jones Index has been substituted for the three-branch fork (consisting of R, C, F) in order to simplify the assessment task. The analyst's assessments for each chance-event fork are shown in Figure 7.5 and he then calculates the path probabilities for each branch as shown on the extreme right of the probability tree, multiplying the appropriate sequence of probabilities together. His probability assessment for a rise (R) in the Index is now determined by summing the path probabilities for the four paths corresponding to R.

Summarizing, anyone who has a clear understanding of probability concepts should be able to assess a prior distribution for discrete outcomes or events. When dealing with outcomes meas-

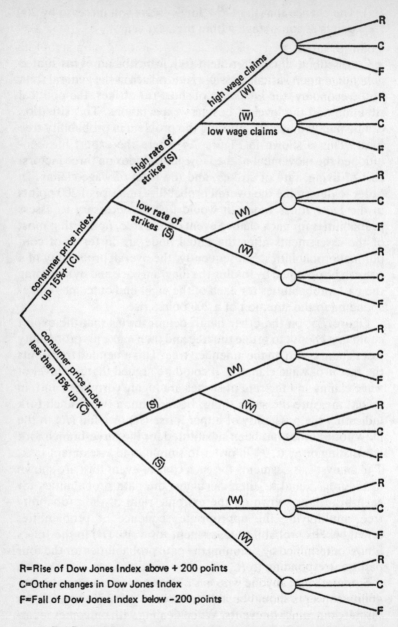

R=Rise of Dow Jones Index above + 200 points
C=Other changes in Dow Jones Index
F=Fall of Dow Jones Index below −200 points

7.4 Probability tree decomposition of Dow Jones Index

ured on a continuous scale, assessment of the prior distribution becomes more difficult as will be seen in chapter 8. The main point for an assessor to keep clear in either situation is that his prior distribution should reflect a judicious blend of his subjective judgement with all the relevant available information about the outcomes of interest.

Exercises

1. Complete the missing entries in Table 7.2.

Table 7.2 Probabilities and odds

situation	probability of success	odds on success
1	0·6	
2		3:1
3	0·8	
4	0·9	
5		2:1
6	1·00	
7		5:1
8	0·25	
9	0·3	
10		1:1

2. The following are three mutually exclusive and exhaustive events:

      A It will rain in Central Park, New York, tomorrow,
      B It will be sunny in Central Park tomorrow,
      C It will snow in Central Park tomorrow.

The probabilities for the first two of these are given as

$$P(A) = 0·2 \quad \text{and} \quad P(B) = 0·6.$$

Calculate (i) $P(C)$
          (ii) $P(B \text{ or } C)$
          (iii) $P(A \text{ or } C)$
          (iv) $P(A \text{ or } B \text{ or } C)$

path probabilities

7.5 Path probabilities for Dow Jones Index assessment

3. Using one of the standard reference devices mentioned in the chapter (i.e. spinner, equivalent urn, etc.) assess your own and some of your colleagues' uncertainty about the following events:

(i) Medical research will produce a complete cure for cancer by the year 2000.
(ii) Oil will be found in commercial quantities off the west coast of Wales by 1995.
(iii) Ireland will become a single united nation in the next twenty years.

Additionally, draw up a list of some further events on which to try out the methods.

4. XYZ Realtors is wondering whether it will be able to sell a certain property. A major complicating factor arises from the possibility that a competitive realtor, BR Inc., is also trying to sell the property. The probability of this happening is assessed at 0·3. If BR is indeed trying to make a sale, XYZ feels that there is a 0·4 chance that it will be successful. However, if BR is not attempting to make a sale, then XYZ believes that it has a 0·95 chance of selling the property.

(i) Draw a probability tree diagram for this situation.
(ii) Determine the conditional probability of XYZ being successful when BR is in competition with it for the sale of the property.

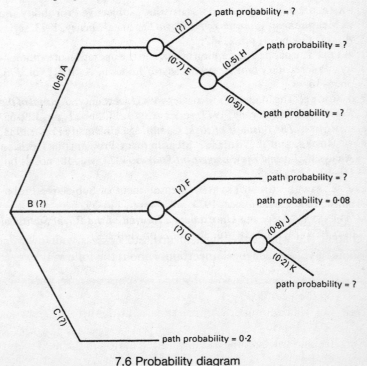

7.6 Probability diagram

(iii) By pruning the probability tree, find the unconditional probability of XYZ being successful.

5. Using the probability diagram in Figure 7.6, derive:

  (i) the missing probability entries (marked with a ?)

 (ii) $P(E/A)$

(iii) $P(F/B)$

(iv) $P(G/B)$

 (v) $P(A$ and $D)$

(vi) $P(F$ and $B)$.

Further Reading

F. R. FARMER, 'Quantification of Engineering and Physical Risks', *Proceedings of the Royal Society of London*, A, 1981, vol. 376, pp. 103–19.

J. HAMPTON, P. G. MOORE and H. THOMAS, 'Subjective Probability and its Measurement', *Journal of the Royal Statistical Society*, 1973, series A, vol. 136, no. 1, pp. 21–42.

T. R. LEE, 'The public's perception of risk and the operation of irrationality', *Proceedings of the Royal Society of London*, A, 1981, vol. 376, pp. 5–16.

P. G. MOORE, 'The Manager's Struggles with Uncertainty', *Journal of the Royal Statistical Society*, 1977, series A, vol. 140, no. 1, pp. 129–65.

P. G. MOORE, *The Business of Risk*, Cambridge University Press, 1983.

P. G. MOORE, and H. THOMAS, 'Measurement Problems in Decision Analysis', *Journal of Management Studies*, 1973, vol. 10, no. 2, pp. 168–93.

C. A. S. STAEL VON HOLSTEIN, 'Measurement of Subjective Probability', *Acta Psychologica*, 1970, vol. 34, pp. 146–59.

A. TVERSKY, 'Assessing Uncertainty', *Journal of the Royal Statistical Society*, 1974, series B, vol. 36, no. 2, pp. 148–59.

8 Probability Distributions

Introduction

The phrase 'continuous event' and 'uncertain quantity' have been used interchangeably. By either we mean a quantity whose value lies anywhere along a specified continuum: e.g. a firm's R and D budget next year, the likely market share for a new product, etc. In many business contexts a decision analysis requires the probabilities of more than just a few events at each fork of the tree (e.g. not just the four sub-ranges for the uncertain

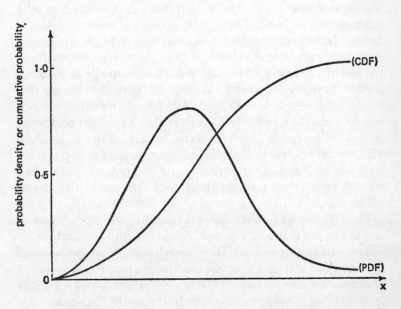

8.1 Probability density versus cumulative probability

quantity, sales level, discussed in chapter 7). Rather than assessing the probabilities of a large number of values of an uncertain quantity, it is generally easier to assess a continuous probability distribution, either in the form of a probability density function (PDF) or in terms of the cumulative density function (CDF) as shown in Figure 8.1. Various methods for obtaining one or other of these forms are now discussed.

The CDF Method

The more commonly used form to describe the uncertainty for some uncertain quantity is the CDF. The horizontal axis of such a distribution shows possible values of the uncertain quantity X, whilst the vertical axis gives the probability that the true value is X or less. In other words, the distribution gives the probability that the true value lies in a range up to X, where values of X are shown along the horizontal axis.

A common method of assessing such a distribution involves first determining a value of X such that the true value of X is estimated to be just as likely to lie above the assessed value as below. The assessor should be equally willing to place a bet on the interval above that value of X as below it. His choice of X is the fiftieth percentile of the distribution (commonly termed the median), usually designated X_{50}. Next, he is asked to assume that the true figure is below X_{50} and is asked to divide that interval into two equally good bets. This gives the 25 per cent percentile X_{25}. Another halving operation can be carried out to give the 12·5 per cent percentile. Similar questions yield the 75 per cent, 87·5 per cent and other percentiles. Plotting these points and smoothing a curve through them gives the cumulative distribution.

The following example shows the interrogation procedure in use to assess a manager's cumulative probability function for his judgement concerning the Dow Jones Index. Suppose we wish to assess the manager's probability distribution for the level of the Index six months hence. The horizontal axis of such a distribution shows possible values of the Index, whilst the vertical axis gives the probability that the true value is that value or less. Hence, for any value X of the Index, this distribution describes the manager's belief that the true value six months from now is less than or equal to X.

The questions might go something like this:

ANALYST: Can you give me a value of the Index, that you feel has a 50 per cent chance of being exceeded six months hence?
  (Note this establishes the value at which the CDF = 0·5.)
MANAGER: I guess I would say 1,000. (Hence 1,000 corresponds to X_{50}.)
ANALYST: Now, suppose that the actual value of the Dow Jones Index in six months' time will be below 1,000, can you give me a value of the Index that you feel has a 50 per cent chance of being exceeded?
MANAGER: Now that's a hard thing to conceive. I suppose about 625.
ANALYST: Are you sure about that? Would you take either side of a bet on the interval above 625 and below 1,000, and that below 625?
MANAGER: I think I'll change my answer; 750 represents my indifference point. (Note that this question establishes 750 as the value of the Index at which the CDF = 0·25, i.e. X_{25}.)
ANALYST: Now, given that the true value of the Index six months hence will be above 1,000, can you give me a value of the Index that you feel has a 50 per cent chance of being exceeded?
MANAGER: Well, I guess that I am beginning to understand what you are after now. My indifference point is about 1,150.
  (Note this establishes 1,150 as the value of the Index at which the CDF = 0·75 or X_{75}.)

From the set of discrete points obtained from these, and some additional questions on the same lines to obtain the credible range for the Index, an approximate curve such as that in Figure 8.2 can be drawn. This is referred to as the CDF curve.

An example of this approach has been given by R. L. Keeney in a study on the development of facilities at the Mexico City Airport. The procedure outlined above was carried out, the quantity to be estimated (in 1972) being the average number of people who would be subjected in 1985 to noise levels of 90

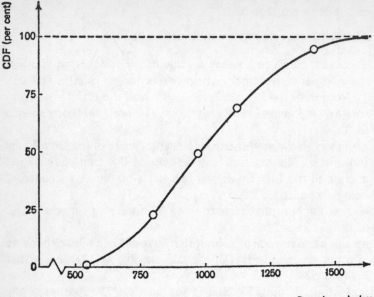

8.2 A CDF assessment for the Dow Jones Index

CNR (Composite Noise Rating) or above. The one major difference was that the first step in the assessment procedure was to
estimate the absolute bounds for the variable X; i.e. the range
within which X would lie. The bounds of the range were estimated to be 700,000 and 1,200,000. Figure 8.3 illustrates part of
the results obtained.

The Tertile Method

People commonly find it easier to judge when they are indifferent between a number of quantities, than to judge the absolute
magnitudes of these quantities. A possible alternative assessment procedure based on such comparisons is illustrated by the
following problem concerning the estimation of the population
of the United States. The person assesses as a start that it is

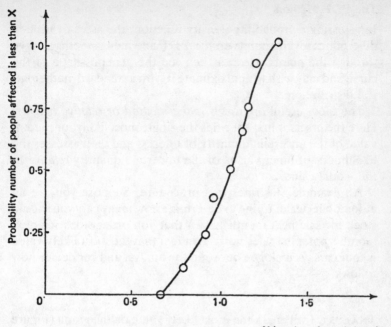

8.3 Cumulative density function for aircraft noise nuisance above 90
CNR

essentially impossible for the population to be less than 90
million or more than 300 million. Two cardboard pointers are
now placed on a scale marked from 90 to 300 million. The
assessor then adjusts the position of the pointers so that he would
consider the three alternative ranges so generated equally likely:
that is, the true value of the variable is felt to be equally likely to
fall above both pointers, between them or below them. The four
points now available are plotted and a smooth curve drawn freehand through them. The object of trisecting the range is to try
to avoid the tendency for assessors to give too narrow a range in
their assessments and also the bias which occurs in the fractile
method when assessors 'anchor' at the median, thus giving too
great a probability value to the central assessment.

The PDF Method

In assessing a probability density function, the assessor usually determines several points on the PDF and then smooths a curve through the points. He can then see the general shape of the curve and may wish to approximate it with a standard mathematical distribution.

The most useful approach is *the method of relative heights*. Here the assessor first specifies the single most likely, or modal, value of the uncertain quantity of interest and then assesses the likelihoods of other values of the uncertain quantity *relative* to the modal value.

An example illustrates this procedure. Suppose you are an automobile dealer trying to determine how many cars you should stock for sale next month, given that you order stock for next month's potential sales now. You feel that the most likely value is four cars. A dialogue between the analyst and car dealer now follows:

ANALYST: I will mark the most likely value on the graph (Figure 8.4) with a height of eight units.

DEALER: OK, I understand that.

ANALYST: Now can you find a value below four cars a month that you feel is half as likely to occur as four?

DEALER: Well, I would say that two cars is half as likely as four.

ANALYST: Right, I will mark the value of two cars as four units on the graph. Now, can you give me a value above four cars a month that is again half as likely as four?

DEALER: Yes, I'd say five.

ANALYST: OK then, I'll mark the value for five as four units on the graph. Can you now give me a value which is a quarter as likely as the four-car value?

DEALER: That's difficult, maybe one car if we do poorly or seven cars if we do well. Can you put the question another way?

ANALYST: Well, is it also four times as likely for you to sell four cars as seven cars next month?

DEALER: Yes, that's also about right.

ANALYST: Right, those points will be marked with two units.

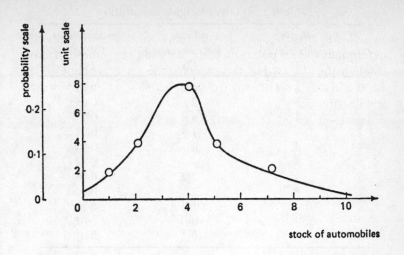

8.4 Relative heights and PDF for automobile stock situation

Finally, what are your minimum and maximum possible sales levels next month?

DEALER: I guess zero and ten.

ANALYST: Let's enter all the relative heights in Figure 8.4 and see how we can derive the probabilities by drawing a smooth curve through the various points and 'normalize' the data to form a PDF.

Table 8.1 shows how the procedure can be inverted by interpolating relative heights for all possible levels of car sales after drawing a graph of the value, and then scaling them by the total of all the relative heights to form probabilities that sum to unity. The probabilities form a slightly asymmetric set with the longer tail to the right.

Indirect Methods

The main indirect method for assessing a continuous (PDF) probability distribution requires the assessor to give estimates of the parameters (e.g. the mean and standard deviation) of some defined form of statistical distribution (e.g. normal, exponential,

Table 8.1 Relative heights calculation

cars (1)	relative heights plotted (2)	relative heights smoothed (3)	probabilities (3)/Σ(3) (4)
0	–	0·7	0·02
1	2	2	0·06
2	4	4	0·12
3	–	7·4	0·22
4	8	8	0·24
5	4	4	0·12
6	–	2·7	0·08
7	2	2	0·06
8	–	1·7	0·05
9	–	0·6	0·02
10	–	0·3	0·01
	totals	33·4	1

etc.). Thus the marketing manager might be asked to assess the mean and standard deviation of the demand for some product next year, and to indicate the assumed mathematical form of the PDF. The analyst would then fit the distribution and read off any individual probabilities required for the decision analysis.

To do this the assessor must have considerable acquaintance with statistical distribution theory. Whilst direct assessment of a distribution is often a difficult task, the indirect approach makes much more severe assumptions and is often difficult to explain to assessors with a limited statistical background. Hence this approach is correspondingly limited in its applicability.

Group Assessments

A major problem exists when we need to evaluate the PDF or CDF from a group rather than from a single decision-maker. Although the problem is discussed here in relation to assessing probabilities for continuous events, the principles apply equally well to discrete events. This problem is commonly described as the *consensus* problem for subjective probability measurements. Basically, the issue is to decide how to aggregate a series of individual probability assessments to give the consensus assessment. A number of schemes have been suggested. The usual way is to aggregate the separate distributions by taking a linear combination of them, the weights not necessarily being equal. Indeed one might expect certain individuals to be better assessors than others and to be given higher weights. Assessors also improve their skill the more often they are given opportunities to make formal probability assessments, which again could affect their relative weighting. In some decision-making situations, e.g. short-term forecasting, it is possible to calibrate probability assessors directly and obtain their appropriate relative weightings from the actual probability assessment performance in the situation concerned.

An alternative approach is the *Delphi technique*. This is essentially a technological forecasting technique, consensus being achieved through controlled feedback of information. Initially, each member of the decision-making group is asked to give his probability assessment for the unknown quantity in terms of the direct percentile approach. Some summary measures (e.g. mean and standard deviation, or median and interquartile range) are then calculated from the initial set of assessments and fed back to the individuals. This feedback process is repeated until the consensus assessment distribution becomes acceptably tight.

Ultimately the group must meet and reconcile any remaining differences in assessments. This process of reconciliation is often much easier when there is agreement amongst the group that certain individuals are well calibrated and, on the basis of past performance, have shown themselves to be good probability assessors.

Consistency

By consistency in probability forecasts we mean the extent to which a probability assessment made in alternative direct ways (for example, odds and point estimates) are consistent between themselves and also with indirect assessment methods (for example, the spinner betting approach or the reference gamble techniques). Empirical evidence concerning consistency is contradictory; statisticians have been found to be more consistent than non-statisticians. For the latter, direct-odds estimates, perhaps because there is no upper or lower limit, tend to be more extreme than direct probability estimates.

There is no obvious criterion to determine which assessment method should be preferred if different assessment methods generate inconsistent assessments for the likelihood of the same event. A possible approach is to present inconsistencies back to the user for interactive resolution. This has the advantage of alerting the forecaster to the fact of their inconsistency which may induce a more considered approach to the judgement.

Coherence

Whatever the technique used to assess the prior probabilities, the derived probabilities must be non-negative and sum to unity. If they are, then the probabilities are said to be *coherent*. The coherence axiom is fundamental to the existence of a rational subjective probability measure. Briefly it states that an individual's subjective probabilities should be sensible in so far as it would be impossible to construct a 'Dutch book', or perpetual money-making machine, against him. D. V. Lindley defends the coherence axiom along the following lines.

Suppose an incoherent person said A is less likely than B, B is less likely than C and then instead of concluding that A is less likely than C, concludes that C is less likely than A. Suppose now you offer him a prize if A occurs, but not otherwise. Keeping the prize fixed, he would prefer to base the receipt of the prize on B, rather than A. Indeed he would pay you a sum of money (or part of the prize) to substitute B for A. You accept the money and replace A by B. The argument can now be repeated so that you receive a further sum of money from him by replacing B with C. Having gained two sums of money, you now offer to replace C by A and the person would accept, since he regards C as less likely than A. A third sum of money now passes and the incoherent person is back to the initial situation where the prize depended on A. The sole difference is that he has already given you three sums of money. The cycle can be repeated if he holds to his uncertainty relations, and the incoherent person provides you with a perpetual money-making machine. This demonstrates that incoherence is unacceptable.

The purpose of the final stage in subjective probability assessment is accordingly to confront the individual with any incoherence in his assessments so that he can reassess them, possibly by making the same set of probability assessments in an alternative manner. This final procedure is commonly referred to as *consistency checking*. Any sensible assessment procedure should give self-consistent results, although some of the methods which do not involve an explicit articulation of probabilities will require a larger number of feedback iterations to achieve a satisfactory level of self-consistency.

In the direct percentile method for assessing a subjective probability distribution, the assessor is asked to give probabilities for percentiles intermediate to those chosen in the original assessment procedure. Achieving self-consistency in these cases is equivalent to obtaining responses which allow a reasonably smooth subjective probability distribution to be drawn. In the more indirect methods, based upon imputing probabilities from betting behaviour, the subject has to be shown whether or not his responses lead to the possible construction of any kind of perpetual money-making machine.

Some interactive computer programs have been developed (e.g. the MANECON suite by R. Schlaifer at Harvard, and those of the Stanford Research Institute) to aid this final stage of confronting the assessor with his inconsistencies. Training and practice in the technique of assessing probabilities will help to reduce inconsistencies in assessments. Self-consistency by itself does not, of course, guarantee the validity of a subjective probability measure. The measure could still contain biases due to other factors, such as incorrect input data to the assessor.

Even when an individual assessor has been taken through consistency checks to ensure self-consistency, and other possible behavioural biases have been eliminated as far as possible, the consensus problem may remain if individual assessors have to agree on a group view. We feel that more understanding of the behavioural factors which operate in group discussions should materially assist in the resolution of the problem of choosing a suitable method for obtaining a decision from an executive group.

Calibration of Probabilities

A probability assessor needs to be well calibrated, i.e., there should be no systematic bias in the assessments made. To test this point, experiments have been carried out with executives to judge their calibration. One such experiment involved asking executives to estimate the value of the percentiles.

$$X_1, X_{25}, X_{50}, X_{75}, X_{99}$$

for some unknown quantity. These percentiles divide the total range for X into six intervals, the probability of the true value falling in each interval being:

0·01, 0·24, 0·25, 0·25, 0·24, 0·01 respectively.

A large number of executives were then asked to assess these particular percentiles for their estimate of some quantity (such as the size of the British National Debt in £m.). Afterwards, the true figure was located as being in one or other of the six assessed intervals. The general tendency was for the results to be unbalanced with regard to the expected probabilities shown above for the six categories. For example, over a large number of different questions and many groups of executives (the questions had to be changed as rumours circulated as to the questions being used) some 31 per cent of results fell in the two end categories against an expected percentage of 2. These results, and others, suggest that assessors do not always correctly appreciate the degree of uncertainty that exists in their knowledge of the quantities that they seek to estimate. Evidence exists to show that even people who assess quite reasonable values for the twenty-fifth and seventy-fifth percentiles of a distribution, usually assess values for the first percentile which are far too high and values for the ninety-ninth percentile which are far too low. As a consequence, the spread of the percentiles is generally too narrowly based, a tendency that can only be overcome by meaningful training of the assessors over a period of time.

This analysis raises the question as to the conditions under which assessors will become well calibrated. Under what conditions might one expect that assessors could achieve this goal? One should not expect assessors to be well calibrated when the explicit or implicit rewards for their assessments do not motivate them to be honest in their assessments. As an extreme example, an assessor who is threatened with beheading should any event occur whose probability was assessed at less than 0·25 will have good reason not to be well calibrated with assessments of 0·20. Although this example seems absurd, more subtle pressures such as 'avoid being made to look the fool' or 'impress your boss' might also provide strong incentives for bad calibration. Any rewards for either wishful thinking or denial could also bias the assessments.

Receiving outcome feedback after every assessment is the best condition for successful training. Under such conditions assessors who are honest and coherent subjectivists will expect to be well calibrated, regardless of the interdependence among the items being assessed. In contrast, in the absence of trial-by-trial outcome feedback, honest, coherent subjectivists will expect to be well calibrated if, and only if, all the items being assessed are independent. This puts strong restrictions on the situations under which it would be reasonable to expect assessors to learn to be well calibrated. Even if the training process could be conducted using only events that assessors believed were independent, there may be good reason to doubt the independence of the real-life tasks to which the assessors would apply their training. Important future events may be interdependent either because they are influenced by a common underlying cause, or because the assessor evaluates all of them by drawing on a common store of knowledge. In such circumstances, one would not want or expect to be well calibrated. This reinforces the view that the receipt of outcome feedbacks after every assessment remains a pre-condition for the successful training of assessors.

Exercises

1. You have acquired a good deal of experience in sales forecasting, and forecast that one of your company's new products will

sell 4,000 units next year. Your superior asks what you can say about the degree of uncertainty in the forecast. To answer this you examine your forecast against performance in the past and feel that:

(i) In the long run sales would turn out to be greater than your forecast about as often as they would turn out to be less.

(ii) On about half of all occasions, sales would be between 20 per cent below and 30 per cent above forecast, and that when they did fall outside this range, they would be equally likely to fall above it as below it.

(iii) On only about one occasion in 100 would sales be less than half your forecast, and on only about one occasion in 100 would they be more than twice your forecast.

Construct a suitable form of distribution to demonstrate to your superior the degree of uncertainty inherent in your forecast.

2. Assess prior probability distributions in both PDF and CDF forms for the following:

(i) The price of General Electric common stock (or some similar stock in your country) six months hence.

(ii) The percentage change in the index of retail prices over the next twelve months.

(iii) The number of new car registrations in your country over the next twelve months.

(iv) The consumption of electricity in your household over the next twelve months.

(v) The number of miles you will travel in your automobile over the next twelve months.

3. Compare the distributions you obtained in question 8.2 (i) to (iii) with those obtained by two or three colleagues, and reach a group agreement as to a single distribution for each item. Is there any pattern of relationship between the combined distributions and the individual distributions from which they were formed?

4. The following table (Table 8.2) gives a marketing manager's prior cumulative probability distribution for the market share percentages, p, for a new consumer product.

Table 8.2 Cumulative probability distribution

p	probability up to p	p	probability up to p
5	0·005	30	0·7
10	0·01	35	0·79
15	0·09	40	0·88
20	0·33	45	0·95
25	0·52	50	0·999

(i) Graph the probability density function (PDF) and cumulative density function (CDF) for the variable p.

(ii) What is the probability that the true value of p
    (a) is less than 40 per cent,
    (b) is greater than 20 per cent,
    (c) lies between 5 and 35 per cent,
    (d) lies outside the interval 15 to 40 per cent?

(iii) By using the graph of the CDF find two values of p, a low value and a high value, which cover 90 per cent of the area of the probability density function for p with 5 per cent of the area remaining outside at each end. (Note the interval between these two values of p is called a 90 per cent *confidence or credible interval*.)

(iv) Find also the 95 per cent and 99 per cent credible intervals for p.

5. (i) Three baseball teams are contesting the overall championship of the American League. A commentator says that there is a 50:50 chance that G will win the championship and also assigns the same chances to teams H and K. Is the commentator making a reasonable set of assessments? Explain your answer.

 (ii) The commentator meets you and says that he will bet even money for any one of the teams, G, H or K. Without knowing anything about the merits or otherwise of each of the teams would you like to bet with him?

*6. Your prior opinion about the likely sales of a new automobile next year is approximately normally distributed with mean 100,000 units and standard deviation 10,000 units.

  (i) What is the probability that sales will be
      (a) less than 75,000 units
      (b) greater than 120,000 units
      (c) lie between 95,000 and 110,000 units?
 (ii) What is the 95 per cent credible interval for automobile sales?†

7. The General Electric Española SA is considering the expansion of its works capacity in Bilbao, Spain, the largest manufacturing and industrial centre of Northern Spain, where sites and labour are currently available at competitive rates. Discuss the nature of the information you would seek, and how you would use it to make a CDF form of estimate of the company's potential turnover in ten years' time from now.

8. Assess probability distributions (drawing both a graph of the discrete PDF and CDF) for the following unknown quantities:

  (i) The number of cars you will buy in the next fifteen years.
 (ii) The number of astronauts who will land on the moon in the next twenty years.
(iii) The number of elections to fill casual vacancies arising in the House of Representatives in the next twelve months.

Further Reading

M. ALPERT and H. RAIFFA, 'A progress report on the training of probability assessors', in *Judgment Under Uncertainty: Heuristics and Biases*, Cambridge University Press, 1982, pp. 294–305.

P. AYTON and G. WRIGHT, 'Assessing and improving judgmental probability forecasts', *Omega*, 1987, vol. 15, no. 3, pp. 191–6.

† This exercise requires a knowledge of the normal distribution; see P. G. MOORE, *Risk in Business Decision*, Longman, 1972.

N. DALKEY and D. HELMER, 'An Experimental Application of the Delphi Method to the Use of Experts', *Management Science*, 1963, vol. 9, no. 3, pp. 458–67.

S. LICHTENSTEIN, B. FISHOFF and L. D. PHILLIPS, 'Calibration of Probabilities: The State of the Art to 1980', in *Judgment Under Uncertainty: Heuristics and Biases*, Cambridge University Press, 1982, pp. 306–34.

P. G. MOORE and H. THOMAS, 'Measuring Uncertainty', *Omega*, 1975, vol. 3, no. 6, pp. 657–72.

D. A. SAMSON and H. THOMAS, 'Assessing Probability Distributions by the Fractile Method: Evidence from Managers', *Omega*, 1987, vol. 15, no. 10.

R. L. WINKLER, 'The Consensus of Probability Distributions', *Management Science*, 1968, vol. 15, pp. 61–75.

9 Assessing Utility

The Utility Concept

Earlier chapters have demonstrated that one of the decision analyst's key steps is the evaluation of payoff (or value) measures at the tips of each of the branches of the decision tree. So far, this has been primarily in terms of cash flow, but the decision-maker's preference may not be strictly and solely monetary. This chapter discusses methods of quantifying and measuring a decision-maker's preference pattern for the alternative outcomes arising from the different courses of action open. This measure is commonly referred to as *utility*.

In the rev counter case-history in chapter 2 (part III), we saw that EMV is not the only criterion which can be used to choose the optimum strategy. The marketing manager proposed the use of maximin, and the accountant suggested the use of minimax regret. Both of these criteria were found to have drawbacks; in the first instance because of its inherent pessimism, and in the second instance because of the conservative nature of the criterion. Chuck Pakin explained that, if the firm is not willing to 'play the averages' (i.e. use EMV), then the maximum expected utility criterion should be used.

Individuals commonly use the same approach as firms. Thus our behaviour in the purchase of house insurance indicates that we do not completely follow EMV principles in our private lives, since strict application of EMV would lead us to reject taking out house insurance (discussed in more detail in the section 'Application to Insurance' below). Again many people, when given a choice between:

  (i) Winning $500 for sure, or
 (ii) Winning $2,000 with probability 0·5

would opt for (i) even though it had the lower EMV. We can explain this behaviour symbolically by using the utility concept as follows:

$$U (\$500 \text{ win}) > 0.5 \ U (\$0 \text{ win}) + 0.5 \ U (\$2,000 \text{ win})$$

where $U(X)$ represents the utility of the sum of money $\$X$ to the decision-maker. This form of equation can be used to show that most people have a utility function $U(X)$ for money which is non-linear, against the value of X.

Most of the case-histories in this book are concerned with situations where the outcomes are satisfactorily described by a single well-understood variable, usually *money*, with a unique scale. In more general decision-making situations, preferences of decision-makers for outcomes can be of two distinct types:

A Direct Preference. An example is given by the statement 'I prefer outcome X to outcome Y.'

B Attitude to Risk. An example is given by the statement 'I prefer to play safe and take the outcome which gives me $1,000 for sure, rather than a strategy which gives me a 20 per cent chance of losing $5,000 and an 80 per cent chance of gaining $4,000.'

Typically, most important commercial decisions involve preference patterns which are a complicated mix of types A and B. Any theory of choice behaviour must explain both direct preferences and attitudes to risk, and utility has been found to be the most acceptable current theory of choice behaviour.

A utility function does no more than associate a relevant set of numbers with a set of outcomes. The principles of decision analysis will still apply; in place of using expected monetary value as the criterion of choice between alternative actions, we now replace money with utility and use expected utility value (EUV) for the choice between alternative actions. Moreover, the role of utility is the same whether the outcomes are monetary or non-monetary; single variable or multi-variable; quantifiable or non-quantifiable. When the outcomes of a decision can be described in terms of one variable, then the utility function is said to be uni-dimensional, or a function of a single attribute. An investor, for example, invokes a single-attribute utility function when choosing between alternative options offering chances of different short-run gains. If, on the other hand, the consequences of a decision have a number of attributes, such as time saved, money saved and convenience, the utility function is described as multi-attributed. Single-attribute functions are discussed here, leaving multi-attribute situations until chapter 10.

Summarizing the discussion so far, a utility function is 'a function defined on the outcomes' with the following properties:

(i) each possible outcome is defined by a single number;
(ii) the outcomes are ranked in preference order by these numbers;
(iii) the optimal decision strategy is to maximize expected utility.

A utility function does not, however, provide absolute value judgements. Outcomes are valued relative to each other and, if the scale of measurement U of a utility function is linearly changed to a new scale V using the formula

$$V(X) = rU(X)+s \text{ for all outcomes } X$$
$$(r \text{ and } s \text{ are constants with } r > 0)$$

then V is essentially the same function as U and will always lead to the same optimal decision being made. The units used on the scale are commonly referred to as *utiles*.

Measuring Utility for Money

The following example illustrates the implementation of the utility concept in practice. The owner of Small Biz Ltd is deciding whether or not to undertake one of two contracts, K and L, that have been offered to him. He cannot undertake both and, to simplify the illustration, suppose that each contract can lead to only three possible outcomes. The probabilities and payoffs are shown in Table 9.1 as follows:

Table 9.1 Probabilities and outcomes

contract K		contract L	
probability	outcome	probability	outcome
0·6	+$80,000	0·5	+$50,000
0·1	+$10,000	0·3	+$30,000
0·3	−$30,000	0·2	−$10,000

If both contracts are refused, it is assumed that the EMV will be zero.

Under an EMV approach, the appropriate calculations are as follows:

$$EMV(K) = 0·6 \times 80,000 + 0·1 \times 10,000 + 0·3 \times (-30,000)$$
$$= 40,000$$
$$EMV(L) = 0·5 \times 50,000 + 0·3 \times 30,000 + 0·2 \times (-10,000)$$
$$= 32,000.$$

On this basis contract K should be accepted. However, since contract K shows a 30 per cent chance of making a fairly large loss of $30,000 whereas contract L has only a 20 per cent chance of a much smaller loss, utility concepts may be relevant. The owner of Small Biz might, for example, be unwilling to consider making such a large loss as $30,000 and would tend to opt out of contract K. This would depend upon a number of factors such as his asset position and cash-flow situation. This suggests that an analysis using expected utility values (EUV) would be appropriate for the problem.

Consider next how this might be done. There are, in decreasing order, seven possible outcomes: +$80,000, +$50,000, +$30,000, +$10,000, $0, −$10,000, −$30,000. ($0 corresponds to taking neither contract.) Because the scale of a utility function is discretionary, the analyst defines

$$U(+\$80,000) = 100 \text{ and } U(-\$30,000) = 0$$

and asks a sequence of questions to determine the utility of the other outcomes. Three possible methods to do this are described, each involving a form of the standard gamble approach.

Method 1. (Illustrative determination of $U(+\$50,000)$.)

ANALYST: Which would you prefer:
(a) Gaining \$50,000 for certain,
(b) Having a 75 per cent chance of gaining \$80,000 and a 25 per cent chance of losing \$30,000?

OWNER: (b) is too risky; I'd prefer to take (a).

ANALYST: Suppose I changed (b) so that you had a 95 per cent chance of gaining \$80,000 and a 5 per cent chance of losing \$30,000, which would you prefer then?

OWNER: (After some hesitation) I'd prefer (b) then.

ANALYST: What if I made (b) an 85 per cent chance of gaining \$80,000 and a 15 per cent chance of losing \$30,000?
etc.

Eventually the decision-maker will be indifferent between (a) and (b). Suppose this happens when he has a 90 per cent chance of gaining \$80,000 and a 10 per cent chance of losing \$30,000. This enables us to write:

$$U(+\$50,000) = 0{\cdot}9U(+\$80,000)+0{\cdot}1U(-\$30,000)$$
$$= 0{\cdot}9 \times 100+0{\cdot}1 \times 0 = 90.$$

The procedure can be repeated for the other four outcome values. Method 2 varies the certain event, keeping the lottery fixed.

Method 2

ANALYST: Which would you prefer:
(a) Gaining \$40,000 for certain, or
(b) A 70 per cent chance of gaining \$80,000 with a 30 per cent chance of losing \$30,000?

OWNER: I'd prefer the \$40,000 for certain.

ANALYST: What if I reduced the certain gain in (a) to \$10,000?

OWNER: Well, then I'd prefer (b).

ANALYST: What if I made the certain gain \$25,000?
etc.

The certain gain continues to be varied until the decision-maker is indifferent between (a) and (b). One point on the utility curve is then known and the percentage chances used in (b) can be changed to determine further points.

Both Methods 1 and 2 have a big disadvantage in that the decision-maker may find it difficult to think in terms of the probabilities being used by the analyst. Indeed, many people cannot directly visualize the difference between say, the probabilities 0·8 and 0·9. Both are just 'pretty likely'. For this reason Method 3 has been devised using only the conceptually simpler 50:50 gambles.

Method 3

The question and answer sequence using Method 3 can be abbreviated as follows:

ANALYST: What certain outcome would you consider equivalent to a 50:50 gamble on outcomes +$80,000 and −$30,000?
OWNER: +$10,000.
ANALYST: What certain outcome would you consider equivalent to a 50:50 gamble on outcomes +$10,000 and +$80,000?
OWNER: +$25,000.
ANALYST: Which outcome would you consider equivalent to 50:50 gamble on outcomes −$30,000 and +$10,000?
etc.

In this way the interval between the best and worst outcomes is bisected repeatedly. Soon the questioner will have enough information to plot the decision-maker's utility function. If, as before, the analyst sets:

$$U(+\$80,000) = 100 \qquad U(-\$30,000) = 0$$

then, from the first two questions above

$$U(+\$10,000) = 50$$
$$U(+\$25,000) = 75 \text{ etc.}$$

Analysis with Utilities

Taking the problem summarized in Table 9.1, suppose that

Method 1 has been used to assess the various utilities with the following results:

$$U(+\$80{,}000) = 100 \qquad U(\$0) = 30$$
$$U(+\$50{,}000) = 90 \qquad U(-\$10{,}000) = 18$$
$$U(+\$30{,}000) = 80 \qquad U(-\$30{,}000) = 0.$$
$$U(+\$10{,}000) = 50$$

These values have been plotted in Figure 9.1 and a freehand curve drawn to illustrate the decision-maker's utility curve.

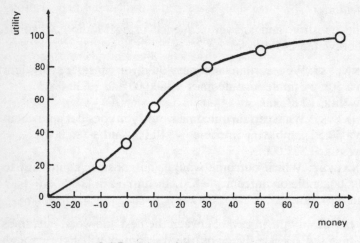

9.1 Decision-maker's utility curve

The EMV analysis used earlier can now be repeated, only using utility values instead of the monetary payoffs. The appropriate calculations are:

$$\text{EUV (contract } K) = 0{\cdot}6 \times 100 + 0{\cdot}1 \times 50 + 0{\cdot}3 \times 0 = 65$$
$$\text{EUV (contract } L) = 0{\cdot}5 \times 90 + 0{\cdot}3 \times 80 + 0{\cdot}2 \times 18 = 72{\cdot}6$$
$$\text{EUV (neither } K \text{ nor } L) = 30.$$

Thus the utility analysis leads to acceptance of contract L rather than contract K as with the EMV approach.

Some basic points about the utility concept can be noted

immediately. First, there is no such thing as *the* utility function for money, either for an individual or for a company. A utility function gives an assessor's relative preferences for money, that is his preferences scaled relative to two arbitrarily chosen reference points. It is only meaningful to compare intervals of utility with one another. Thus one interval of utility may be expressed as being twice that of another interval; but it is not right to say that one amount of money has twice the utility of some other amount of money.

Secondly, utility may change over time. A utility function assessed today at Lockheed Aircraft Corporation would probably look rather different from one assessed in 1980. If you go home tonight to discover you have inherited a fortune, tomorrow's personal utility function may well reflect tomorrow's greater willingness to take monetary risks.

Thirdly, every utility function should be identified with a horizon date. In other words, you are assessing today what you think money will be worth to you at some future defined date.

Utility Functions of Executives

A number of studies have been carried out to measure the utility functions of executives. All used variations of the standard gamble methods described earlier, and some are presented here to give an insight into the results obtained and the practical problems encountered.

The first study presented oil executives with a series of hypothetical drilling opportunities and asked them whether they would accept or reject each one. Most of the oil executives readily accepted the general concepts of decision trees, but they were wildcatters in the sense that they would accept some apparently unfair gambles, although differing on how great the possible rewards had to be before they would do this. There was only moderate success at introducing the oil-men to the formal concept of utility, because they seemed to distrust the idea of using formal graphs to replace judgement. This highlighted the need for more effort to be devoted towards demonstrating the value and practicability of such an approach.

The next set of studies asked executives from one company a

common set of questions, using an averaging procedure to obtain a corporate utility function. One of these studies attempted to determine the utility functions of sixteen executives from a large chemical company, both as private individuals and as business executives. Another study, possibly the largest ever attempted, used 100 executives with different backgrounds, from a number of companies, and produced a variety of different utility plots. All the studies showed that different executives have utility functions of varying shapes so that obtaining a corporate utility function is a particularly tricky task. In practical terms, there are three basic shapes for utility functions: risk-averse, risk-neutral (EMV) and risk-seeking. They are graphed in general form in Figure 9.2. In general, most executives seem to be slightly risk-averse, and also find it difficult to conceive of utility for negative cash flows, perhaps because of an adverse emotional reaction to tight financial situations.

Recent advances in behavioural decision theory have emphasized the role of reference or target levels in the analysis of risky choices. Current evidence reveals that a majority of individuals exhibit a mixture of risk-seeking and risk-averse behaviour, with the range of returns, where these two risk preferences are the predominant modes of behaviour, being intimately connected with the notion of a target return. For returns below target, a large majority of individuals appear to be risk-seeking; for returns above target, a large majority appear to be risk-averse. This is consistent with one of the main predictions of prospect theory, namely that the risk-return relationship has a non-linear functional form.

Another difficulty which emerged with the use of standard gamble methods was that many managers found it hard to distinguish on the one hand between events with probabilities such as 0·2, 0·1 and 0·05 and, on the other hand, between events with probabilities such as 0·8, 0·9 and 0·95. To them these were simply classifiable as very unlikely and very likely events respectively. This means that the utility function will be inadequately determined at the upper and lower ends of the range. Some analysts have attempted to overcome this by using Method 3 with only 50:50 gambles – but on a variety of outcomes instead of just the

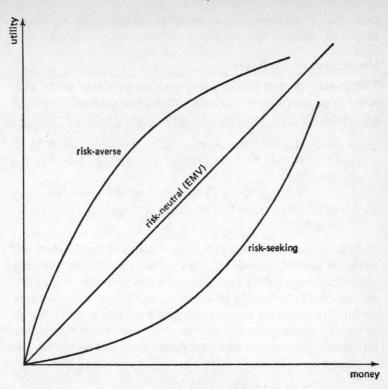

9.2 Specimen utility functions

best and the worst. This makes the problem conceptually a great deal more simple for the decision-maker, but it can have disadvantages. The oil executives, for example, could reply, 'but we never get drilling opportunities with odds as good as 50:50'. On the other hand, the reaction on occasion was 'but we never accept investments unless the odds are much better than 50:50'.

Ideally, in deriving utility functions, executives should always be presented with the kinds of decisions they are used to in real life, posing questions phrased in the familiar language of the decision-maker's own environment. Preliminary studies should be undertaken to determine what these decisions are, and how small differences in probability can be made meaningful to the executive. Only then are the procedures likely to be successful in that situation.

Non-Monetary Attributes

The principles used earlier could also be used where the outcomes are described by variables other than money. We could ask:

(a) a panel of consumers whether they would prefer a 70:30 gamble on soap powder brands A and C, to brand B for certain; or

(b) businessmen travelling to Sydney, Australia whether they would prefer to save five hours for certain or ten hours with a probability of ½.

Often, however, these kinds of questions are too far removed from the sort of real-life situations that respondents normally know (the soap powder example above shows this well). For this reason, other approaches to assessing utility functions are often useful. These usually involve asking the subject directly, either to rate his preferences for outcomes on a scale, or to compare differences between outcomes. Typical questions would be:

(i) How would you rate brand B powder on a scale stretching from brand A to brand C?

(ii) Which is greater: the difference between soap brands A and B or the difference between soap brands B and C?

(iii) Consider the benefit you would obtain from speeding up planes to Sydney by five hours; how much extra would planes have to be speeded up for this benefit to be twice as large?

Questions such as (i) and (iii) are examples of the use of *direct rating* methods. Enough similar questions of this type would enable an appropriate utility function to be established. The method is conceptually simple and of great practical importance where the outcomes are discrete and not readily lending themselves to any other sort of quantification. In a consumer survey, for example, housewives might be asked to rate different brands of soap powder on a scale from 0 (worst brand presented) to 10 (best brand presented). The answers would then provide direct numerical data for the housewives' utility structures. There are a number of variations on this method: the origin and unit of measurement can be fixed in different ways and to differing extents by the form of the question; individual ratings can be requested immediately after each brand is presented or all at the end; the decision-maker can be asked to represent his answer by a number, or by a point on a straight line, etc.

Direct rating has, however, serious drawbacks when there are other scales of measurement describing the outcomes. Imagine attempting to measure the utility of a decision-maker for money ($) by asking him to rate $-2,000$, $-1,000$, 0, $1,000$ and $2,000$ on a given scale, say from 0 to 100. The questioner would either be met by a blank expression, or else receive answers reflecting the magnitude of the numbers in the question rather than the decision-maker's attitude to risk.

Equally unadvisedly, the standard gamble methods described earlier have been used in a market research study when direct rating would have been more appropriate. Sample customers were offered a choice between:

(i) Receiving a frozen turkey with an unknown brand name, or

(ii) Having a probability P of receiving a frozen turkey with a well-known brand name, and $1 - P$ of receiving a certain sum of money (less than the value of the turkey).

The results were interesting, but had serious limitations as to their interpretation. The general disadvantage of all such methods is that some individuals, because of social or religious convictions, might be biased towards alternatives involving no gambling, while for others the very act of indulging in a gamble may have a positive utility. For this reason it is doubtful whether it is a good idea to introduce risk artificially into a normally riskless situation. The object of the experiment was, after all, to determine a pricing policy for frozen turkeys rather than to investigate some aspect of the consumer's risk behaviour, and hence a direct rating approach might have been more reliable.

The Oil Wildcatter Situation Again

The utility procedure is now demonstrated by adapting the example on page 97 concerning the oil wildcatter. The decision he had to make was to choose one of three possible actions: to withdraw, to drill without a seismic sounding, or take a seismic sounding before making his final decision. Suppose now that it has been possible, using the methods from the section 'Measuring Utility for Money', for the oil wildcatter to establish his utility function on a scale from zero to one as in Figure 9.3. We can then substitute the appropriate utilities in place of his various monetary payoffs at the ends of the relevant branches to give the decision tree shown in Figure 9.4.

Each branch is evaluated in turn. For the upper branch at point W the expected utility corresponding to decision D is:

$$EUV = 0.5 \times 0.16 + 0.25 \times 0.64 + 0.25 \times 1 = 0.49.$$

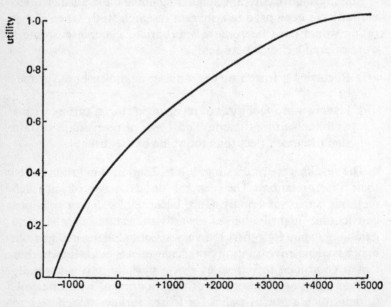

9.3 Oil wildcatter's utility function

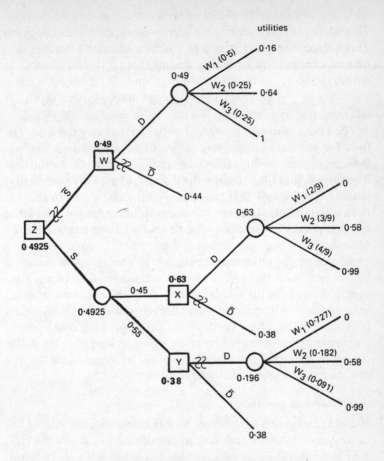

9.4 Oil wildcatter's decision tree

Hence D, with its utility of 0·49, is a better decision than $\bar{D}$. At decision point W, the utility of 0·49 is now entered and decision route $\bar{D}$ is barred. A similar analysis at point X gives the value 0·63, corresponding again to option D.

For the lower branch at point Y the decision D, to drill, leads to an expected utility of:

$$\mathrm{EUV} = 0{\cdot}0 \times 0{\cdot}727 + 0{\cdot}58 \times 0{\cdot}182 + 0{\cdot}99 \times 0{\cdot}091 = 0{\cdot}196.$$

This is lower than the utility of 0·38 corresponding to decision $\bar{D}$, and, hence, the latter figure is entered at point Y and decision $\dot{D}$ is barred. Our next step is to combine the two branches into one expected utility as before, giving:

$$0·45 \times 0·63 + 0·55 \times 0·38 = 0·4925.$$

The initial comparison now is between an expected utility of 0·49 for the decision to proceed without a seismic sounding, 0·4925 to proceed with a seismic sounding, and 0·44 to withdraw. The seismic sounding result is the highest, albeit very marginally, leading to a decision that is contrary to the one found in chapter 6. In this particular instance the decision-maker might argue that the two results are so close that he really has no preference for either of the two possibilities, and other factors, e.g. convenience, might influence his decision. The changed situation has arisen from the effect of the decision-maker being risk-averse, in that the oil wildcatter now finds the purchase of extra information before making a final decision more worthwhile than previously. If his utility curve were of the opposite form, namely a concave curve showing him to be a risk-seeker, then his desire to purchase extra information would be diminished by the change from monetary values to utilities.

Application to Insurance

We next examine a case where we are faced with the risk of fire destroying our home and wish to consider disposing of the risk. This illustrates the unconscious use of utility in practice. In return for an annual premium from the home-owner, an insurance company will compensate him in the event of a fire calamity. The decision situation which faces the owner is shown in Table 9.2. Let C be the home-owner's total assets, m the amount of the annual premium for fire insurance, and h the cost of reinstating the home if it is destroyed by fire. Insurance is assumed to leave the owner where he would have been financially without the fire. If he does not insure and there is a fire, he could however be much worse off, since m is considerably less than h. (In what follows we simplify by considering only the total loss, as opposed to a partial loss situation, and ignore interest on the premiums or assets.)

Table 9.2 Decision outcomes in fire insurance

	outcome	
decision	fire	no fire
insure	inconvenience, but no real loss $(C-m)$	*loss of premium* $(C-m)$
don't insure	loss of capital $(C-h)$	no losses $(C$

(Home-owner's capital is shown in brackets.)

The decision 'don't insure' leads to a situation whose consequences are probabilistic. Clearly, part of the decision whether or not to insure is governed by the premium quoted by the insurance company, and part by the risk of fire as the owner assesses it. Suppose that he assesses the probability of a fire during the year at p. The home-owner would be indifferent between the two possible decisions if p is the probability of a fire and

$$U(C-m) = pU(C-h) + (1-p)U(C). \qquad \text{(equation 9.1)}$$

Let us first suppose that the owner's utility function is given by $U(x) = x$. In other words, the owner is neutral towards risk. Then we have, from equation 9.1, that

$$C-m = p(C-h) + (1-p)C$$

or $\qquad m = ph.$

This is the premium calculated from a straight expected monetary value approach and illustrated by line AB in Figure 9.5. Now the home-owner is likely to be risk-averse and hence have a concave utility function such as curve XY. This gives

$$U(C-m) > pU(C-h) + (1-p)U(C)$$

and the corresponding acceptable premium is greater than
before. If equation 9.1 is solved to give this revised premium, m'
say, then the difference $m'-m$, or $m'-ph$, represents the excess
that the decision-maker is prepared to pay above the strict
expected monetary value cost for insuring his home. (The revised
premium m' is sometimes termed the owner's *certainty equivalent* value for the risk situation.) Alternatively, the premium can
be found graphically by projecting a horizontal line from point
W on Figure 9.5 until it cuts the utility function at point V. The
length VW then represents the excess premium $m'-ph$ which
the owner is willing to pay.

The situation from the insurance company's point of view is
rather different. If their assets are K, then the possible asset
positions for the company after offering the insurance, are
$K-h+m$, K, and $K+m$, according to whether or not a claim is

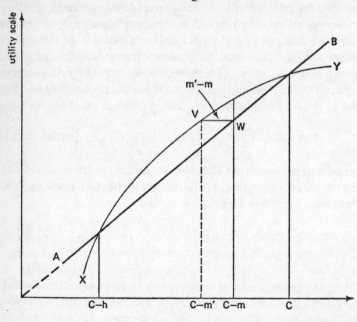

9.5 Insurance premiums

made and/or the policy is taken out. These three quantities will be not very different from one another in *relative* terms as the company's assets, K, will be very large. Thus, for the company, a very close approximation to their utility function can be obtained by assuming it to be linear over the range from $K-h+m$ to $K+m$. If this utility curve is linear, this is equivalent to taking utility to be the same as money, albeit with a scale factor. Hence, the company will be quite content to work with expected monetary value as its decision criterion. Consequently, a 'pure' premium of $m = ph$ as calculated earlier would be acceptable to the company, plus a loading to cover expenses and profit. Thus, a premium somewhat in excess of the pure premium ph is acceptable to both the policyholder and the insurance company. This attractiveness of insurance applies because of the concave nature of the home-owner's utility function. It follows as a corollary that if the curvature of the individual's utility function is very small, or even reversed in direction, he will not be able to obtain attractive premiums. Again, the argument demonstrates that it does not pay an individual to insure against small losses, only against large ones, because an individual's utility function is effectively linear over a small range. In such circumstances the insurance company cannot offer the individual an attractive premium.

Group Utility

So far, we have assumed the existence of one decision-maker with a single utility function. In many practical situations this is unrealistic; often it is necessary for groups of people, or even the whole firm, to choose between alternative outcomes. There are a number of possible voting procedures for accomplishing agreement between group members, and bargaining procedures can be devised where individuals 'give way' on the evaluations of some outcomes in return for their own evaluations being accepted. There is, however, no reason to suppose *a priori* that there exists any voting or bargaining process which will result in a single unique group utility enabling the group, whatever the decision procedures it adopts, to act as a whole 'rationally', and maximize the expectation of a single consensus utility function.

The measurement of group utility is clearly an important practical problem, particularly because utility evaluations of individuals cannot be simply aggregated to obtain a group utility – it being a relative and not an absolute measure. As an illustration of a possible procedure consider the formulation of a risk policy for making capital investment decisions in a corporation. A general procedure is then as follows:

(a) Present a number of executives in the company with a series of hypothetical investment decisions and, from their answers, plot utility functions (one for each executive) using the methods discussed earlier in this chapter.
(b) Agree with the help of further questioning on a functional form to fit the utility plots (the same functional form, but with different parameters being used for each executive).
(c) Re-interview, allowing each executive to spend a great deal of time on a few questions, and determine each executive's parameters for the functional form from the results.
(d) Present the results to top management, attempting to form in discussion with them the best parameters for a corporate risk policy.

In essence, step (d) argues that a group utility is best obtained by thrashing out the inconsistencies of individual decision-makers at the level of the top decision-making group. In most cases it is found that, at all levels of investment, the final corporate utility function is far less conservative than the average for the individual executives interviewed. (This can be regarded as a particular example of the 'risky shift phenomenon' i.e. the willingness to be more risky in group situations, which has been well documented by psychologists.)

The main identifiable advantages accruing from a study like the one discussed above are first that it is educational in the sense that executives are forced to consider their individual risk attitudes; second, that the premature rejection of risky projects by middle management is avoided; and finally that it allows the development within the corporation of a way of communicating risk by means of utility evaluations, and of thrashing out a rational corporate risk policy.

There appears to be little doubt that the only realistic and practical approach for obtaining a group utility structure is for the group to meet, and 'thrash out' a group utility view. The method of conducting such a meeting is, however, of crucial importance in order to ensure that the final view which emerges is indeed that of the group.

Exercises

1. A decision-maker has the following utilities over the relevant portion of his overall assets scale, his current total assets being $70,000:

assets ($000)	50	60	70	80	90
utility	0·32	0·46	0·59	0·67	0·72

(i) He is offered a place in the lottery where he has a chance of 0·6 of winning $10,000, together with a complementary chance of 0·4 of losing $10,000. Should the decision-maker accept the offer?

(ii) If the decision-maker were offered participation in a series of two independent plays of the lottery with the same prizes and probabilities in each play, would this affect his decision? (Note that entry implies participation in both plays of the lottery.)

2. An international mining company with substantial assets is faced with decisions on a large number of separate projects each year.

(i) For what sorts of decisions on projects would it seem reasonable to maximize the expected monetary value?

(ii) How might one set about determining the size of the sums of money involved before expected monetary value is no longer a suitable criterion for choice amongst projects?

*3. A firm is offered a contract to develop a special turbine engine. The contract stipulates that, if the engine is not developed within two years from date of contract, the contract is void. If the engine is developed in time, the expected profit is $1.0

million; if not, the expected loss is $5.0 million. The firm's current assets are $6.0 million. The research and development department assesses the probability of successful development within the two-year period as 0·9.

(i) If the firm uses expected monetary value as its criterion, what is the optimal action?
(ii) Suppose the firm has the following utility function for its assets, x(in $m.)

$$U(x) = 0·25x - 0·0125x^2 + 150.$$

What is now the optimal action? For what range of values is this utility function likely to be reasonable?
(iii) Would you expect there to be any difference in reaction to this contract as between a large firm (e.g. Westinghouse) and a small research and development engineering firm? If so, why?

4. Imagine that you are personally invited either to take part in a gamble having a prize of $2,000 with probability p, or a loss, b, with probability, $1-p$, or, alternatively, to receive a cash sum $\$X$ with certainty. Give the value of p (for yourself) at which you would be indifferent between these two alternatives for the values of b and X specified below, and hence draw out a portion of your own utility function. (For the purposes of this exercise you should abandon any moral scruples you may sensibly have against gambling.)

$X = 250, 500, 1,000, 1,500,$ combined with each b_i value listed

$$b_1 = -50 \qquad b_4 = -500$$
$$b_2 = -100 \qquad b_5 = -1,000$$
$$b_3 = -250$$

5. A mutual fund manager sells to another a block of shares in the XYZ Company. Both men agree, without telling the other, that the share block has a 60 per cent chance of increasing in value to $600,000 and a 40 per cent chance of decreasing in value to $400,000. The selling price agreed by the pair is $520,000.

Neither is in immediate need of cash. Discuss the behaviour of each mutual fund manager.

6. The following is a dialogue between a consultant (C) and a decision-maker (D).

C: Suppose that you are currently committed to a contract which gives you a 50 per cent chance of a $100,000 profit and a 50 per cent chance of a $20,000 loss. If you were forced to sell the contract, what is the minimum amount you would accept for it?

D: About $70,000.

C: Suppose that you are also committed to a contract which gives you a 50 per cent chance of a $70,000 profit and a 50 per cent chance of a $20,000 loss. What is the minimum price you would take for this one?

D: Well, it's not as good as the first contract. Let's say roughly $40,000.

C: Now, let's try just one more. Suppose also that you have a firm contract which gives you a 50 per cent chance of either a $70,000 profit or a $100,000 profit. What would you ask for this one, if you had to sell?

D: $90,000.

 (i) Use the above responses to graph D's utility function for money.

 (ii) From the graph determine D's utility measure for $80,000.

 (iii) Is D a risk-avoider? Explain.

 (iv) Comment on C's attempt to elicit D's utility function.

*7. Mr Bull currently has assets of $50,000 and is presented with a deal which, in his opinion, has a probability of ⅓ of resulting in a loss of $50,000, but a probability of ⅔ of resulting in a profit of $50,000. Mr Bull's utility function is as follows:

Assets ($000)	0	12·5	25	50	75	100
Utility	0	0·45	0·65	0·85	0·95	1·00

 (i) Should Mr Bull accept the deal?

(ii) Suppose that five people with utility functions exactly like Mr Bull's and each with assets of $50,000, all assign the same probabilities to the possible consequences of this deal. If they agree to share the profit or loss equally, does the deal become attractive for all of them as a syndicate?†

Further Reading

R. M. HOGARTH, *Judgment and Choice*, Wiley, 1980.

J. C. HULL, P. G. MOORE and H. THOMAS, 'Utility and its Measurement', *Journal of the Royal Statistical Society*, 1973, series A, vol. 136, no. 2, pp. 226–47.

D. KAHNEMAN and A. TVERSKY, 'Prospect Theory: An Analysis of Decisions Under Risk', *Econometrica*, 1979, pp. 262–91.

R. L. KEENEY and H. RAIFFA, *Decisions with Multiple Objectives: Preferences and Value Trade-offs*, Wiley, 1976.

† This exercise requires some knowledge of the binomial theorem in probability, see P. G. MOORE, *Risk in Business Decision*, Longman, 1972.

10 Multi-Attribute Utility

Introduction

In many decision problems the outcomes cannot be immediately characterized in terms of a single value, such as monetary cost or profit. Business organizations commonly need to take account of a number of outcome dimensions, such as orderly industrial relations or the company image, which go beyond simple monetary assessments of value. The same is true of public sector agencies, where relevant consequences might include consideration of national prestige, political implications, social implications, value to the community, etc. Examples of the kinds of situation envisaged are:

(i) What is the value to a busy executive of using supersonic jets on the London–Sydney route if they reduce journey time by five hours, or ten hours, but increase the cost by 20 per cent?

(ii) How does a company choose its promotional strategies when each possibility will change asset position, market share, and turnover in different ways and amounts?

(iii) How does an individual choose an apartment, the most important factors to him being price, accommodation, location and journey time to the office? (Note the difficulties of quantifying location on a relevant scale.)

(iv) The need for, and the location of, an additional airport to serve a large city.

Several ways have been suggested for obtaining and handling multi-attribute utility measures for the consequences which result from such situations. In this chapter we review some of the more useful methods that have been proposed, giving examples of their application to problems involving both companies and governmental agencies.

Multi-Attribute Situations

The following simplified example illustrates the issues involved. A manufacturer of heavy engineering goods is running behind schedule on an important export order. He now has to choose between continuing to work normally (when the goods will be ready to leave the factory in thirty days) and working overtime (when they will be ready in twenty days). Later he will have to choose between shipping by sea or by air. The delivery date fixed for the order is in thirty-six days' time and goodwill will be lost for every day it is late, but there are no penalty clauses as such in the contract.

Table 10.1 gives the net profits which the manufacturer can expect under the four strategies open to him. Table 10.2 gives assessed probability distributions for the transport times by air and sea.

Table 10.1 Strategies and profits (π)

	work normally	work overtime
ship by sea	12,000	9,000
ship by air	11,000	8,000

Table 10.2 Probability distributions of transport times

	days taken to reach customer from leaving factory (D)									
	2	4	6	8	10	12	14	16	18	20
by sea	–	–	0·1	0·1	0·2	0·2	0·1	0·1	0·1	0·1
by air	0·1	0·3	0·2	0·1	0·1	0·1	0·1	–	–	–

Four different decision combinations are open to the manufacturer. Each can lead to a number of different outcome combinations as shown in Table 10.3.

Table 10.3 Possible outcomes

work normally ship by ship		work normally ship by air		work overtime ship by sea		work overtime ship by air	
prob	outcome π D	prob	outcome π D	prob	outcome π D	prob	outcome π D
0·1	12,000　　0	0·6	11,000　　0	0·8	9,000　　0	1·0	8,000　　0
0·1	12,000　　2	0·1	11,000　　2	0·1	9,000　　2		
0·2	12,000　　4	0·1	11,000　　4	0·1	9,000　　4		
0·2	12,000　　6	0·1	11,000　　6				
0·1	12,000　　8	0·1	11,000　　8				
0·1	12,000　10						
0·1	12,000　12						
0·1	12,000　14						

Suppose the manufacturer's utility function is $U(\pi, D)$ (i.e. a function U of the two variables π and D). It would be possible to evaluate this function by using adaptations of the methods for assessing simple attribute functions discussed in chapter 9. The best and worst possible outcomes would first be determined and then the manufacturer asked a number of questions where he had to choose between:

(a) a lottery on the best and worst outcomes, or
(b) some other intermediate outcome.

The two-dimensional nature of the problem would, however, make this a very long and tedious procedure. For this reason we consider another approach. Suppose we make the assumption that

$$U(\pi, D) = U_1(\pi) + U_2(D)$$

This implies that π and D are independent in the sense that value judgements on π are independent of D and vice versa. It is a reasonable assumption as we would not expect the decision-maker's relative feelings about different values of D to be affected by the value of π and vice versa.

We can then use the methods of the previous chapter to determine:

    (a) the utility function for 'profit made' (assuming 'days late' is kept fixed), and

    (b) the utility function for 'days late' (assuming 'profit made' is kept fixed).

Suppose the results expressed on a utility scale of 0 to 100 utiles for each variable are as shown in Table 10.4.

Table 10.4 Utility functions

	profit made ($)				
	8,000	9,000	10,000	11,000	12,000
utiles	0	25	50	75	100

	days late							
	14	12	10	8	6	4	2	0
utiles	0	5	10	20	30	40	60	100

Next we ask the decision-maker to make a trade-off between the two variables. A typical question used might be: 'Consider the situation where π is 8,000 and D is 0. To what value would π have to be increased in order to compensate for D increasing to 6?'

Suppose the answer to this question is $10,000. We then know that 70 utiles on the 'days late' scale is equivalent to 50 utiles on the 'profit made' scale, i.e. that the π-scale is 40 per cent more important than the D-scale. It is now possible to define U_1 and U_2 as shown in Table 10.5 and to treat the two variables π and D as additive when expressed on the utility scales.

The expected utility of each of the four courses of action can now be calculated in the usual way. Thus E U V (work normally, ship by sea)

$$= 0\cdot1 \times 240 + 0\cdot1 \times 200 + 0\cdot2 \times 180 + 0\cdot2 \times 170$$
$$+ 0\cdot1 \times 160 + 0\cdot1 \times 150 + 0\cdot1 \times 145 + 0\cdot1 \times 140$$
$$= 173\cdot5.$$

Table 10.5 Utility functions

π	8,000	9,000	10,000	11,000	12,000
$U_1(π)$	0	35	70	105	140

D	14	12	10	8	6	4	2	0
$U_2(D)$	0	5	10	20	30	40	60	100

By similar calculations, EUV (work normally, ship by air) is 180, EUV (work overtime, ship by air) is 125, EUV (work overtime, ship by sea) is 100. The best strategy is, therefore, to work normally and to ship by air.

This example illustrates the kind of assumptions that commonly have to be made in assessing multi-attribute utility structures. Here it was assumed that value judgements on profit for the heavy engineering manufacturer are independent of value judgements on days late. The two-attribute utility structure $U(π, D)$ was thereby collapsed into a function of the two single-attribute utility structures $U_1(π)$ and $U_2(D)$ for each of which the methods described in the previous chapter could be used.

Collapsing Several Criteria into One Criterion

The general point which already emerges is the need to reduce the attributes of a multi-attribute structure into a convenient form for assessment. Several approaches are available, but we concentrate on the most practically useful one which aims to collapse several criteria into one. This approach is satisfactory for decision problems in which there is a single clear objective which dominates all the others. In many business contexts, for example, the attainment of a high level of profit is the most important objective, even though the firm would also like to maintain satisfactory labour relations and a viable corporate image.

To illustrate the approach, consider the situation facing Harman Merchants† who had to decide whether and how to rationalize some associated companies in a medium-sized manufacturing city. The results were presented to a board meeting, using as a background illustration the partial decision tree shown in Figure 10.1 (where some of the possible branches of the tree have been eliminated for clarity).

The methods of analysis used were fully discussed with the executives. It was pointed out that the various sources of uncertainty had been taken into account through their subjective probability assessments and that the alternatives had been evaluated in money terms, adjusting them to allow for the decision-maker's time preference for money through discounting. They were fascinated by the analysis but, in discussion, raised a number of other factors, in addition to money, by which the alternatives should be judged. For example, the ease of access to one of the sites and the existence of better housing facilities for employees near one of the other sites were frequently mentioned.

The basic decision analysis showed in expected monetary value terms that the best decision was immediate amalgamation of the three existing subsidiaries at a new site on the south side of the town. The difference in expected value between this strategy and the next most preferred EMV was of the order of 3 per cent in relation to a $2m. payoff. A number of board members felt that, as the margin was so narrow, they should look more closely at all aspects of the preferred strategy. They argued that the figure for rebuilding all three on one site straight away was under-valued and that it should be adjusted upwards for:

(i) rationalization savings – common ordering, stock control etc.;
(ii) greater effectiveness of transportation and distribution from the south site;
(iii) better employee relations – housing, access etc. – in relation to the south site.

After discussion it was agreed that the better employee relations factor could be valued at about ½–1 per cent of total

† See P. G. MOORE, H. THOMAS, D. W. BUNN and J. HAMPTON, *Case Studies in Decision Analysis*, Penguin Books, 1976, chapter 2.

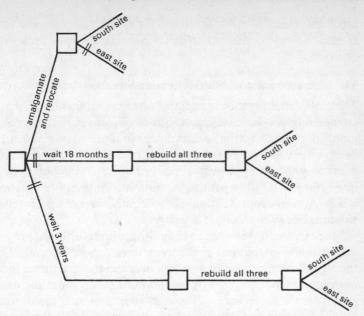

10.1 Harman Merchants decision tree

payoff. The combined effect of immediate rationalization savings would also be of the same order but no more, since these savings had already largely been accounted for in the existing financial calculations. Item (ii) had already been accounted for in the analysis. Thus, a range of 1–2 per cent of total payoff was added to the financial value of the preferred alternative which widened the difference between it and the next most preferred strategy to about 5 per cent, even when the effects of these other factors on the other alternative strategies were taken into account.

The basis of this approach is that the less tangible separate factors are 'collapsed', expressed in money terms and added to the existing expected value for the various strategies. This is really no more than using an additive utility function, as in the earlier example, and giving equal weighting to each of the factors – i.e. money, rationalization savings, etc. – in the multi-attribute objective function. As a rapid calculation for handling multiple attributes there is much merit in this approach, provided that there is a single dominant attribute amongst the set of relevant attributes.

The Characteristics of Multi-Attribute Situations

The earlier multi-attribute example on the manufacture of heavy engineering goods, raises questions of objectives that are commonly in conflict, further achievement in terms of one objective being achievable only at the expense of a reduction of achievement on some other objective. For example, a reduction in days late results in a fall in profits. A multi-attribute utility function is a quantitative representation of a decision-maker's preference structure for such multiple objectives.

Much of the development of multi-attribute utility theory is recent, and operational procedures have lagged behind. The theory has been primarily based on deriving the functional form of utility function implied by assumptions made about the decision-maker's preferences. These assumptions are then crosschecked and parameters assessed for the assumed functional form. To assist in this process some assumptions are commonly made about the possible nature of the utility function. Two particular assumptions, namely those of *linearity* and *additivity*, permit application to a wide range of problems. Moreover they require the decision-maker to make only a relatively few straightforward assessments.

Linearity is the simplest assumption that can be made, implying that each attribute can be quantified in terms of a common scale of measurement, say money. Formally, linearity states that

$$U(x_1, x_2, \ldots) = \sum_{i=1}^{n} a_i x_i \qquad (10.1)$$

where U is the utility function, x_1 is the value of the variable corresponding to the ith attribute, and the a_i are constants. This assumption defines a constant rate of trade-off between one attribute and another. For example, suppose that a corporate decision-maker is establishing his preferences for alternatives in terms of three attributes: asset position, market share and turnover. Linearity would imply a series of statements of the form: 'No matter what the value of my asset position, market share and turnover I would always consider a 1 per cent unit increase in market share as valuable as a $100,000 increase in assets.'

The case-study of the cost-benefit analysis of a new rail link between the main Heathrow airport (some twelve miles west of Central London) and the centre of London in the next section uses this linearity concept.

Additivity is a more general assumption. Linearity can be regarded as a special case of additivity. Formally it states that:

$$U(x_i, x_2, \ldots) = \sum_{i=1}^{n} U_i(x_i) \qquad (10.2)$$

Additivity thus implies that the rate of trade-off between two variables may depend upon the values of those two variables, but will not depend upon that of other variables. The corporate decision-maker would subscribe to a series of statements of the form:

(i) 'Whatever my turnover, increasing my market share from 10 to 11 per cent would always have the same value to me as increasing my asset position from $2.0m. to $2.2m.'

(ii) 'Whatever my turnover, increasing my market share from 20 to 21 per cent would always have the same value to me as increasing my asset position from $5.0m. to $5.3m.'

The example on the manufacture of heavy engineering goods illustrated such a situation, where constant rates of trade-off were used to develop the utility formulation. Structures based upon strict additivity rather than linearity have been put to relatively little practical use. The main reason is that the difficulties of assessing variable trade-off rates for outcomes in a business problem with several attributes can become extremely complex. An illustration of the complexities that can arise is given in an article by Lock (see Further Reading, p. 212), in a situation where Bally Shoes were considering how to counter the long-term decline in their men's shoe business. Experiments were designed to elicit multi-attribute preference structures, but encountered resistance from the decision-makers concerned. Nevertheless, their use yielded valuable information into managerial preferences.

The Heathrow Rail Link

The aim of this study, carried out in the early seventies, was to produce recommendations on the construction of a rail link between Central London and Heathrow airport. Four possible schemes were identified:

LT: An extension of the Piccadilly Line (on the London Underground system) to Heathrow with the present airline coach services continuing.

BR1: A British Rail (overground railway) link between Victoria main line station and Heathrow, with a check-in option at Victoria.

BR2: A similar link to BR1, but with the coach services continuing.

BR3: A similar link to BR1, but without a check-in at Victoria and with coach services continuing.

A twenty-five-year planning horizon (1970–94) was used and all costs and benefits were considered with reference to continuation of the present 'coaches only' system. The costs and benefits were identified and, with the help of appropriate models, e.g. for the forecasts of air traffic, five items were assessed for each year in the planning period. These were:

 (i) capital costs (mostly incurred in the first four to five years);
 (ii) annual operating costs;
(iii) 'time saved' benefits for various sections of the community;
(iv) congestion benefits (due to a reduction in coaches and private cars travelling to and from Heathrow);
 (v) private and public resource savings (from fares and private vehicle running costs in London).

All costs and benefits were first translated from their present scales to a single money scale. Items (i) and (ii) were already in monetary terms. For item (iii) passengers were split into business passengers, leisure passengers and airport workers, a different value of time being hypothesized for each. In item (iv) an average value of time for road users was used whilst item (v) presented little problem when costs per mile of travelling in Central London had been evaluated.

Net present values in 1970 with a 10 per cent discount rate were used for each cost and benefit to convert the twenty-five individual monetary values in the period to a single figure. The results are shown in Table 10.6 where NPV cost and benefits in £m. are calculated with respect to the present 'coaches only' situation, increases in costs being positive and decreases negative. The total NPV cost is taken as the sum of the five individual factors and NPVs. The ranking obtained is LT, BR3, BR1, BR2.

Table 10.6 Cost-benefit summary (£m.)

	LT	BR1	BR2	BR3
capital costs	+11·9	+22·6	+21·7	+15·9
annual operating costs	−6·6	−5	+4·2	−3·7
time saved	−27·4	−19·2	−19·2	−32·3
congestion benefits	−1·6	−0·2	−0·2	−3·1
resource savings	−7·8	−0·9	−0·6	−0·6
Total cost (NPV)	−31·5	−2·7	+5·9	−24·1

A sensivity analysis was then carried out where the value of business time, traffic estimates, coach times, etc. were systematically varied with 'reasonable penalties' being introduced for such items as the lack of an in-town check-in. This was shown to have no effect on the ranking of the schemes. The unquantified factors were then expanded upon and discussed with the help of the ratios in Table 10.7. However, it was concluded that these factors did not have sufficient impact to destroy LT's clear-cut cost advantage in Table 10.6, and LT was recommended without assessing the precise monetary value to be assigned to each of the factors in Table 10.7. It is worth commenting that LT was accepted, and the link was operating by summer 1977 and has now been extended to cover the expanded Terminal 4 on the south side of Heathrow.

Table 10.7 Unquantified factors

factor	LT	BR1	BR2	BR3
choice of two public modes	high	low	high	high
option of check-in Central London for rail link passengers	low	high	high	low
comfort	fair/good	good	good	good
baggage handling	fair	v. good	v. good	fair/good
reliability	v. good	good	good	good
town planning	acceptable	acceptable	acceptable	acceptable

This study is an example of a public policy decision where, although there are several attributes (such as cost, comfort, convenience, time saved, etc.), the outcomes are to a close approximation deterministic. In retrospect, the further assumption of constant rates of trade-off between the attributes may not have been fully justified. More effort could perhaps have been usefully concentrated on the estimation of certain variable rates of trade-off.

A Multi-Attribute Retailing Example

A second case-history, drawn from the shoe retailing industry, is presented as an illustration of multi-attribute screening concepts. The company, Bally UK Ltd, is well established and its major interest lies in the shoe industry. In addition, it has related investments in fashion accessories such as handbags. It also has an established reputation as a high-quality, premium price manufacturer and retailer of shoes.

The British company, a wholly owned subsidiary of the Swiss parent, operated both as a wholesaler and retailer in the shoe business. Their strategic concerns focused around the problem of how to arrest the long-term decline in their imported men's shoe business owing, in part, to exchange rate problems. The concern was made even more relevant given the parent company's desire to expand its range of retail shoe stores in the United Kingdom.

The environment of declining sales and rising prices affected the wholesale business as well as Bally's men's shoe retailing operations. Below a given volume the percentage of markdowns increases sharply and this, coupled with a reluctance to deal in small volume lines, makes the product much less attractive to the independent retailer. Furthermore, retailers tend to define themselves as trading in a given price bracket and, as Swiss shoe prices rose faster than locally manufactured shoes, they fitted into the ranges of increasingly fewer independent retail outlets. Indeed, if London with its overseas visitor trade were excluded, the decline would have appeared even more serious.

In an effort to keep retail prices competitive, the temptation was to cut margins in Bally's own outlets. However, such action was likely to have a severe effect on the wholesale trade, and hence on the company's ability to sustain the Bally brand of high fashion and quality in the market-place as a whole. Furthermore, the action was likely to undermine the exclusive nature of the Bally outlets and diminish their special appeal in contrast to other retail chains. For all these reasons, it was seen as important to sustain a position in the men's shoe market.

The company also needed the men's shoe business to support the expansion of its retailing operations. A new store requires a lower share of the market to achieve viability if it obtains that share in both the men's and ladies' market rather than in the ladies' market alone. Moreover, the men's market has higher net margins in value terms than the ladies' business and is much less price sensitive.

The company had already decided to import a limited number of men's shoes from Italy and brand them with the Bally name. Although this had been done previously for a number of ladies' product lines, it was considered an exceptional decision because of possible deleterious effects on both the Bally brand image and the cannibalization of the sales of Swiss shoes.

A range of further options emerged in discussions with the decision-making group:

(i) Do nothing, i.e. continue with the sale of Swiss men's shoes and limited imports from Italy;

(ii) Expand the sales of bought-in Italian shoes;

(iii) Persuade the Swiss parent company to reduce the transfer price;

(iv) Import shoe parts from Switzerland for assembly in England, thus increasing the UK value-added component;

(v) Manufacture men's shoes in their existing UK factory, which would involve an increased plant investment;

(vi) Subcontract to an existing UK manufacturer; this might involve a loss of business skills, technology, and expertise and lessen the organization's competitive edge;

(vii) Purchase a small shoe manufacturer.

These strategy alternatives were not necessarily mutually exclusive and were complicated by important decision variables such as price and manufacturing capacity. Moreover, any strategies selected would be subject to ultimate approval by the Swiss parent.

A similar process, involving lengthy discussion and debate, was followed which identified the following set of criteria by which the options should be judged:

(i) Contribution and its distribution through time;

(ii) Investment requirements (including working capital);

(iii) Market share (in terms of pairage);

(iv) Speed of erosion (i.e. rate of loss) of pairage and rate of recovery;

(v) Bally image: the brand and its survival;

(vi) Feasibility of manufacture of Bally shoes;

(vii) Impact on retail business (e.g. expansion);

(viii) Impact on Swiss parent;

(ix) Impact on wholesale business;

(x) Ability to present a range of men's shoes;

(xi) Bally UK Ltd., corporate objectives;

(xii) Demands made on management resources and skills.

The chief executive also specified a cut-off hurdle rate of return for acceptance of any policy option.

Some of these criteria involved a certain amount of overlap. In order to clarify the nature of these potential overlaps, it was necessary to identify measures for each decision criterion.

The first two criteria, contribution and investment requirements, were combined into net cash-flow measures through time (over a five-year planning horizon). They were divided, however, into wholesale and retail cash flows, since the decision-makers wished to evaluate them separately. This also covered criteria (vii) and (ix). The market share criterion was measured in terms of the distribution of the total sales volume per annum (again over a five-year planning horizon). These three criteria (or attributes) and their configuration through time, were used as dominant criteria in the subsequent analysis. The next state was to structure the options further, screen them and obtain an insight into preferred policy options.

Each of the policy options involved many variables which were probabilistic in nature, for example, future exchange rates and demand levels. A simulation model was therefore developed for each policy option. It produced such output variables as net present value, net cash flow, and sales volume for each option for each year of the five-year planning horizon.

At the same time, the group chief executive rated the various policy options by using a two-stage rating approach of the Churchman–Ackoff type. This is a matrix approach in which the matrix consists of a set of subjectively assessed scores for each option (defining the rows) against each relevant dimension (defining the columns). By using estimates of importance as weights for each dimension, the weighted score can then be computed for each option. In formal terms, if s_{ij} denotes the score of option i on the jth attribute, and w_j the weight given to attribute j, then the score S_j, where

$$S_j = \sum_j s_{ij} w_j$$

is used to rank the options.

The main value of two-stage rating procedures is in their intuitive appeal as a simple formalization, and this probably accounts for much of their popularity. A rating procedure also provides an overview of the problem and its issues, and a sensitivity to the nature of the trade-offs which may exist between the problem attributes. As a decision model, however, it assumes that the attributes are considered independent and that preferences are adequately represented by the implicitly linear scoring measure. There is also the problem that ratings for a policy on the various dimensions may reflect its overall attractiveness to a particular decision-maker.

The experimental process adopted for the chief executive's ratings was to ask him to give the twelve decision criteria (attributes) a rating from zero to ten, where zero would represent no importance whatsoever, and ten would denote a vitally important attribute. He was then asked to rate seven alternatives (policy options) on a scale between zero and ten, where ten would imply that the criterion requirements were wholly met, five that they were adequately satisfied and zero that they would not be satisfied at all. The scores for each alternative were multiplied by the importance rankings for each alternative and summed for each option. The resultant scores are shown in Table 10.8 showing option 6, linking with another company, as the leading choice.

Table 10.8 Two-stage policy rating scores

policy option		score	rank
1	Continue as before	372	6
2	Expand branded imports	462	5
3	Reduction of Swiss transfer price	523	2
4	Assemble in existing plant	520	3
5	Manufacture in existing plant	518	4
6	Link with another company	586	1

This analysis was performed before the chief executive was aware of the results of the simulation model. Once these results were obtained, further discussion amongst the decision-makers provided additional insights about the characteristics of the policy alternatives and the more important decision attributes.

It had originally been intended to use a combined measurement approach for a whole set of attributes. Difficulties were encountered in persuading the decision-makers to perform the required ranking exercises, so it only proved possible to use the combined analysis approach for the configurations of three criteria: retail and wholesale cash flows, and sales volume over the first five years. Rankings for these criteria were obtained from another of the main decision-makers. Three different levels on each attribute were defined to generate the hypothetical alternatives. A full design of three levels on three attributes yields 27 alternatives. The highest and lowest values on each attribute were taken from the ranges of simulation results. The middle level was chosen as approximately bisecting the interval between highest and lowest. The combinations were examined to check that ranking them required genuine trade-offs to be made. The attribute levels for the composite model linking the major quantified attributes are shown by way of illustration in Table 10.9.

Table 10.9 Attribute levels for the composite subset

	level 1	level 2	level 3
Wholesale/manufacturing, year 1	−£500,000	−£200,000	£50,000
Retail cash flows, year 1	£270,000	£400,000	£530,000
Sales volume, year 1	£85,000	£135,000	£180,000

Where it was possible to identify best and worst alternatives for a subset, these were numbered 1 to 27 respectively. This provided a useful anchoring. The rest of the alternatives were allocated unique numbers between 2 and 26 on a randomized basis. The alternatives were printed on cards, shuffled, and presented to the subject with a set of instructions. It was anticipated that the linear additive model would prove more than adequate and, on this basis, linear models were immediately found to give excellent fits for the sales volume and composite rankings. For the wholesale outcome rankings, the fit of the linear model was only moderate, and this was only marginally improved by the addition of extra terms in the equation.

The cash-flow rankings yielded unsatisfactory fits with counter-intuitive signs, whichever metric model was fitted. Further examination showed, however, that one could reproduce the rankings almost perfectly with a simple set of ordering rules. The first was to choose, irrespective of actual magnitudes, options where the cash flows increased from year to year. The alternatives were then ranked within these sets on the basis of the final year's outcome, followed by the next to last and so on. For the purpose of the analysis, a linear model with modified weights was used for the retail cash flows. Table 10.10 shows the broad results of the derived composite model in the final column.

Table 10.10 Broad description of model output[1]

policy option (alternative)	two-stage ratings (1st decision-maker)	qualitative[2] ratings (2nd decision-maker)	linear model
1 continue as before	7	5	7
2 manufacture elsewhere in UK	–	2	4
3 reduction of Swiss transfer price	2	7	6
4 assemble in existing plant	3	4	1
5 manufacture in existing plant	4	1	5
6 link with another company	5	6	2
7 purchase another company	1	3	–
8 expand branded imports	6	–	3

(1) Synthesis has collapsed several cases for each option (e.g. mixes of price and manufacturing capacity). Rank correlations were calculated using **all** case information.
(2) The data show the ranks given to options (with 1 being the most preferred). Only the first seven options were rated.

The optimal policy option was to assemble Swiss parts in England. This was compatible with continuing to market shoes imported from Italy, but did not involve cannibalizing Swiss sales.

The combined analysis rankings (and associated qualitative ratings) were assessed by one of the two chief executives. His colleague used the two-stage rating model as a preliminary screening model. Whilst the combined analysis (and qualitative ratings) favour manufacturing options, a two-stage rating procedure pointed to the purchase of another company as a dominant option.

One immediate explanation for the difference lies in the basic interest base of the two chief executives. Rating methods would seem to be most effective in assessing the importance of attributes rather than the actual attribute scores in the context of complex strategic decisions. Apart from response biases and halo effects associated with the use of rating approaches, it would seem to be a gross under-utilization of the potential information available, particularly given the potential value of a decision analysis approach in this type of situation.

The general level of agreement in the combined preference models does not justify the use of equal weighting models in strategic decisions with multiple criteria. It would appear that, in the majority of business situations, problems being discussed usually involve a distinct hierarchy of relative weights. Indiscriminate application of equal weight models might well lead to markedly non-optimal decisions where the attribute values were disparate.

By the end of the decision process, the decision-makers were enthusiastic about the options that involved further manufacturing. They wished to retain a degree of flexibility that would not have been possible had they committed capital to the policy suggested by the combined analysis. Discussions were therefore opened with a UK company about initially selling that company's products, and possibly later training and licensing the company to produce shoes to be sold under the Bally brand name.

Exercises

1. Suppose that you are offered an exactly comparable job in

terms of responsibility, conditions of service and interest as you hold now. How much of a salary increase (or decrease) would you need (or accept) if you found out that this job was in Wellington, New Zealand, or London, England, instead of New York? How did you reach your conclusions?

2. The Churchman–Ackoff approach attempts to deal with multiple-objectives by developing an index (or weighted score) which the decision-maker uses to discriminate between alternative strategies.

Suppose an R and D manager lists five objectives which are important in evaluating the worth of four R and D projects. A, B, C and D: (1) profitability, (2) growth and diversity of product line, (3) offensive research mounted to anticipate competition, (4) increased market share, (5) maintenance of technical capability. Table 10.11 shows the manager's worth assessment for the projects on each of the objectives. Note that a rating scale of 1 (low) to 10 (high) is allowable for each of the objectives.

Table 10.11 Objective worth measurements for projects

	objectives				
projects	(1)	(2)	(3)	(4)	(5)
A	8	6	5	7	7
B	6	7	6	6	7
C	4	6	8	8	6
D	5	9	7	7	6

Instead of giving the objectives equal weight the manager feels that he should assess weights which reflect his view of the relative importance of each objective. He undertakes a measurement process which involves ranking the objectives in order of importance and then transferring this ranking into a numerical weighting. The results of this process are as follows:

weights given to objectives					
(1)	(2)	(3)	(4)	(5)	Total
0·6	0·1	0·05	0·2	0·05	1·0.

(i) Develop a weighted index score to discriminate between projects.
(ii) What problems do you foresee in using this method in practical situations?
(iii) Can financial comparisons of A, B, C and D be obtained as a check on the reasonableness of the weighted average score? List what additional information you would require.

3. Dave Rosenberg is contemplating moving house within Los Angeles. He can buy more expensive houses with smaller accommodation in fashionable areas, or much bigger houses at a more reasonable price in less fashionable areas. He decides that the relevant criteria by which he should judge the available alternatives are: price (including any necessary structural alterations or renovation), profit realized if he sells over a five-year time horizon, size of home and area.

He assesses for each of three alternative houses monetary values for price and profit, and preference scores (between 1 (low) and 10 (high)) for size and area as shown in Table 10.12.

Table 10.12 Money values and scores for A, B and C

house	price	profit	size	area
A	$400,000	$56,000	6	8
B	$240,000	$78,000	7	7
C	$376,000	$20,000	5	9

(i) Can you suggest a procedure by which Dave can come to a choice between A, B and C? What should he decide to do?
(ii) Dave Rosenberg decides that his main criterion is profit. Will this affect the choice of preferred house?

*4. The planning department of Allied American Shipping Lines has been asked by its chief executive to assist in formulating a five-year strategy for the company. The chief executive has identified eight areas of activity for the company: (1) conventional passenger cruise shipping, (2) container shipping, (3) road haulage, (4) portfolio investment, (5) hotels, (6) property development, (7) offshore facilities for North Sea oil and (8) cash. He has also identified three criteria by which the different possible avenues his company may take over the five-year planning horizon could be judged: earnings potential, asset potential and compatibility with the company's image. With the aid of the head of the planning department, he has given weights for the relative importance of each of these three criteria on a scale 0–10 as summarized below.

criterion	weight
earnings	10
assets	8
compatibility	5

He then identified those factors which contributed to earnings potential, asset potential and compatibility, and assigned relative weights to each of these contributory factors. Thus, for earnings potential the factors considered important were:

  (i) Risk of earnings fluctuations,
 (ii) Knowledge of area within company,
(iii) The existence of competition,
 (iv) Speed of technical obsolescence,
  (v) Possibility of currency and exchange rate fluctuations,
 (vi) Inflexible earnings base.

For asset potential similarly the crucial factors were:

  (i) Risk of ruin if activity collapses,
 (ii) Disposability of assets in severe economic situation,
(iii) Amount of capital investment required.

Finally, compatibility with existing areas of activity was assumed to be uni-dimensional.

To obtain relative weights, the chief executive then asked senior managers within the company to cooperate with the planning department and assign values (on a scale 0 to 10) to each of the factors within the three main criteria of assets, earnings and compatibility. For this purpose, managers were given a scale divided into five equal areas with the mid-point of each evaluated as follows:

interval mid-point	*real-world interpretation*
1	dreadful
3	poor to fair
5	average
7	good
9	outstanding

The table of criterion weights thus obtained is given in Table 10.13 *for one option* (container shipping) where it should be noted that the weights within categories are normalized to sum to the weights given in Table 10.13. Similar tables were obtained for each of the other seven possible areas of activity.

Table 10.13 Criterion weights for container shipping

(*a*) *earnings potential*	
risk of fluctuation	1
area knowledge	0·5
existence of competition	5
speed of technical obsolescence	0·5
possibility of currency fluctuations	2
inflexible earnings base	1
total	10

(*b*) *asset potential*	
risk of ruin	1.5
disposability of assets	1.5
capital investment	5
total	8

(*c*) *compatibility*	
strong	5
(could be average or low – weight would then be 3 or 1 respectively)	

Similar scores were obtained for each of the eight areas and a ranking of the eight activities was thus obtained. Comment upon:

(i) the strengths and weaknesses of the procedure, and
(ii) the extent to which a measure of riskiness of each of the activities may emerge.

Would you recommend the adoption of such a procedure if you were in control of the planning activity?

Further reading

P. W. ABELSON and A. D. J. FLOWERDEW, 'Roskill's successful recommendation', *Journal of the Royal Statistical Society*, 1972, series A, vol. 135, no. 4, pp. 467–502.

A. ARBEL and R. M. TONG, 'On the Generation of Alternatives in Decision Analysis Problems', *Journal of the Operational Research Society*, 1982, vol. 33, pp. 377–82.

R. L. KEENEY, 'Utility Functions for Multi-attributed Consequences', *Management Science*, 1972, vol. 18, part A, pp. 276–87.

A. R. LOCK, 'A strategic business decision with multiple criteria: the Bally men's shoe problem', *Journal of the Operational Research Society*, 1982, vol. 33, pp. 327–32.

R. DE NEUFVILLE and R. L. KEENEY, 'Use of Decision Analysis in Airport Development for Mexico City', in *Analysis of Public Systems* (ed. by A. W. Drake, R. L. Keeney and P. M. Morse), MIT Press, 1972.

'Report of a study of Rail Links with Heathrow Airport', HMSO, London, 1970, parts I and II.

R. K. SARIN, 'Screening of Multi-attribute Alternatives', *Omega*, 1977, vol. 5, no. 4, pp. 481–9

K. D. TOCHER, 'Planning Systems', *Philosophical Transactions of the Royal Society*, 1977, series A, vol. 287, pp. 125–41.

11 Risk Analysis

Introduction

Risk analysis, a technique widely used in management science and operational research, provides a way to assess the effects of uncertainty that has been widely used, particularly in capital investment decisions and strategic planning generally. Assessments are made by finding the probability distribution of the worth measure concerned, taking into account the varying degrees of uncertainty affecting the input variables.

There are a number of commonly used worth measures, e.g. net present value (NPV), internal rate of return (IRR), and payback. We outline here the risk analysis procedure in terms of NPV and then discuss areas to which it can usefully be applied. In conclusion, the role of sensitivity analysis is examined and an example is presented of the use of strategic risk analysis in the context of new product diversification.

The Basic Procedure

In risk analysis the decision-maker has first to make subjective probability assessments of the uncertain quantities which are important. Consider an investment decision about an R and D project. If the firm knew with certainty the cash-flow pattern which would occur over the project's life-cycle, a definite value could be calculated for the NPV. Uncertainty impinges, however, with unpredicted fluctuations occurring in the various elements making up the cash-flow pattern for the project. The decision-maker needs a mechanism which allows him to characterize the effects of these uncertainties on the NPV measure. This is achieved by deriving the probability distribution of the NPV from the inputs, so that the variability or spread about the expected value of NPV can be evaluated.

The steps in the risk analysis procedure are as follows:

(i) Identify the key uncertain factors for the investment decision under consideration (e.g. investment cost, raw material costs, selling price of final product, level of sales, etc.).

(ii) Obtain estimates of the range of values within which each of these factors is expected to lie, and the likelihood of occurrence (possibly in bands) of each value within the range. For example, raw material costs are expected to lie within the range $25–$50 per ton but the decision-maker might assign probabilities of 0·6 that the price will be $40, of 0·1 that it will be $25, of 0·2 that it will be $45, and of 0·1 that it will be $50. Note that some of these key factors may be interdependent. In such a situation estimates of the correlations between them must be obtained and introduced by means of conditional probability distributions.

(iii) Select by some random procedure a value for each of the key factors from the appropriate probability distributions assessed in stage (ii). If some of the factors are interdependent, the value obtained from the distribution of one key factor will determine which of several conditional distributions should be sampled to give the value of another key factor.

(iv) Calculate in the usual manner the value of NPV obtained from the values of each factor found in (iii). Repeat the procedure in (iii) and (iv) a large number of times, obtaining a set of NPVs. The distribution of NPV values thus obtained can be used to calculate the mean and variability of the NPV. (The whole procedure is sometimes referred to as the *simulation* [or *Monte Carlo*] method.)

Illustrative Example

An R and D project is being evaluated for which the basic economic factors to be considered are:

(i) development cost per year of the project's life;

(ii) production and sales costs at the point of commercial sale;

(iii) the price at which the product will be sold;

(iv) the quantity which will be sold per year of the project's life.

To avoid introducing the complication of assessing correlation effects between factors, we assume that the net cash flows in successive years of the project's life are independently distributed. All the four factors are estimated in relation to the decision-maker's estimate of the project's life-cycle, namely seven years, with the following results:

(i) (a) First-year development cost: mean: $80,000
standard deviation: $5,000

(b) Second-year development cost: mean: $115,000
standard deviation: $5,000

(ii) Production and sales costs in years three to seven. These are assumed to be a proportion of the revenue (price × quantity sold in each year); the assessed proportion is 65 per cent with a standard deviation of 2 per cent.

(iii) Price for years three to seven: mean: $4,000
standard deviation: $250

(iv) Quantities sold of final product:

year 3 mean 240 units; standard deviation 24 units
,,   4   ,,   275 ,,   ,,   ,,   30 ,,
,,   5   ,,   280 ,,   ,,   ,,   20 ,,
,,   6   ,,   250 ,,   ,,   ,,   25 ,,
,,   7   ,,   200 ,,   ,,   ,,   20 ,,

In each instance the assessment is made in terms of a normal distribution defined by its mean and standard deviation (see the section 'Indirect Methods' page 142). By means of random selection a set of values can be obtained for each of the four factors. (The exact procedure is not considered here, but the book by D. B. Hertz and H. Thomas, listed at the end of this chapter, gives further details.) Suppose that on the first round of such selection the following results emerge:

(i) (a) Development cost first year $75,000
(b) Development cost second year $125,000
(ii) Production and sales costs   70 per cent

(iii) Price for years three to seven	$3,500
(iv) Quantities sold year 3	220
year 4	280
year 5	260
year 6	250
year 7	200.

The net cash flows in each year can then be calculated and are shown in Table 11.1. The final column gives the overall NPV for this particular set of values. Further sets of combinations of values from the distributions could now be selected. For each of these sets the net cash flows and NPV are calculated. In this way a series of values for NPV is obtained which would enable us to determine the approximate shape of the distribution for NPV.

Table 11.1 Net cash flows – one sample run

year	cash flows	net cash flows (discounted at 10 per cent p.a.)
1	−$75,000 *or* −$75,000	−$75,000
2	−$125,000 *or* −$125,000	−$113,625
3	+0·3×(220×3,500) *or* $231,000	+$190,805
4	+0·3×(280×3,500) *or* $294,000	+$220,795
5	+0·3×(260×3,500) *or* $273,000	+$186,455
6	+0·3×(250×3,500) *or* $262,500	+$163,010
7	+0·3×(200×3,500) *or* $210,000	+$118,440

total +$690,880 (NPV)

Figure 11.1 shows some possible shapes for such NPV distributions. Typical questions that a decision-maker would ask in relation to the NPV distribution are:

(a) What is the probability of making a loss? (i.e. NPV < 0).
(b) What is the expected or mean value of NPV? (i.e. the value for NPV that we would get on average).
(c) What is the probability of making a gain greater than some specified level L? (i.e. NPV > L).
(d) How risky is the project? Is the variability or spread in the NPV distribution large in relation to the mean?

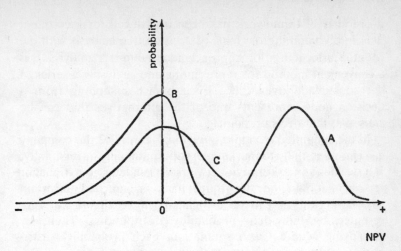

11.1 Possible shapes for NPV distributions

Looking at the shapes in Figure 11.1, we note that Project C has about a 50:50 chance of an NPV exceeding zero and is fairly risky. Project A always gives rise to a positive value for NPV. Project B has about an 80 per cent chance of an NPV below zero and a decision-maker is unlikely to get a positive NPV with this project.

Knowledge of the shape of the NPV distribution helps the decision-maker to assess whether the expected NPV by itself gives a good indication of the final outcome. The shape necessarily depends, however, for its validity upon the degree of accuracy with which decision-makers assess subjective probability distributions for the key factors in the decision problem. The basic methodology of decision analysis, which we developed earlier, is more meaningful than the risk analysis method, in that it looks at the sequential multi-stage nature of decision-making. Risk analysis in the form outlined above reduces decision-making to a single-stage analysis in which later decisions are not considered.

Stochastic Decision Tree Analysis
To overcome the difficulty just mentioned, the 'stochastic

decision tree' framework has been introduced for investment decisions combining the logic of decision tree analysis with the Monte Carlo simulation approach adopted in risk analysis. It is a convenient method for representing and analysing a series of decisions made over time. Each branch extending from a decision node represents one of the alternatives that can be chosen at that decision point.

In the simplified example shown in Figure 11.2 the company can choose initially to market a product nationally or regionally. If it decides to market regionally first, it can later go national or remain regional. Once the product has been launched, uncertain cash-flow patterns can be associated with each branch, represented by individual probability distributions. Then, by employing Monte Carlo simulation, each probability distribution on the various paths of the decision tree is sampled. The process of sampling is repeated and the net cash flows resulting are accumulated to give separate frequency distributions for each of the four possible end net cash-flow patterns in the tree. Management can then choose the most favourable decision sequence on the basis of these results. However, as we saw in risk analysis, choosing one from a set of distributions is a difficult task which reflects the risk attitude of the decision-maker.

Sensitivity Analysis

With both risk analysis and stochastic decision tree analysis we can carry out a sensitivity analysis in response to questions from management. For example, in the R and D situation discussed earlier, the manager may want to know the effect on the NPV probability distribution of a catastrophic 50 per cent fall in demand for the product. The demand figure in the input for the analysis can be altered and the amended risk model run to obtain a new risk profile. From this profile relevant statistics, e.g. the probability of a negative NPV, can be estimated.

In this way, with different questions from management, a whole range of sensitivity analyses and resulting risk profiles can be built up. Given this information, management can then use its experience, intuition and judgement to guide it in choosing amongst alternative projects. Note, however, that the input

net cash flows

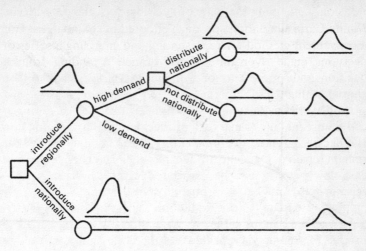

11.2 Stochastic decision tree for market launch

changes examined are not chosen arbitrarily, but reflect management's view as to meaningful changes that should be examined.

Interpretation

The output of both the risk analysis and stochastic decision tree approaches is a PDF curve of Net Present Value for each strategy. In order to choose between strategies, we must choose between their associated NPV density curves. As a consequence, it is often helpful to express these curves not in the form shown in Figure 11.1, but as cumulative (or CDF) forms. This is done in Figure 11.3 for a decision problem in which there are two alternative strategies A and B. We note under (a) that the cumulative curve for A is always to the right of the payoff curve for B. We can therefore always do better financially with A than B and can say that A probabilistically dominates B. However, if (b) represents the situation where the curves A' and B' cross, then one strategy does not always dominate the other. In these latter situations the utility concept is valuable, because it allows us to measure the decision-maker's preference for money

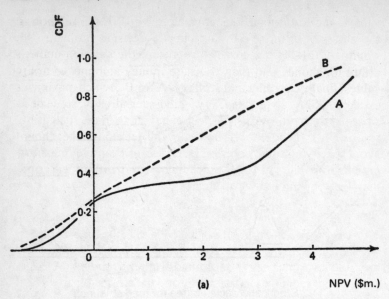

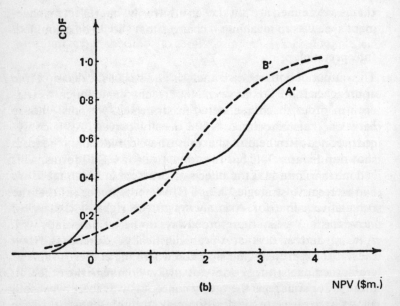

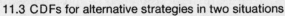

11.3 CDFs for alternative strategies in two situations

values, and to formalize his attitude towards risk in relation to the amounts of money at stake in the decision problem. We would try to obtain a curve to represent the decision-maker's utility for money and then translate money amounts to utility values, finally choosing that strategy, A′ or B′, which maximizes expected utility. In practice, as we have seen already, some decision-makers baulk at the prospect of having to make such utility assessments. In those cases, however, the decision-maker cannot avoid specifying some criterion (such as, for example, maximizing the probability of NPV exceeding zero) in order to discriminate between alternative strategies.

New Project Diversification Example

This case reviews a problem faced by a US chemical company when they had to decide whether or not to diversify into a related area and invest in a newly developed synthetic product. Management had a seemingly attractive product, but was unsure about its longer-term competitive viability, its cash-flow generation potential and its fit in relation to corporate growth and return goals. Given the high capital investment required there was particular concern about the decreasing prices of competitive products and the increasing possibilities of additional firms entering the market.

It was decided to undertake a decision and risk analysis based on an evaluation of the diversification opportunity. The key assumptions of the model including clear statements about key marketing, manufacturing, R and D and financial factors, were incorporated into the flow chart shown in Figure 11.4. Management decided they wanted the new product opportunity evaluated in terms of a series of indicator variables or criteria, rather than in terms of a single rate of return, performance measure such as internal rate of return, or net present value. Six performance measures were suggested and each was calculated over its entire range of probable values. The following measures were calculated for the opportunity's assumed time horizon; total dollar sales; cash flow; gross profit as a percentage of sales; net profit after tax; annual return on investment, and overall discounted return on investment. The probability profiles of each of these

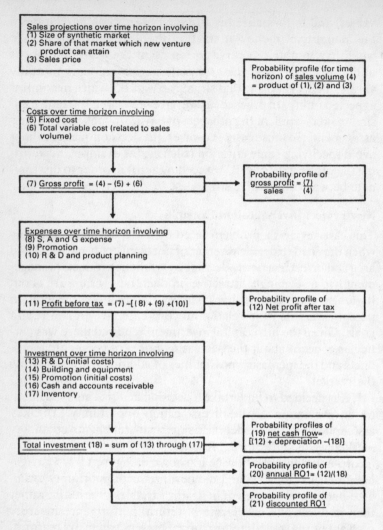

11.4 Flow chart of the initial diversification investment model

performance measures were generated, with the cash-flow pro
file shown as an illustrative item in Figure 11.5.

The assessments made of the probability distributions for the
key uncertain variables in the decision problem were a necessary

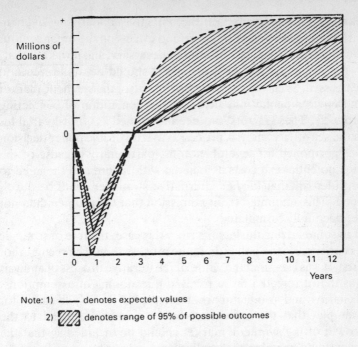

Note: 1) ——— denotes expected values

2)  denotes range of 95% of possible outcomes

11.5 Illustrative cash-flow profile.

input for the calculation of these probability profiles. The distributions for later years (not shown here) were much more diffuse or 'spread out', confirming the expectation that the management team was less uncertain about the longer-term future.

The probability profiles for the six performance measures were examined and discussed by the management team. The team decided to undertake further sensitivity testing, even though it was felt that the cash generation potential and the Discounted Cash Flow return of the project were both satisfactory. The sensitivity analysis showed that the critical factors for success were the size of the synthetic market, the share of that market which the new product was likely to obtain, the sales price of the final product, the variable costs and the financial resources involved in capital investment.

On the basis of these findings, it was decided that attention should be firmly focused on the objectives underlying diversification moves as well as the portfolio effects on the organization. Further re-analysis was considered necessary, and it was felt that, in the meantime, the critical factors should be monitored and reassessed. Such factors included the size of the synthetic market and environmental influences on the generation of competing products. These factors had been identified as critical variables in the sensitivity analysis process. An irrevocable policy decision was postponed for several months, particularly because of the high potential exit costs associated with failure and the need to consider whether further alternative strategies could be developed. This amounted to an admission that the problem had not yet been fully formulated.

In summarizing the lessons from this case, the role of strategic risk analysis in the policy dialogue process should be recognized. First, it was clear that the value of the iterative process of analysis was that it forced a more focused questioning of assumptions, scenarios and product/market concepts. It was decided, for example, that the extreme 'what-if' scenarios related to the growth of the synthetic market should be included so that the team could examine the challenging project assumptions. Secondly, the value of sensitivity analysis lies in relation to its simplicity and the speed and economy with which it is undertaken. It can quickly highlight crucial uncertain areas, focus attention on conflicting viewpoints and stimulate problem redefinition. It thus forms a complement and a necessary adjunct to the application of decision analysis. Thirdly, the dialogue process concerning the six performance measures recognizes that there is no single 'best' criterion, or set of criteria, by which the management of the firm's strategic diversification can be handled. Rather, it encourages all members of the management team to understand the policy alternatives more fully before a choice decision has to be made. Fourth, the dialogue and debate process encourages conflicting viewpoints to emerge, and recognizes the need for appropriate problem reformulation through creative development of new alternatives. Although such dialogue and debate took place in the context of a decision-making group representing several different functions and disciplines, the common denominator was the will to examine the problem from a wide range of viewpoints and perspectives.

Exercises

1. Table 11.2 gives the results of a risk analysis of five alternative strategies for a property development company. Only one of the five strategies can be adopted because currently the firm is in a tight cash-flow position with total liquid assets of about $⅔m.

Table 11.2 Net present values for alternative strategies

	total NPV	
strategy	mean ($ thousand)	standard deviation ($ thousand)
1	700	20
2	800	18
3	1,250	45
4	500	10
5	680	15

Which strategy should the firm undertake in its present position? (Hint: you should consider the most appropriate decision criterion in the light of the firm's current attitude to risk.)

2. Analyses for the stochastic decision tree shown in Figure 11.2 (in terms of a one-year time horizon after the introduction of the product) are obtained by simulation for each of the four possible paths through the tree (see Table 11.3 overleaf).
As the managing director of the company, what initial decision would you make? Explain your answer, discussing particularly any drawbacks you consider exist with the stochastic decision tree approach.

*3. Pethow Inc. have developed a new aerosol touch-up spray paint for automobiles. The investment cost for putting the product on the market is not known with certainty, and there is also considerable uncertainty about market variables and manufac-

Table 11.3 Net cash flows

path		net cash flow ($000) (over a 1-year time horizon)		
		mean	standard deviation	probability of occurrence of the path
A	introduce regionally, high demand, distribute nationally	250	40	0·25
B	introduce regionally, high demand, no national distribution	180	35	0·5
C	introduce regionally, low demand	140	60	0·15
D	introduce nationally	320	60	0·4

turing costs. The managing director has consulted relevant experts within the company and they have produced probability assessments for the uncertain quantities as shown in Table 11.4.

The managing director reckons that there will be a five-year life for the product and that inflation will be about 10 per cent per annum over the period. In addition, as a first approximation he suggests that the factors in the table can be considered to be independent of each other.

Use a simulation approach with random numbers to carry out an analysis, considering in particular:

(i) the factors you will include in your risk model,
(ii) the criterion (e.g. NPV) whose probability distribution you will generate in the risk analysis procedure, and
(iii) the possibility of examining the sensitivity of the final criterion distribution to changes in the distributions associated with the factors on the table.

What decision would you recommend to the managing director of Pethow Inc.? Comment on the realism of the analysis.

Table 11.4 Probability assessments

factors		probability	value
investment cost	low	0·2	$125,000
	medium	0·7	$200,000
	high	0·1	$220,000
total yearly market for	low	0·2	200,000 units
aerosols	medium	0·6	300,000 units
	high	0·2	500,000 units
market share	low	0·1	10 per cent
	medium	0·8	15 per cent
	high	0·1	20 per cent
price (per unit)	low	0·2	$1·50
	medium	0·7	$2·00
	high	0·1	$3·00
manufacturing production	low	0·1	$0·35
and sales costs (per unit)	medium	0·8	$0·55
	high	0·1	$0·90

*4. Carry out a simulation sensitivity analysis on Pethow Inc.'s decision problem discussed in Exercise 3 by developing a grid such as the one shown below, in Table 11.5.

Table 11.5 Sensitivity analysis

factor	amount of sensitivity change in each factor (say)	effect on NPV distribution
investment cost	+20 per cent	
total market	±20 per cent	
market share	±5 per cent	
price	±5 per cent	
marginal manufacturing + sales costs	±10 per cent	

The table indicates that you could change a single factor, say investment cost, by +20 per cent, or else change one or more factors simultaneously. There are, therefore, a large number of possible sensitivity analyses that can be carried out.

What conclusions do you draw from your analysis? What criticisms would you make of the sensitivity analysis approach?

Further Reading

C. P. BONINI, 'Risk Evaluation of Investment Projects', *Omega*, 1975, vol. 3, no. 6, pp. 735–50.

E. E. CARTER, 'What are the Risks in Risk Analysis', *Harvard Business Review*, July 1972, pp. 72–82.

D. COOPER and C. CHAPMAN, *Risk Analysis for Large Projects*, Wiley, 1987.

D. B. HERTZ, 'Risk Analysis in Capital Investment', *Harvard Business Review*, Sept. 1979, pp. 169–81.

D. B. HERTZ and H. THOMAS, 'Decision and Risk Analysis in a New Product and Facilities Planning Problem', *Sloan Management Review*, 1983, vol. 24, no. 2, pp. 17–31.

D. B. HERTZ and H. THOMAS, *Risk Analysis and its Applications*, Wiley, 1983.

C. W. HAFER and D. E. SCHENDAL, '*Strategy Formulation: Analytical Concepts*', West Publishing Company, 1978.

12 Implementation

Introduction

Decision-theory analysis should be regarded foremost as an approach to problem solving. In this chapter we consider first some problems in the methodology of decision analysis which require further development to improve its overall serviceability. Secondly, we outline a number of situations in which decision analysis techniques have been, or are being, applied. Thirdly, we discuss the pros and cons of decision analysis and indicate the ways in which its promise can be fulfilled. Finally, we provide some guidelines for readers who might themselves wish to get started on decision analysis in their own firms – hopefully to help them avoid some of the more obvious pitfalls which occur.

Organizational Implications

In most business decision-making situations choices, or recommendations about choices, are made on the basis of some analysis – formal or informal, quantitative or qualitative. Very often the various forms of analysis used lead to inconsistencies when they are applied to a series of decision situations. For example, a long-term strategic decision may be made very informally, whilst a new product launch may be the subject of long and detailed scrutiny utilizing NPV concepts.

Decision analysis should be regarded as a general system for making decisions which will ensure a consistent treatment of varying decision situations, handling the different degrees of uncertainty which exist in such situations. Our experience is that its most effective position in the corporate situation is at the planning level of strategy and policy formulation. In some large companies decision analysis is operated from within the corporate planning department. In others, particularly smaller firms, the decision analysis approach will tend to be most useful at board level.

The close connection between decision analysis and planning is important and meaningful. Decision analyses carried out for short-run decisions, however, have to be made within the constraints of overall corporate policy. This will dictate the current assumptions employed with regard to cost evaluation, cost of capital, overall economic trends, employment prospects, etc. In the long term the analysis itself may equally well change the direction of corporate policy. The paper by Wells (see references at the end of this chapter) gives some illustrations of planning decisions made through decision analysis in the Imperial Group.

The excitement of decision analysis lies in its ability to formalize wide-ranging policy, planning and decision situations, while at the same time enabling communication between the interested parties in the organization to be effectively maintained.

Applying Decision Analysis to Ill-Structured Problems

The decision analysis approach is normally applied in terms of a series of distinct steps or stages (see Figure 12.1).

(i) Structuring the problem; definition of the set of alternative strategies: the key uncertainties; the time horizon and the attributes or dimensions by which alternatives should be judged.

(ii) Assessing consequences; specification of impact or consequence measures for the decision alternatives.

(iii) Assessing probabilities and preferences; assessment (or definition) of probability measures for key uncertainties and utility measures to reflect preference for outcomes.

(iv) Evaluating alternatives; evaluation of alternatives in terms of a criterion for choice, such as the maximization of expected utility.

(v) Sensitivity analysis in relation to the optimal strategy, possibly leading to further information gathering.

(iv) Choice of the most appropriate strategy in the light of the analysis and managerial judgement.

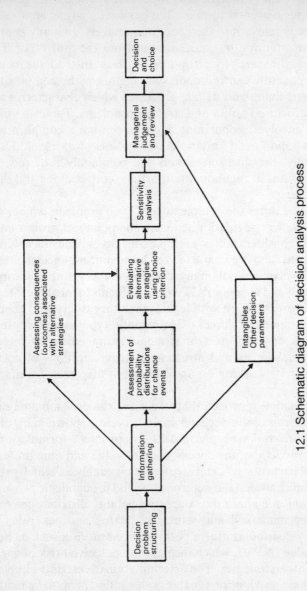

12.1 Schematic diagram of decision analysis process

Since this basic paradigm was proposed, experience has generated changes designed to make the decision analysis approach more directly relevant to the needs of managers. In many applications the attention has moved away from the 'purity' of the analysis and the search for an optimal solution. Instead, the focus is more frequently centred upon such factors as the complexity and the bargaining and debate processes which characterize so many ill-structured policy and strategy problems. Typically, the problems involved concerning high stakes have complicated structures and need multiple viewpoints for resolution. Additionally, the decision-makers are commonly required to justify decisions to regulatory authorities, corporations and the public at large.

Figure 12.2 notes the complexities of such problems which, as a result of law or regulation, concern many impact groups and involve the consideration of multiple objectives. They have long time horizons, and are characterized by significant uncertainties and the involvement of many decision-makers with differing backgrounds and viewpoints. Typical problems involve the interface of the organization with legal, regulatory, social and economic environmental forces. Cost/benefit type analyses used require a keen awareness of strategic management of inter-organizational forces and are familiar to generations of cost-benefit analysts working on applications in the area of welfare economics.

An alternative approach that structures the decision analysis process in terms of the decision analysis cycle is shown in Figure 12.3. The *deterministic phase* calls for problem formulation, structural modelling, the specification of value and time preferences and, particularly, extensive sensitivity analysis, which provides the link between the deterministic and probabilistic phases. The *probabilistic phase* introduces probability distributions for certain key numerical and structural factors and generates a probability distribution for a performance criterion such as net present value (NPV), which displays the perceived risk of various alternative strategies. The determination of certainty equivalents for these distributions enables value judgements to be made in relation to risk. The *informational phase* stresses the economic structure

Identify the alternatives

Specify relevant impact groups

Determine the objectives

Define measures of effectiveness (attributes) for each objective

Step 2. Assess the possible consequences of the alternatives

Quantify consequences in term of attributes

Assess judgements of experts

Collect data and update estimates

Quantify uncertainty, using probability

Determine the general form of the utility function to quantify the value structure

Assess the single attribute utility functions

Assess the value trade-offs to indicate relative importance of different objectives

Verify the consistency of the value judgements

Step 4. Evaluate and compare the alternatives

Integrate the previous information to evaluate alternatives

Conduct a sensitivity analysis with respect to preferences and consequences

Re-examine aspects found to be crucial to the decision

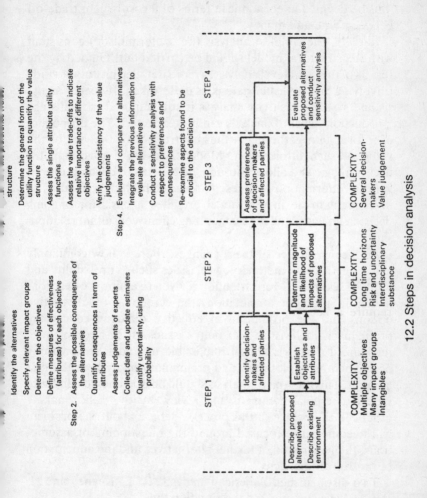

STEP 1

COMPLEXITY
Multiple objectives
Many impact groups
Intangibles

Describe proposed alternatives
Describe existing environment

Identify decision-makers and affected parties

Establish objectives and attributes

STEP 2

COMPLEXITY
Long time horizons
Risk and uncertainty
Interdisciplinary
substance

Determine magnitude and likelihood of impacts of proposed alternatives

STEP 3

COMPLEXITY
Several decision-makers
Value judgement

Assess preferences of decision-makers and affected parties

STEP 4

Evaluate proposed alternatives and conduct sensitivity analysis

12.2 Steps in decision analysis

value to be obtained from reducing the uncertainty characterized in the probabilistic phase. Additional information gathering may thus be deemed uneconomic in terms of a cost/benefit trade-off between time and money.

Initially, the simplest analysis (i.e. deterministic) consistent with the structural model should be carried out. Guided by the results of this pilot level analysis, a more detailed prototype study (involving probabilistic analysis) is undertaken. If deeper analysis and system sensitivity analysis is still required, a final stage 'production' level of analysis can be generated. The economics of information gathering is thus controlled by analyses of the value of such information. Models provide a road-map for decision logic and allow, through the process of decomposition, various information sources to be specifically targeted. The investment made in the model provides a basis for ongoing decision analyses and for a continuing client-consultant relationship.

As a consequence of these changes, there is now commonly less concern about methodological issues such as probability and utility assessment. More attention is given to aiding the decision-maker in problem formulation, the screening of alternative options and the promotion of effective dialogue concerning problem characteristics and policy issues. It has come to be recognized that it is almost impossible to undertake anything other than an exploratory and preliminary analysis at the first attempt. This 'first-pass' analysis should be documented and subjected to critical comment and review by the policy-making group. In the course of this process, debate about the problem will become more focused around the questioning of assumptions, the generation of further alternatives and the anticipation of future contingencies.

Two distinguished American analysts, R. L. Keeney and H. Raiffa, have summarized the situation thus:

The major role of formal analysis is 'to promote good decision-making'. It is meant to serve as an aid to the decision-maker and not as a substitute for him . . . As a process, it is intended to force hard thinking about the problem area: generation of alternatives, anticipation of future contingencies, examination of dynamic secondary effects, and so forth.

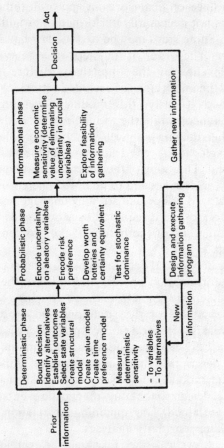

12.3 An alternative scenario

Furthermore, a good analysis should illuminate controversy – to find out where basic differences exist in values and uncertainties, to facilitate compromise, to increase the level of debate and undercut rhetoric – in short, to promote good decision-making.

This modified decision analysis is an approach rather than a technique, and is not necessarily performed in a rigid series of sequential steps. Some steps may be excluded or handled in an informal manner. The order of the steps may be varied and, indeed, the relevance of the objective structure, problem assumptions and the importance of excluded factors may be continually reassessed. Clearly, this modified decision analysis approach can still incorporate the techniques outlined in Figure 12.1. Indeed, when dealing with well-structured problems (such as oil and gas exploration), the traditional and modified paradigms are identical. The value of the new paradigm is embedded in its flexibility, which is needed to deal with increasingly complex and unstructured policy and strategic management issues. It requires deliberate and disciplined use, but yields a greatly enhanced understanding of the nature of the problem and the available options.

Recent studies in personal decision-making give much greater emphasis to the formulation process and much of the value of decision analysis seems to come from the structuring phase when subjects' representations of the situations and problems are developed. The aim is to generate an acceptable decision analysis model which concisely captures the problem elements and provides a problem description that can be discussed with the decision-makers to aid understanding. Subjectivity and creativity are required in model design so that only diagnostic events and critical trade-offs are retained. The remaining information gathered may be used in later sensitivity analyses.

The process is a cyclical one, in which the technology is a structuring aid in itself. This process of formulating ill-structured strategic problems may also require specialized aids. A number of aids have been proposed to assist this process: for example the concepts of devil's advocate (DA), dialectical inquiry (DI) or Delphi decision analysis. Approaches such as the devil's advocate and dialectical inquiry involve the introduction of conflict into the corporate problem formulation process. In particular three activities exist which can improve the quality of problem formulation in uncertain environments. The first is the generation of conflict between the decision-making group or within a decision-maker. The second is the identification of assumptions about the nature of the problem, and the impacts of the internal and external decision environments. The third is the challenging of assumptions.

Decision-makers may resist adoption of such processes because of the continual need to re-examine assumptions, even when a solution has been proposed. This continual re-examination imposes a time requirement which may not be feasible or acceptable and may open up areas which are regarded as particularly politically sensitive.

Having arrived at an appropriate initial problem structure, assessment of the probabilities and preferences identified within the representation of the structured decision problem can proceed using appropriate encoding aids. Ultimately the 'first-pass' analysis has to be useful to decision-makers, and they have to feel confident about it. The presentation of a single best option does not always inspire this confidence. Strict optimization is less attractive than the ability to explore the problem by the policy dialogue of several 'passes' through the analytic model, involving varying assumptions about problem elements. A major role for computer-based decision support models exists in facilitating manager-based sensitivity analyses and the ability to respond to 'what-if' questions. Decision-makers acquire commitment to the solution by feeling both that they have some control over the policy recommendations and that they have contributed to its development.

The goal of this modified approach should be judged in terms of its contribution to organizational processes, rather than concentrating on the adoption of a specific course of action. Very often, the understanding derived from the process of structuring the problem and the information related to outcomes and actions may significantly influence the quality of the decision process.

The Initial Contract

During the intial stages of the decision analysis process, the analyst must explain the requirements of the process in terms of information requirements and the preferred degree of access to organizational decision-makers. In the more politicized organizations, sponsoring coalitions or individuals may attempt to control access to the analyst, or the analyst's access to other decision participants. This should be recognized in developing the initial structuring of the problem and deciding which groups' views are essential in devising acceptable strategies and representing preferences. Interested groups could include a wide range of stakeholders, including owners (the state, shareholders, community, etc.), employees, consumers, managers and society. However, the incorporation of the views of various groups can lead to a decision analysis model rather different from that anticipated by the sponsor.

The analyst may interface with clients in a spectrum of possible roles, ranging from the 'expert' at one extreme to the 'trainer' at the other extreme. In the expert role, the structuring and analysis is largely performed by the analyst, without significant organizational involvement. In contrast, the trainer role aims to teach organizational decision-makers to structure analyses and evaluate alternative strategies on their own, thus developing the ability to use the techniques in the absence of the analyst. The involvement and resulting commitment on the part of the decision-makers will increase as the analyst moves from the 'expert' to the 'trainer' role. The tendency for the conventional decision analysis paradigm to follow the first path, partially explains the resultant low commitment to conclusions and recommendations that arises in a number of situations.

One view of the decision analyst is that of a passive encoder of client-provided information. This view assumes that the organizational decision-makers have a fully developed understanding and representation of the decision problem. In complicated applications, problem formulation is frequently the most time-consuming phase. Despite the apparent critical importance of problem structuring and formulation in the strategic decision process literature, mainstream decision analysis texts have tended to bypass it, suggesting that the process is more art than science.

Implementation

The main elements in devising an implementation strategy relate to identifying the key groups and individuals, how they can be induced to contemplate change, and how they will respond to any particular proposals. The person with the perceived responsibility for the decision should be in charge of the implementation strategy rather than the decision analyst. Nevertheless, the analyst must help to instil confidence in clients and avoid imposing their own values and perceptions, operating in a creative milieu.

It is clear that decision-makers often dislike conflicts, particularly highly personal ones, and seek to avoid them. In many situations, changes and decisions are postponed until they are imposed by an external agency. By this time, the organization's survival may even be threatened. The alternative is to consider to what extent it is possible to improve the client's or the client organization's ability to deal with conflict. In cases where conflict is not directly resolvable, it may be feasible to assist people to handle overt conflict and to confront political issues openly. This is a development strategy that may require a longer time horizon than is usually available in a decision analysis study.

Applications

One question that will be in the mind of executives who have read this far is 'Where have these techniques been successfully applied?' The list of applications is always growing, amongst which the following are illustrative:

investment: new plant, expansion of plant, etc;
plant rationalization;
new product introduction;
sales force deployment;
scale and use of market research information;
research and development policy;
distribution methods;

oil and gas exploration decisions;
nuclear power plant site selection;
pricing strategies;
competitive bidding tenders;
control of quality and production;
negotiation and bargaining;
property litigation;
cash-flow management;
the pricing of acquisitions;
structuring and evaluation of career choice options;
planning corporate strategy and growth;
diagnosis and treatment of heart disease and psychiatric disorders;
energy forecasting and modelling.

We believe that routine decisions about such diverse items as medical diagnoses, macro-economic policies and governmental decisions will be made in the near future using decision analysis techniques as guidelines. Indeed we would speculate that in the future decision analysis is likely to be used increasingly as a planning tool for strategy formulation and policy analysis at the corporate level, both in the public and private sectors of business activity.

Pros and Cons

After the foregoing discussion, it is useful to attempt some summary of the main arguments for and against the use of decision analysis. These are presented in tabular form.

pro	*con*
(i) Systematic and logical approach to decision-making.	(i) Time consuming and unsuitable for snap decisions.
(ii) The views from experts in other areas are more readily incorporated in decision-making.	(ii) Lack of acceptance of principles by all decision-makers.
(iii) Permits a thorough analysis of alternative options.	(iii) Assessments of probabilities and utilities are difficult to obtain and therefore felt to be unreliable.

(iv) Separation of preference assessment for outcomes from probability assessments for uncertain quantities.

(v) Allows decision-maker to judge how much information to gather in a given decision problem.

(vi) Assists in the communication of a decision to all concerned.

(iv) Decisions are more readily handled in terms of available 'hard data', and hence areas for which only 'soft data' are available are overlooked.

(v) Organizational obstacles in situations with defined responsibilities.

Study of this brief summary suggests that the logic of the technique must be balanced against a number of measurement problems. Great strides have been made in resolving the major measurement problems in decision analysis and, if you are able to accept the step-by-step logic of the procedure, you should join the increasing band of managers applying decision theory. Experimental studies in probability and utility assessments and the publication of real-life case studies of application of decision analysis have significantly contributed to the increasing acceptance of the approach.

Getting Started

For those readers who feel able to apply decision analysis themselves in their own firms, the following guidelines are suggested, based on the authors' experiences:

(i) Make sure that your colleagues are enthusiastic about decision analysis and see the merit of the approach and the pay-off to be obtained. Educational programmes have great value in developing an awareness of decision analysis within an organization – often at a relatively low cost.

(ii) Ensure that the decision problem to be studied is defined correctly.

(iii) Try several alternative decompositions and decision trees for the problem before going through the assessment process. It is often useful to hire the services of a decision analyst for your first decision analysis; he can guide you and discuss problem structure as a non-involved third party.

(iv) Before obtaining probability assessments from decision-makers, make sure that they are fully trained in the concepts and meaning of probability. This training is best done by a series of informal tutorials on probability in the context of the firm.

(v) In asking decision-makers to assign probabilities for some uncertain quantity, e.g. price, you must give those decision-makers all the objective, quantitative information about price levels which is available in the firm (e.g. from accounting records, past sales data, etc.)

(vi) Stick to EMV as the decision criterion on the first analysis. Bring in the utility concept gradually and indicate how to assess a utility-for-money function. Consult with a decision analyst if the utility concept is found difficult to implement, when the concept of certainty equivalence is an alternative.

Finally, the note on which to conclude is to emphasize that the successful implementation of decision analysis by you, the reader, to a problem of your own, will have made study of this book worthwhile. We have all experienced that feeling of emptiness when long and tedious debates and discussions over some decision have ended, and the die has been irrevocably cast. Is our conclusion right, or are we storing up further problems? Decision analysis will not eliminate such feelings of apprehension, but the knowledge that we have made optimal use of all the information and resources at our disposal in coming to the conclusion whose outcome we now await with mounting excitement, gives a sense of satisfaction that would otherwise be absent from the decision process.

Further Reading

L. ADELMAN, 'Involving users in the development of decision-analytic aids: the principal factor in successful implementation', *Journal of the Operational Research Society*, 1982, vol. 33, pp. 333–42.

G. M. KAUFMAN and H. THOMAS, *Modern Decision Analysis – Selected Readings*, Penguin, 1977.

A. D. PEARMAN, 'The application of decision analysis: a US/UK comparison', *Journal of the Operational Research Society*, 1987, vol. 38, no. 9, pp. 775–84.

H. THOMAS, 'Strategic Decision Analysis: The Role of Applied Decision Analysis in the Strategic Management Process', *Strategic Management Journal*, 1984, vol. 5, pp. 139–56.

S. R. WATSON and R. V. BROWN, 'The valuation of decision analysis', *Journal of the Royal Statistical Society*, 1978, series A, vol. 141, pp. 69–78.

G. E. WELLS, 'The use of decision analysis in the Imperial Group', *Journal of the Operational Research Society*, 1982, vol. 33, pp. 313–18.

Bibliography

The short list below gives a few books that can usefully be studied to follow up and expand upon the material presented in this book. They are additional to the references (mainly journal or monograph) given on specific topics at the end of some chapters.

General Introduction

B. F. BAIRD, *Introduction to Decision Analysis*, Duxbury, Mass., 1978.

R. V. BROWN, A. S. KAHR and C. R. PETERSON, *Decision Analysis: An Overview*, Holt-Blond, 1974.

W. G. BYRNES and B. K. CHESTERTON, *Decisions, Strategies, and New Ventures: Modern Tools for Top Management*, Allen & Unwin, 1973.

H. THOMAS, *Decision Theory and the Manager*, Pitman-Times Management Library, 1972.

Psychological and Behavioural Insights

R. M. HOGARTH, *Judgment and Choice: Strategies for Decisions*, Wiley, 1987.

D. KAHNEMAN, P. SLOVIC and A. TVERSKY, *Judgment Under Uncertainty: Heuristics and Biases*, Cambridge University Press, 1982.

W. LEE, *Decision Theory and Human Behaviour*, John Wiley, 1971.

Decision and Risk Analysis Texts

J. AITCHISON, *Choice Against Chance*, Addison-Wesley, 1971.

D. W. BUNN, *Applied Decision Analysis*, McGraw-Hill, 1984.

D. B. HERTZ and H. THOMAS, *Risk Analysis and its Applications*, Wiley, 1983.

C. A. HOLLOWAY, *Decision Making Under Uncertainty*, Prentice-Hall, 1979.

D. V. LINDLEY, *Making Decisions*, Wiley, 1985.

P. G. MOORE, *The Business of Risk*, Cambridge University Press, 1983.

H. RAIFFA, *Decision Analysis*, Addison-Wesley, 1968.

R. L. WINKLER, *An Introduction to Bayesian Inference and Decision*, Holt Rinehart & Winston, 1972.

Case Studies

R. V. BROWN, A. S. KAHR and C. R. PETERSON, *Decision Analysis for the Manager*, Holt Rinehart & Winston, 1974.

D. W. BUNN, J. HAMPTON, P. G. MOORE and H. THOMAS, *Case Studies in Decision Analysis*, Penguin Books, 1976.

D. B. HERTZ and H. THOMAS, *Practical Risk Analysis*, Wiley, 1984.

Statistical Tables

D. V. LINDLEY and J. C. P. MILLER (eds), *Cambridge Elementary Statistical Tables*, Cambridge University Press, 1984.

Glossary of Terms

This list gives descriptions, but not formal definitions, of the distinctive terms used in this book. Further information can be obtained from the text, the number in brackets indicating the page where each term is first introduced in the text.

Action (p. 30) One of a set of alternative decisions that can be made at a particular point in time.

Additivity (p. 167) An assumption which enables a multi-attributed utility function to be simplified in terms of summarizing a number of single-attribute utility functions.

Attribute (p. 135) Measured characteristic appertaining to some specified situation.

Bayes's theorem (p. 66) A fundamental theorem which revises initial probabilities in the light of further information to form revised probabilities.

Binomial probability (p. 74) A probability distribution for the number of successes in a series of independent trials at each of which the probability of success is the same.

Certainty equivalent (p. 182) A decision-maker's single equivalent value for a variable and uncertain outcome in a decision problem.

Chance event (p. 45) A possible, but not entirely predictable, consequence of an action.

Coherence (p. 158) A decision-maker obeying the axioms of coherent behaviour ensures that subjective probabilities conform to the usual rules of mathematical probability.

Conditional probability (p. 71). The probability of some event A, given that a defined further event B has occurred.

Consensus assessments (p. 136) An assessment for utility or probability that has been agreed upon amongst the members of a group.

Consistency (p. 159) A decision-maker who is consistent reaches the same probability estimate for the recurrence of a defined event whatever method of assessment is used.

Credible interval (p. 163) A C per cent credible interval for a PDF (q.v.) of an uncertain quantity implies C per cent confidence that the true value of the uncertain quantity lies within that interval.

Cumulative density function (CDF) (p. 150) Function expressing the probability that a continuous variable is less than or equal to some defined value.

Decision tree (p. 43) A method of displaying the flow of possible courses of action and outcomes in the form of a branching network.

Delphi technique (p. 157) A method for consensus assessment (q.v.) where in each round summary information from earlier rounds is fed back to all members of the group.

Direct rating (p. 176) A procedure for directly assessing a multi-attribute utility structure.

Discounting (p. 50) A method of allowing for the precise timing of income and expenditure items in a series of transactions (commonly referred to as Discounted Cash Flow).

Event (p. 30) The consequence of an action; it may be known with certainty or have a chance element associated with it.

Expected Monetary Value (EMV) (p. 36) A weighted average of the values of the possible outcomes of some action, the weights being the respective probabilities.

Exponential (p. 119) A standard statistical distribution of a J-shaped form.

Folding-back (p. 46) A principle of analysing decision trees which involves proceeding from the final action choices back to the initial action choice (see Rollback).

Fractiles (p. 153) The percentiles (q.v.) expressed as fractions rather than percentages.

Judgemental probability (p. 131) A probability whose estimation requires some element of human judgement.

Likelihood (p. 35) The input in Bayes's theorem (q.v.) which expresses the probability of the 'evidence' or 'new information' being observed.

Linearity (p. 196) A simpler assumption than additivity (q.v.) concerning the form of multi-attributed utility structures.

Marginal probabilities (p. 103) The probability of some event A summed over all the states of some other possible event B that may or may not be linked to A.

Maximax gain (p. 33) The principle of choice whereby the action selected is the one whose maximum outcome is maximized.

Mean (p. 156) The arithmetic average.

Minimax loss (*or maximin gain*) (p. 32) A principle of choice whereby the action selected is such that the maximum loss in taking a wrong decision is minimized.

Minimax regret (p. 34) A principle of choice whereby the action selected is such that the maximum regret (q.v.) in taking a wrong decision is minimized.

Monte Carlo method (p. 214) An alternative name for simulation (q.v.).

Mutually exclusive (p. 71) Two events A and B are mutually exclusive if they cannot occur simultaneously.

Net present value (NPV) (p. 199) See Present value.

Node (p. 45) A point in a decision tree where a choice of action has to be made, or alternative outcomes may occur.

Normal distribution (p. 155) A continuous bell-shaped probability distribution defined by its mean and standard deviation and arising very commonly in practice.

Objectives (p. 29) The aim or aims that underlie consideration of alternative courses of action.

Odds (p. 132) An alternative way of expressing the probability of some event. Odds of r:1 are equivalent to a probability of $r/(r+1)$.

Only possible (p. 71) A series of events are said to be only possible if no other can occur as the result of some process or experiment.

Opportunity loss (p. 34) The cost of a lost opportunity in goods, services or investments forgone.

Option (p. 30) One of a set of possible actions.

Outcome (p. 30) See Event.

Payoff (p. 31) The consequence of an outcome (or series of outcomes) measured in terms of the objective.

Percentile (p. 150) The series of cut-off points that divide the total frequency of some uncertain quantity ordered by value into 100 equal parts.

Pie diagram (p. 140) A circular diagram divided into segments that correspond in area to the frequency of each attribute amongst a set of only possible attributes.

Posterior probability (p. 66) The revised probability assigned to some event when the prior probability is modified in the light of further information.

Present value (p. 199) The value now of receipts and payments that occur at later points of time (see Net present value).

Prior probability (p. 66) The probability assigned to some event at a particular moment in time.

Probability (p. 35) The mathematical language of uncertainty.

Probability density function (*PDF*) (p. 150) Function expressing the probability that a continuous random variable takes any defined range of values.

Probability diagram (p. 142) Branching network diagram for analysing probability inter-relations.

Regret (p. 34) Difference between the payoff achieved under a given action and that which would have been achieved had the optimal action been taken in relation to the outcome which subsequently resulted.

Relative heights (p. 154) An assessment technique for obtaining the PDF of an uncertain quantity using relative odds (or likelihood) assessment procedures.

Risk analysis (p. 213) An analysis of a decision problem using simulation to form PDFs of the outcomes corresponding to the various alternative actions.

Risk-averse (p. 175) A term to express the risk attitude of a decision-maker who would pay a positive premium to avoid the risk in an uncertain situation.

Risk-neutral (p. 175) A decision-maker for whom expected value is an adequate guide to action, in which case the expected value and the certainty equivalent value coincide.

Risk-seeking (p. 175) An attitude towards risk such that the decision-maker's certainty equivalent value is always greater than his expected value, i.e. he would be willing to pay to take part in the uncertain situation.

Rollback (p. 46) A principle of analysing decision trees which involves proceeding from the final action choices back to the initial action choice (see Folding-back).

Simulation (p. 214) A sampling procedure which derives the PDF of some outcome through consideration of the PDFs of the various inputs relating to that outcome.

Stochastic decision tree analysis (p. 217) A multi-stage decision analysis approach which uses a series of simulations.

Subjective probability (p. 131) See Judgemental probability.

Tertile method (p. 152) A method for assessing the CDF of an uncertain quantity which overcomes possible anchoring bias in probability assessment.

Time horizon (p. 198) The planning period over which a decision problem is structured.

Uncertain quantity (p. 149) See Chance event.

Utile (p. 168) A measurement scale for utility (q.v.).

Utility (p. 31) Relative values for the possible outcomes of a decision, taking into account the preferences of the decision-maker.

Notes on Exercises

Chapter 3 (p. 38)

1. (i) 10, (ii) 22, (iii) 14, (iv) 16, (v) 16.
2. 0·20.
3. (i) A, (ii) A, (iii) B, (iv) B.
4. Buy 30, EMV is $186.
5. (i) B, (ii) A, (iii) C.
6. EOL is $248.
7. (i) Use device; expected cost is $28·25 per unit.

Chapter 4 (p. 60)

2. Keep old car, minimum expected cost is $196·1.
3. Buy 1,000 ton cargo, EMV is £32,800.
4. Buy one plot and test for subsidence.
5. Go to Singapore, manufacture if political climate proves secure, otherwise establish agency; EMV is $3·94m.

Chapter 5 (p. 84)

1. (ii) (a) Don't buy, (b) Buy if C < A, otherwise don't buy.
   (iii) Take test, buy if test result positive, don't buy if test result negative.
2. Take test, expected cost $200.
3. ABC9, ACB6, BCA3, BAC6, CAB3, CBA1 (in twenty-eighths).
4. (i) 0·526, (ii) 0·342.
5. (i) No. (ii) 30:0·023, 40:0·231, 50:0·514, 60:0·232. (iii) 0·4955.
6. (i) 0·72, 0·01; (ii) 0·991, 0·009.
7. Market new cake mix without test.
9. (i) $(\frac{1}{2})^{n+1}$ divided by $[(\frac{1}{2})^n + 1]$; (ii) 8.

Chapter 6 (p. 115)

1. (i) With no further information M. Borel should reject the offer $(EMV = -5m.NF)$.

(ii) Given the opportunity of obtaining more information, M. Borel should inspect one ship and accept the offer if it passes, and reject otherwise (EMV of this strategy is 17·9m. NF).

2. Optimal strategy is not to test (EMV = 350).

3. Use the juvenile hormone.

4. EMV of sampling is $1·26×10^4$ (rule is to accept offer if two or more customers purchase); EMV of not sampling is $1·25×10^4$; hence it is marginally best to take sample before deciding whether or not to accept offer.

5. (i) Best strategy, using EMV, is to drill without seismic soundings (EMV is $52,800).

(ii) Note that chance of finding oil is less than one in five, and there is a ⁴/₅ chance of making a loss of $100,000 or more.

Chapter 7 (p. 145)

1. In order of situations, 3:2, 0·75, 4:1, 9:1,0·67, ∞:1, 0·83, 1:3, 3:7, 0·5.

2. (i) 0·2 (ii) 0·8 (iii) 0·4 (iv)1.

4. (ii) 0·12 (iii) 0·785.

5. (i) B:0·2, C:0·2, D:0·3, path probabilities 0·18, 0·21, 0·21, 0·02.

(ii) 0·7 (iii) 0·5 (iv) 0·5 (v) 0·18 (vi) 0·10.

Chapter 8 (p. 161)

4. (ii) (a) 0·88, (b) 0·67, (c) 0·785, (d) 0·21

(iii) 13 to 45 per cent.

(iv) 12 to 48 per cent, 10 to 49 per cent.

5. (i) The commentator is being inconsistent.

(ii) Yes; he is making a 'Dutch book'.

6. (i) (a) 0·00621

(b) 0·02275

(c) 0·5328.

(ii) 80,400 to 119,600.

Chapter 9 (p. 185)

1. (i) No (ii) Yes

3. (i) Accept (EMV is $0·4m.).

(ii) Reject (EUV is 151·05 versus 151·0475 for acceptance).

6. (ii) 0·6 (iii)No.

7. (i) No (ii) No.

Chapter 10 (p. 207)

2. (i) 7·4.
3. (i) B (ii) No, will still choose B.

Chapter 11 (p. 225)

1. Strategy 4: has minimum risk, i.e. standard deviation smallest in relation to mean NPV. Strategies 2 and 5 are good alternatives.
2. Strategy D with EMV of $128,000. Has a low standard deviation in relation to mean, but not the lowest possible which is B, although with a very low EMV.
3. The simulated mean for the authors' trials NPV were positive, suggesting that the aerosol should be marketed.
4. Final column of table reads:

Investment	−$37,400
Market	±$52,500
Share	±$13,000
Price	±$18,000
Marginal costs	±$120,000

   Worst position is decrease in mean NPV of $120,000; best position is an increase of $100,000. These are results from the authors' simulation, other readers' figures may be slightly different.

Index